AF505442

The Development of the International Book Trade,
1870–1895

The Development of the International Book Trade, 1870–1895

Tangled Networks

By Alison Rukavina

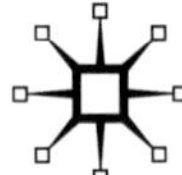

First published 2010 by
PALGRAVE MACMILLAN

Palgrave Macmillan in the UK is an imprint of Macmillan Publishers Limited, registered in England, company number 785998, of Houndmills, Basingstoke, Hampshire RG21 6XS.

Palgrave Macmillan in the US is a division of St Martin's Press LLC, 175 Fifth Avenue, New York, NY 10010.

Palgrave Macmillan is the global academic imprint of the above companies and has companies and representatives throughout the world.

Palgrave® and Macmillan® are registered trademarks in the United States, the United Kingdom, Europe and other countries.

ISBN 978–0–230–27563–8   hardback

This book is printed on paper suitable for recycling and made from fully managed and sustained forest sources. Logging, pulping and manufacturing processes are expected to conform to the environmental regulations of the country of origin.

A catalogue record for this book is available from the British Library.

Library of Congress Cataloging-in-Publication Data

Rukavina, Alison.
   The development of the international book trade, 1870–1895 : tangled networks / by Alison Rukavina.
        p. cm.
   Includes bibliographical references and index.
   ISBN 978–0–230–27563–8 (alk. paper)
1. Book industries and trade—History—19th century.   I. Title.
   Z280.R85 2010
   070.5'09034—dc22   2010034428

10   9   8   7   6   5   4   3   2   1
19 18 17 16 15 14 13 12 11 10

Printed and bound in Great Britain by
CPI Antony Rowe, Chippenham and Eastbourne

Dedicated to my mother, Carol Rukavina

Contents

Acknowledgements

I would like to thank Ian MacLaren, Julie Rak, Heather Murray, Stephen Slemon, and Merrill Distad for their input and advice regarding my dissertation and all the individuals at the University of Alberta who helped me complete this project. In particular, I offer thanks to Ian MacLaren and Julie Rak who encouraged me and acted as sounding boards as I developed my project and later as I revised and added to my doctoral research when I wrote this book. I would also like to acknowledge the Social Sciences and Humanities Research Council of Canada, which provided funding for this research, and the University of Alberta, which provided travel grants and bursaries. I would also like to thank the National Library of Australia (Petherick Collection), Ontario Archives (Kirby Collection), and ProQuest (*Archives of the British Publishers*) for permission to use the archival sources I quote in the book. I would also like to thank the editors and journals, *Angles on the English Speaking World*, *Book History*, and *Script and Print*, for permission to reuse material and for giving me input on early versions and drafts of my work that ended up in this book. I am grateful to HarperCollins for granting permission to reproduce the 'Commercial Map of the World' from *The Century Atlas and Gazetteer* as part of the book cover. Without the assistance of Bonnie Gallinger and the librarians at the University of Alberta Cameron Library and William C. Wonders Map Collection I would not have found this map. Finally, I would like to thank my mother, Carol Rukavina, for listening to me tell stories about the international book trade and for encouraging me to write them down.

Introduction[1]

In a letter dated 3 April 1885, Macmillan's New York manager George E. Brett wrote to Frederick Macmillan about meeting with Edinburgh publisher A & C Black's agent, who was passing through New York on his way to Australia: 'he tells me that there is quite a little boom in England in regard to Australian business. Would you let me remind you that Australia is not a great distance from San Francisco where George occasionally goes.'[2] Brett believed that in an already competitive business, Macmillan's American branch was in a unique position to utilize the transcontinental rail system that had been completed in 1869 and to develop a Pacific shipping route to the Australian colonies. Brett did not want the British firm to fall behind other publishers scrambling to increase their share of the thriving international trade in English-language books and the Australian colonies in particular, as this market accounted for a large percentage of British book exports.[3] Consequently, Brett proposed that his son, George P. Brett, could travel to the colonies the subsequent year to investigate ways of expanding Macmillan's portion of the Australian textbook market and the book trade in general.[4]

In 1886, George P. Brett echoed his father's sentiments and reminded Frederick Macmillan that the firm could not rely on the continuing success of the American and British offices.[5] Brett and his father both considered that the future of the business lay in supplying books for the growing number of readers worldwide, and Macmillan needed to seize the opportunity to expand their overseas business. Thus, George P. Brett added that the publisher should also think about sending him to scout other Asian Pacific markets, including Japan. In a letter dated 22 June 1886, George P. Brett wrote to Frederick Macmillan that he had spoken to '[a] member of the firm of Iveson AJM of this city [New York] … and I learn[ed] from him that their Japanese trade is growing larger year by year and

I obtained from him the promise of a list of their customers there, without intimating however that we purposed making a visit to the country'.[6]

Frederick Macmillan did not need convincing and agreed that George P. Brett should travel to Japan, Australia, and New Zealand. Macmillan's brother, Maurice, had visited India and Australia, between 1884 and 1885, meeting 'many of the most influential men' and reported on the flourishing book trade in the colonies and Asia.[7] Both brothers were interested in expanding the house's overseas capabilities. Maurice Macmillan ran the publisher's Indian office in London and the firm was already competing with other publishing houses like Richard Bentley and Son for a share of the growing Indian market in English-language books. In 1886, George Bentley complained to Alexander Macmillan about his company's actions in asking authors – with agreements with Bentley – to sell their 'Indian & Colonial' copyrights to Macmillan.[8] Both Bretts hoped Macmillan could take advantage of the new transpacific distribution route and cultivate the contacts Maurice Macmillan had made during his earlier visit to the colonies.[9] Generally, the publishing house was willing to make the most of the firm's assets – whether those advantages were letters of introduction to 'influential men' in the Australian colonies or a legal department able to spot loopholes in other publishers' contracts that allowed Macmillan to appropriate colonial copyright – in order to gain purchase in the international book trade.[10]

After one of his regular visits to booksellers in cities and towns in Canada and the United States, George P. Brett returned to New York in October 1886 and reported to Frederick Macmillan that he was making 'many inquiries as to the best methods of making the trans-Pacific trip'.[11] Brett recognized that expanding into foreign markets was a risk but he believed the possible benefits outweighed that risk. Still, upon learning about a cholera epidemic in Japan, Brett informed Frederick Macmillan that visiting the country would be 'dangerous beyond precedent' and suggested he postpone this portion of his trip: 'I write to ask if you will allow me to give up, for next year, the Japanese portion, and devote the time at my disposal to Australia and New Zealand only, leaving Japan and possibly some of the Chinese Posts to the following year if you so desire.' However, the primary reason he gave for rearranging his plans was that 'the time during which I can be spared from the house here [New York] is insufficient to accomplish the trip entire'. If he could focus on Australia and New Zealand, it would allow him 'to give the cities of the Australasian Colonies the attention and time they deserve'.[12] Brett estimated he had three months to make his trip and in practical terms it made sense for him to spend all three months in the two largest markets for English-language books in the Pacific rather than dividing his time between the colonies and the much smaller Asian markets. Frederick Macmillan agreed to the change of plans and that Brett's limited time would best be spent developing the publisher's contacts and business in the colonies and investigating the possibility of opening distribution agencies in Australia and New Zealand.

Both George E. Brett and George P. Brett felt it was imperative that Macmillan continue to invest in the emerging international book trade and gain an advantage over others developing overseas branches, as well as transnational distribution routes. One individual who actively expanded his company's international capabilities was London-based Edward Petherick, who worked for Australian publisher, bookseller, and distributor George Robertson. As Robertson's London manager, Petherick experimented with the various distribution channels between Britain and the Australian colonies, trying to determine the fastest and most reliable for his employer.[13] Petherick also pioneered using the Suez Canal route to ship books between Britain and the colonies. Moreover, contrary to George E. Brett's belief that he was the first to suggest developing a transpacific route, in 1877 Petherick wrote to his father about the possibility of a new distribution channel between the United States and the Australian colonies that utilized the port of San Francisco and he had in 1878 travelled across the Pacific from Melbourne to San Francisco to test the viability of such a route.[14]

Macmillan shipped and distributed the majority of their Australian-bound book orders with George Robertson. While Macmillan had to this point been happy to cooperate and work with Robertson and Petherick, both George E. Brett and George P. Brett believed there would come a time when the publisher would compete with firms like George Robertson and Company for a share of not only the colonial book trade but also the international marketplace. In particular, George P. Brett argued in his letters to Maurice Macmillan reporting his findings from his trip to the Australian colonies that the British house might be best served by opening colonial stock agencies and distributing its own publications overseas. While initially it had financially made sense for Macmillan to entrust transnational distribution to colonial and foreign firms like George Robertson and Company, as the number of book buyers in emerging markets increased, the potential economic value of the still largely underserviced international market to the house demanded more of Macmillan's attention. Whereas British publishers had not at first been that interested in supplying the overseas trade, by 1886 Brett noted that these once overlooked markets were too valuable to ignore and the firm needed to position itself to compete for and to capture as large a market share of the international book trade as possible.

Increasingly book trade agents like George P. Brett and Edward Petherick accepted that their business incorporated both the circulation of books between and among countries in Europe, North America, Asia, Africa, and Australia and the production of English-language books for this burgeoning worldwide market. This book provides a history of the development of the international book trade between 1870 and 1895 and select agents like Brett and Petherick who anticipated the shift from agents primarily focusing on their local and national markets to firms competing on a global stage. It is important to acknowledge the fact that books and people have always circulated not only within but also between and among countries. During the fifteenth century, booksellers and publishers, such as Anton Koberger, sold books throughout Europe on 'a grand scale' that was equivalent to 'the international [book] cartels and trusts of the era of "early capitalism"'.[15] The history of the book trade is not about the linear progression from a local to international business; instead, the print economy has often incorporated transnational commerce. However, while printed matter had circulated throughout Europe and the Mediterranean for centuries, it was only in the late nineteenth century that a truly international book trade – the precursor of the modern global book economy – developed.

During the late nineteenth century a combination of social, cultural, political, economic, and technical advances were transformative catalysts for not only the international trade in English-language books but also a transnational economy. For example, George P. Brett made use of improvements in transportation and communication, such as the telegraph, which shrank the world and made it easier to buy and sell goods across vast distances. Jan Aart Scholte explains that '[t]he hundred years after 1850 saw the advent of the first global communications technologies, the consolidation of the first global markets, some elements of global finance, and a degree of globality in certain organizations'.[16] Two essential developments of this period of incipient globalization that were also fundamental to the development of the transnational book trade were an international gold standard and a free trade system, which 'helped to spread global thinking to more contexts and to wider circles of people from the mid nineteenth century onwards'.[17]

In 1821, the British Currency Commission, chaired by MP and later Prime Minister Robert Peel, introduced the idea of a gold standard as a 'particular solution to the problem of exchange currencies'.[18] The international gold standard fully emerged in the 1870s following its adoption by

Germany, France, the United States, and other countries. Before the gold standard, transnational trade was complicated by the fact that there was not a set currency exchange rate between countries. In an international gold-standard system, the currencies of member countries 'are fixed to gold, but can move in relationship to each other'.[19] The establishment of the gold standard 'facilitated the movement of money from one country to another ... [and] the nineteenth century saw the beginning of very large capital flows through the international system'.[20] The second development in the nineteenth-century international system vital to the book trade was 'the appearance of the doctrine and practice of free trade'. Free trade was a theory developed by David Ricardo, a British Member of Parliament in the early nineteenth century, who 'suggested that by specializing in the product that you make best and engaging in free trade you can benefit even if other people make the products better than you do'.[21] The government promoted free trade on a unilateral basis rather than in terms of reciprocity, and these unilateral trade policies were accompanied by 'unprecedented imperial expansion', which in turn created new markets for British goods.[22]

Both the gold standard and free trade supported British businesses, including publishing, interested in selling commodities overseas. However, while the gold standard 'gave certain national currencies transworld circulation ... [a]part from limited sums of money wired by telegraph, currencies at this earlier time lacked the supraterritorial mobility made possible on a large scale later in the twentieth century by airborne shipments and transworld electronic fund transfers'.[23] In other words, in the late nineteenth century business still lacked a secure system of transferring payments overseas. The Bretts saw an opportunity to send George P. Brett to investigate opening local branches of the company in the Australian colonies and other Asian Pacific markets that would be able to circumvent one of the last barriers to a truly globalized economy, which was paying bills and making payments across immense distances.

In the late nineteenth century Macmillan and other book trade agents overcame various obstacles that constrained the development of the global economy. The book trade had to develop reliable transportation and communication strategies and channels. Book trade agents also had to find solutions to the lack of financial transfers between countries. However, other barriers were not as easily overcome; social and political impediments to the international circulation of books and commodities, such as book piracy, or illegal reprinting, and a lack of international copyright protection, stymied growth. The fear of piracy intensified throughout the nineteenth century and book trade agents generally viewed it as a pervasive and pernicious problem, whether a book trade was under assault from inexpensive reprints or not: publishers, authors, printers, and others were anxious that the pirates were invading their markets and threatening their livelihood. George P. Brett repeatedly worried that the international book trade would become a battleground between pirates and established firms like Macmillan and that the publisher's ambitious global plans would never get off the ground until strong international copyright protection existed.[24]

Another deterrent to the development of the international book trade was that British publishers, even Macmillan, initially declined to produce and distribute publications for the emerging colonial and foreign markets in the early nineteenth century. The steep costs associated with transnational distribution and the widespread belief that there was not a large enough market to justify these expenses led British publishers to refuse to take a risk on such a speculative venture. As a result, they ceded the market to their overseas counterparts who took advantage of transportation advances such as the opening of the Suez Canal in 1869 and developed their own transnational distribution routes to facilitate the circulation of books. For instance, Edward Petherick tried to position George Robertson and Company, between 1870 and 1887, as a transnational distributor for not only British publishers but also European and American firms as well.

British publishers resisted entering the international marketplace until their counterparts like Robertson and Petherick had not only established transnational distribution channels but also demonstrated the economic viability of selling books overseas. When British publishers finally realized the potential value of these new markets they found it necessary to work with colonial and foreign firms. British houses, such as Macmillan and Richard Bentley and Son, had financial and cultural capital but lacked knowledge of overseas markets; in contrast, colonial and foreign firms, such as George Robertson and Company and later Edward Petherick's Colonial Booksellers' Agency, were deficient in financial and cultural capital but had knowledge of international markets and distribution practices. However, as British publishers reaped the economic benefits of selling their publications overseas and learned about these new markets, the knowledge gap that had led the firms to cooperate and collaborate with their counterparts narrowed. By 1886, when plans for George P. Brett's trip to the Australian colonies were being discussed, British publishers were increasingly more likely to compete for a share of the international market rather than work with colonial and foreign businesses. Still, Macmillan continued to support firms like Petherick's Colonial Booksellers' Agency until the 1890s and was one of ten leading British publishers who provided loans and stock to launch the international distribution company.

The history of Petherick's Colonial Booksellers' Agency is largely unknown. One possible reason for the lack of knowledge about Petherick and his transnational distribution company is that the field tends to focus on the actors and events within a nation's borders, and in order to trace the history of Petherick's company, as well as the history of the international book trade, one has to make connections across borders. Sydney Shep observes that 'the construction and deconstruction of nationhood and nationalism rarely appear to be central preoccupations for book historians', yet research and projects, such as large-scale collaborative history-of-the-book surveys, are often played out against a national backdrop.[25] For example, in the *History of the Book in Canada* (*HBiC*) *Beginnings to 1840*, editors Patricia Fleming, Gilles Gallichan, and Yvan Lamonde link the book to the development of British North America: 'Products of the same technical and intellectual revolution, the printed book and the exploration of the New World were destined to nourish each other.'[26] Eva Hemmungs Wirtén argues that academics need to examine the effects of large-scale projects, such as *HBiC*, on book history and 'what *kind* of knowledge they produce'.[27] Both Shep and Wirtén note that these projects, reflecting the field in general, sometimes lack self-reflexive awareness of the assumptions and structures that organize their construction. Book history often assumes and overemphasizes the importance of national geography as the 'given investigative point-of-departure'.[28]

This absence of critical engagement results in a potential national bias or fallacy that threatens the field, as academics, influenced by the work of Benedict Anderson, stress 'the close connections between print culture and the invention of modern nations'.[29] Anderson contends that the development of print-capitalism in the nineteenth century enabled the imagining of nations 'as a deep, horizontal comradeship' that promoted and underscored the 'fraternity that makes it possible, over the past two centuries, for so many millions of people, not so much to kill, as willingly to die for such limited [national] imaginings'.[30] However, the nation cannot be defined as simply a shared national identity or narrative. Homi Bhabha argues that national identity is fractured and always mutating. Print does not support a single all-encompassing timeless cultural and political identity. Bhabha believes that print provides the tools for reimaging affiliations.[31] Accepting that a symbiotic relationship exists between the rise of nation and the growth of national book trades, print historians who start with this premise guarantee that the resultant product will conform to a national mould and potentially limit their findings to a history that is confined by the borders of the nation.

There is even a tendency to privilege the role of nation in international histories of print culture and the book trade. At the Society for the History of Authorship, Reading, and Publishing's annual conference in Lyon, in 2004, Simon Eliot argued that future international studies of the book could only develop after the completion of national-history-of-the-book projects.[32] National-history-of-the-book surveys are then seen as providing a staging ground for future international comparative studies. There are two 'implicit structures' and assumptions wrapped up in this belief: national-history-of-the-book studies are a necessary and foundational precursor to an international history and a comparative method is the appropriate means by which an international history will be developed.[33]

Putting aside the idea that a comparative approach is not necessarily the best way to examine the international book trade for the moment, there are a number of problems with regard to international histories of the book as consolidating projects. Once again nation is the 'given investigative point-of-departure', and the emphasis is on comparing a series of histories rather than considering the international trade as a complex and integrated system.[34] Also, it is a slippery slope from simply viewing national surveys as the initial projects that will be followed by an international history to thinking about the book trade as evolving from a national concern into a transnational print economy. For example, in *Les Mutations du Livre et de l'Edition dans le Monde*, Jacques Michon suggests that the internationalization of the print economy is a further development of national book trades in the twentieth century and that books first circulated locally and nationally before becoming commodities in the international realm.[35] It is easier to construct a linear narrative that starts with the national before moving to the international sphere; however, this method risks constructing a false geography of the book trade that in turn produces an inaccurate history of the circulation of books and print matter. Borders 'were immaterial to the drive for profits' and distributors like George Robertson and Edward Petherick simultaneously developed their businesses at local, regional, and international levels.[36]

Eliot has remarked that participants in history-of-the-book studies often recognize the paradox at the heart of these projects; however, even though books and manuscripts may have always been 'relentlessly and inescapably international', research still tends to focus on or start with the national stage.[37] Even if academics recognize books are international objects as Eliot argues, recognition is not the same as critical engagement and consideration of the assumptions that organize and structure the field. The insular privileging of the nation in book history can lead to a host of problems, including academics paying little or no attention to the booksellers, printers, publishers, distributors, and authors who either worked outside the national stage or had companies that spanned the local, regional, national, and international markets. I am not arguing that nation should be elided from international book histories but that academics need to be aware of the limitations of a national focus. Petherick is primarily remembered by academics in a national context as a librarian and a collector of rare Australiana and as one of the main donors who helped to establish the National Library of Australia.[38] Neglected is Petherick's influential role in the expansion and promotion of an overseas book trade in the late nineteenth century.

This national fallacy or preoccupation also tends to 'reinforce Book History's own inherent theoretical and methodological assumptions'.[39] While existing models have served the field well and provided tangible maps that helped academics trace the production, distribution, and consumption of books, these models, like Robert Darnton's communications circuit, were designed for the study of books in a national setting. Darnton developed his communications circuit as a purposeful model to chart the 'life' or history of a book.[40] The communications circuit is a synthetic model where the 'life cycle' of a book is condensed and works best in a national setting where the book follows an orthodox prescribed path that starts with the author, moves to the publisher and select other agents, and finishes with the reader. However, the communications circuit becomes a problematic model once the book circulates internationally; it is too linear to account for interactions that resulted in colonial distributors working with British publishers or distributors collaborating with authors to produce books that were suitable for the overseas market. Book history risks stagnation if we do not pay more attention to how the linking of the rise of nations and national book trades limits the field's development. At the same time, we cannot move forward without new models and tools that allow us to trace the history of the book trade across borders.

'Heedless of borders', book trade agents negotiated, collaborated, and competed as the international book trade developed, and a potentially useful conceptual model for this activity is to think of it as a social system or network.[41] Increasingly book trade agents like George P. Brett and Edward Petherick thought about the world not as a vast geographical expanse but as a negotiable space in which commodities and ideas circulated. In the first chapter I develop a social network model that is a decentred system that has three principal components – connection, multiplicity, and rupture – and is best imagined as one of its organic rhizomic counterparts like a potato plant. Once planted, a potato quickly grows by a subterranean network of nodes and roots into a larger system. Similarly, the international book trade expanded rapidly, like its organic counterpart, as transportation and communication innovations improved the speed and cost of trade flows and as agents interacted and intersected with others interested in selling books in the transnational sphere. The Bretts, Petherick, and Robertson were part of this social network and their surviving correspondence documents the growth of the system as British, European, American, and colonial publishers, authors, and other agents vied for a portion of the international marketplace.

In 1872, Petherick in a letter to his father described the world in terms of a social network of 'ante-rooms' through which authors, publishers, and other book trade agents communicated and negotiated.[42] Petherick recognized that he was a node within a growing international network continually connecting and reconnecting with other agents in processes of production and consumption as he bought books and sold books, as he wrote to authors and publishers to persuade them to sell books overseas, and as he signed agreements with authors and publishers to produce colonial and foreign editions. In his memoir he described the scope of his duties as Robertson's London manager and later as owner of the Colonial Booksellers' Agency as almost overwhelming at times: 'correspondence, reports, lists, invoices, shipments, and shipping details, banking and cash accounts, – accounts with over 300 houses in this country [Britain]'.[43] As Petherick's purchases, packages, and correspondence circulated, they were bought, received, and responded to by other agents. Petherick believed that the connections he made to agents in the trade would result in increased and regular book supplies to meet the growing demand overseas and improved transportation times, methods, and routes. He could not have foreseen when he wrote his letter to his father in 1872 that because of his position within the social network, and as a result of all the connections he made to other agents as he expanded Robertson's distribution business, his ambitious dream to own his own company would eventually come true. In 1887, Petherick launched the Colonial Booksellers' Agency, an international distribution and publishing firm, that was financially backed by ten British publishers, including Macmillan, Bentley, Longman, Blackwoods, and Smith Elder.

However, within eight years Petherick's Colonial Booksellers' Agency would be in bankruptcy. A social network can rupture. As it expands or changes, the social network can break and start up again, creating new networks or re-establishing old ones. Petherick's company replaced Robertson's business, and British publishers supplanted Petherick's agency with their own distribution systems. By 1895, the knowledge gap that had prevented British houses entering overseas markets earlier was erased. A result of British publishers engaging representatives, or opening foreign and colonial branches, was that they no longer needed the wholesale firms and middlemen like Edward Petherick to sell and distribute their publications overseas. Consequently, British publishers were reluctant to offer Petherick any financial help when the Australian federal bank called in an outstanding loan and let his company slip into bankruptcy.

A social network is an organic and fluid model that can illustrate the complexity of connections and social acts of meeting, reading, writing, talking, printing, etc. that link agents within the network and cause it to develop, contract, and split. While organic is a loaded term, in regards to a social network it simply references the potential elasticity of a rhizomorphic model that does not privilege either the book as the primary object of study or view national geography as the obvious 'point-of-departure' of book history.[44] A social network model also does not presume there is a set starting point or beginning; an academic can choose to start with any agent and trace the connections that make up that particular line within the larger network.

As the subtitle of this book suggests, I conceive of an entangled history in which the international book trade is made up of a complicated array of connections and interactions. There are three suggested methods for producing global or international histories: comparative, transfer, and entangled. Shep does an excellent job summarizing the strengths and weaknesses of each option in 'Books Without Borders' and considering whether the field can use any of these approaches or whether we should 'develop our own structural grammar to shift book history from a field of study to a discipline'.[45] I believe entangled history or *l'histoire croisée* is perhaps the best platform, though I think the field requires more specific tools than currently offered by this option, which is why I develop a social network model. Still, as entangled history complements a social network, it is important, as well as useful, to highlight the benefits of the approach.

Jürgen Kocka argues that historians of entangled history are 'much less interested in similarities and differences ... but rather in the processes of mutual influencing in reciprocal or asymmetric perceptions, in entangled processes of constituting one another'.[46] He defines entangled history as 'in tension with basic principles of comparative history', which is the method many book historians argue needs to be used to construct an international history of the book.[47] While Kocka suggests that '[i]t is not necessary to choose between *histoire comparée* and *histoire croisée*' and the aim should be to combine the two approaches,[48] Michael Werner and Bénédicte Zimmerman argue that

> *Histoire croisée* breaks with a one-dimensional perspective that simplifies and homogenizes, in favor of a multidimensional approach that acknowledges plurality and the complex configurations that result from it. Accordingly, entities and objects of research are not merely considered in relation to one another but also *through* one another, in terms of relationships, interactions, and circulation. The active and dynamic principle of the intersection is fundamental in contrast to the static framework of a comparative approach that tends to immobilize objects.[49]

Werner and Zimmerman view entangled history as providing a method of studying the international sphere where 'the transnational cannot simply be considered as a supplementary level of analysis to be added to the local, regional, and national levels [but] ... as a level that exists in interaction with the others, producing its own logics with feedback effects upon other space-structuring logics'.[50]

Kocka is correct in that comparison and entanglement are not necessarily mutually exclusive. What I find particularly compelling about an entangled history approach to international history is that it stresses the dynamic act of intersection and is 'in favor of going beyond reasoning in terms of micro versus macro, emphasizing instead their inextricable interconnections'.[51] Constructing an international history of the book and book trade that brings together and compares the various projects examining the national book trades in Canada, the United States, Australia, and elsewhere once again risks producing an inaccurate narrative, because the originating studies do not account for the agents who moved between and among countries as they plied their trade. An international history of the book should not be 'reduced to the sum of the[se] histories' as the 'relationships, interactions, and circulation' that took place in transnational spaces can be lost.[52]

An international history of the book needs to take 'into account the diversity of transactions, negotiations' and connections of agents like George P. Brett, who crisscrossed the globe as Macmillan's 'traveling salesman'.[53] Still, the complexity and diversity of the international book trade can be overwhelming and leave an academic wondering where do I start and what connections should I trace. In order to write a coherent history of the international book trade I believe one should begin with a couple of agents, such as George P. Brett and Edward Petherick, and disentangle and trace their connections to other agents that make up lines or branches within the larger network. Any comparison of and between agents is secondary because what matters is letting their narratives intermingle and intersect in order to exemplify the larger sphere in which they operated – the international book trade – and the importance of connections and connectivity in this social network.

In correspondence with his father, Petherick described the international book trade as 'a wonderfully comprehensive business and a vast amount of trouble', and George P. Brett, his father, and others involved in overseas book distribution and production would have likely agreed that it was a complicated business.[54] A social network privileges connection. In order to convey the intricate array of interconnections and interactions between and among agents that make up the international book trade, I do not attempt a comprehensive history but a representative one that in focusing on certain individuals and companies illustrates the wider field in which books circulated and the change in attitudes towards transnational trade in the late nineteenth century. This project starts with Edward Petherick and follows the connections he made to other book trade agents during the course of his career working for George Robertson and later himself. Petherick led to Macmillan, and Macmillan led to the Bretts, and it is the agents I focus on who limit the scope of this history.

In 1870, Petherick travelled to London to work in Robertson's office. His correspondence quickly establishes his enthusiasm for developing the firm's transnational distribution system and business and his ability to convince British, American, and European publishers to work with Robertson so that their publications could be distributed overseas. I could have started the history in 1869 when Macmillan launched the New York office and the Suez Canal opened to shipping traffic, or I could have picked another date. My history ends in 1895, the year Edward Petherick was discharged from bankruptcy. What is important is not the specific date range but that the late nineteenth century is a period when the international circulation of books grew exponentially as publishers, distributors, and other agents capitalized on their individual advantages, developed new distribution routes and markets, and engaged in processes of negotiation, collaboration, and competition.

This volume traces the connections between agents and surveys select branches of the social network between 1870 and 1895. While Chapter 1 develops a social network model, the remaining chapters illustrate that book trade agents engaged each other repeatedly as books were produced, distributed, and consumed and in doing so these connections added to the rapid growth of the international book trade. Chapter 2 examines both how the growth of the social network rapidly accelerated as the necessary physical infrastructure for an international book trade developed and Edward Petherick's role in utilizing new technology in order to improve upon and cultivate transnational distribution routes. Petherick's correspondence also reveals the number of connections he made with others in the trade and his impact on the growing interest of British publishers in the Australian colonies and in other overseas markets for English-language books. Robertson and Petherick capitalized on the central location of the London agency and on the firm's existing Australian and developing overseas distributing system in order to position themselves as middlemen whom larger British publishers like Bentley needed to work with to expedite the sale of their books in the colonies.

In Chapter 3 I demonstrate how three different branches of the social network end up intertwining and connecting around the issues of book piracy and a lack of international copyright. The fear of piracy fostered cooperation among publishers, wholesalers, authors, booksellers, and others in the trade, though the nature of that cooperation varied around the world. In 1855, William and George Robertson exploited the industries' widespread fear of book piracy to pressure British publishers into developing the trade between Britain and the Australian colonies, which would lead to George Robertson, in the 1870s and 1880s, working with British publishers, like Bentley, to produce books specifically for the colonial market. In the 1870s, the publishing history of William Kirby's novel *The Chien d'Or* demonstrates a different response to the fear of book piracy, but another branch of the social network that debated the effects of and potential cures for book piracy. Finally, correspondence and articles in *The Publishers' Weekly*, from 1879, provide insight into another branch of the social network and the fear and anger caused by Canadian pirates flooding the American market. George E. Brett's and George P. Brett's letters to Frederick Macmillan provide an interesting counterpoint to the discussions in *The Publishers' Weekly* regarding copyright law and book piracy. Father and son were eager to defeat the reprinters but realistic that until the development of international copyright law Macmillan's New York branch, as with the rest of the trade, would struggle with or at least fear the spectre of book piracy. By the 1880s, book trade agents were organizing associations that lobbied for changes to copyright legislation that would protect the trade from pirates. Increasingly, agents defined cooperation in terms of transnational literary and industry associations that lobbied for some sort of international copyright law.

The last two chapters document the shift in the late nineteenth century from British publishers willing to cooperate with and to support their colonial and foreign counterparts to British houses directly competing with overseas firms. Chapter 4 surveys the development of Richard Bentley and Son's Foreign and Colonial Department, and the British firm's growing interest in selling books overseas, particularly in the United States, India, and Australia. Also, I recount Macmillan's foray into the American, Indian, and Australian markets. In particular, I focus on George P. Brett's trip, in 1887, to Australia, Tasmania, and New Zealand. While at first George P. Brett advocated Macmillan working with colonial and foreign firms to increase the British house's share of the book market, particularly the educational sector, after travelling in Australia, he recognized that Macmillan could establish local distribution offices in Australia and New Zealand and compete directly with colonial firms.

Chapter 5 examines the rupture that led to Edward Petherick leaving Robertson and opening the Colonial Booksellers' Agency and the role Bentley, Macmillan, and other British publishers played in supporting the launching of the company and in eventually destroying it. When Petherick's bank loans came due in 1892, his investors refused to help him. Bentley, Macmillan, Longman, and other backers realized that they no longer needed to cooperate with distributors, like Petherick, to gain access to the international book market, and so they allowed Petherick's company to fail. This chapter documents the shift in the 1890s away from established British publishers eager to work with and to support colonial wholesalers and booksellers to British firms more likely to compete with their colonial and foreign counterparts for access to and a share of the international market in English-language books.

Book production, distribution, and consumption fuelled the growth of the international book trade in the late nineteenth century. One connection led to another as books were produced, distributed, and consumed and the social network expanded as agents engaged with one another in order to facilitate the transnational circulation of books. While the flow of people, books, and ideas increased between 1870 and 1895, it is important to recognize that this development was not inevitable. Connections produce further connections and the network grows, but the nature of this growth is not necessarily in one direction or correlated to physical expansion. In the 1890s, a series of depressions led to a global economic downturn and contraction in the international book trade. This reduction did not mean that the social network stopped or disappeared; instead, the development of the social network slowed and the network ruptured, splitting into new systems. The capacity of the international book trade would not return to 1890 levels until the second half of the twentieth century, when other structures necessary for a global economy would also appear that would eventually lead to increased and wider-reaching book circulation as part of a global print economy.

1
Social Networks[1]

Upon arriving in London in August 1870 to take up a management position in the London office of Melbourne bookseller, distributor, and publisher George Robertson, Edward Petherick, in a letter to his younger siblings, described the distance between Australia and Britain as vast and daunting.[2] He included a sketch with his letter of the globe that illustrated the distance between himself and his family: the sketch is of the earth with two ships and two men, where one man and ship are 'on opposite sides of the world' from the other man and ship (Figure 1). However, by 1875 Petherick's attitude had changed and he proudly claimed in a letter to his father that he could get books from anywhere in the globe shipped to the Australian colonies and that 'it is very rarely that we have to reply "can't find"' to a customer's order for new publications or 'for books out of date and circulation for generations'.[3] Moreover, Petherick thought nothing of travelling in 1877 to Australia for a short visit home before going to the United States and Canada to meet with leading publishers about expanding Robertson's distribution business.[4]

Petherick's correspondence provides a wealth of information about how rapidly attitudes regarding distance changed in the late nineteenth century and how a combination of social, economic, political, and technical advances were catalysts for the growth of the transnational book trade between 1870 and 1895. More importantly his letters also illustrate that this international book trade was a social network made up of agents intersecting and communicating as they negotiated the sale and circulation of their publications. In a letter to his father dated 13 June 1872, Petherick described the world in terms of a series of interconnected rooms in which one eventually meets everyone: 'After all what is this world? Only a lot of ante-rooms in which we dodge about before entering the next. In that we can all meet, be it soon or

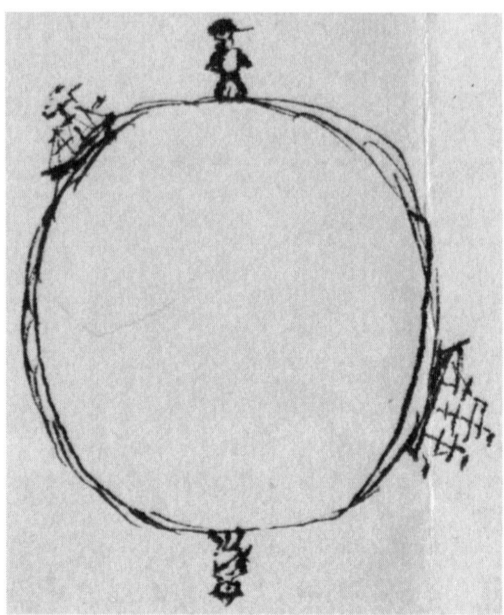

Figure 1 Petherick's drawing from 1870 letter to siblings. Petherick Collection, National Library of Australia.

late.'[5] Petherick's architectural metaphor illustrates his understanding of the world as a negotiable space and the book trade as a social network through which authors, publishers, and others who were interested in the international circulation of books could exchange ideas and commodities. Distance did not impede Petherick's ability to communicate and work with other book trade agents because they were only conceptually a room away from one another.

Reading his letters motivated me to think about what a system of 'anterooms' or a social network might entail. As I started to think about networks, a second source of inspiration, Gilles Deleuze and Félix Guattari's *A Thousand Plateaus*, helped me to realize that a social network is rhizomorphic in design and as such can act as a general model for the complicated, decentred, and explosive growth of foreign and colonial markets for English-language books in the late nineteenth century. In this chapter, I want to define and explore the possibilities of a social network, while outlining the three principal components of this model: connection, multiplicity, and rupture. However, before describing what a social network entails, it is important to outline why a new model is necessary.

While existing models have served the field well and provided tangible maps that helped academics trace the production, distribution, and consumption of books, these models like Robert Darnton's communications circuit cannot capture the circulation of books and book trade agents in an international arena. Darnton argues that as book history took 'on a distinct scholarly identity', it needed 'a general model for analysing the way books come into being and spread through society' that could also act as a potentially unifying methodological starting point for the new discipline.[6] He adds that he is 'not arguing that book history should be written according to a standard formula but trying to show how its disparate segments can be brought together within a single conceptual scheme'.[7] Darnton develops his communications circuit, which represents a book's 'life cycle', as a purposeful model to chart the 'life' or history of a book as it moves within a linear communications circuit from the author to the reader.[8] The communications circuit is a synthetic model where the 'life cycle' of a book is condensed to a coherent, unified account that elegantly traces the path a book takes as it moves between agents.

Darnton acknowledges that all models 'have a way of freezing human beings out of history'.[9] In order to 'put some flesh and blood' on his communications circuit, he applies it to the publishing history of Voltaire's *Questions sur l'Encyclopédie*. While the model works in this specific case, the communications circuit is neither general nor flexible enough to apply to every textual case study. It works best in a national setting where the book follows an orthodox prescribed path that starts with the author, moves to the publisher and a limited number of other agents, and finishes with the reader.

Similarly, modified versions of the communications circuit, such as Thomas Adams and Nicholas Barker's system or Michael Winship's model, are also problematic. Adams and Barker propose a modified circuit where the cycle of a bibliographical document, a term that includes any printed or written text,

> becomes the centre: the indirect forces are seen outside it, looking and pressing inwards. Instead of six groups of people who make the communications network, we have five events in the life of a book – publishing, manufacturing, distribution, reception and survival – whose sequence constitutes a system of communication and can in turn precipitate other cycles.[10]

Within the five events are further agents or parties that operate as other circuits within each respective event. Adams and Barker attempt to account for the whole socioeconomic history of a text, while providing a 'map' for the future of the history of the book.[11] However, Adams and Barker still envision a cycle where the text moves in a single direction from event to event. Michael Winship's model both emphasizes activities, not the people who perform them, and stresses the business relationships over the life of a book as it passes from hand to hand.[12] Winship's model accents the role of the publisher as *entrepreneur*, a role he argues that is of central importance in the study of the business and economic history of the American book trade. Whether the original communications circuit or one of its progeny, these models are still too linear and predicated on the study of book trades within local, national, or regional geographical spaces to account for the varied interactions between agents interested in buying and selling books in the transnational sphere.

In order to 'put some flesh and blood' on my critique of existing models of print production and circulation, one need only consider the relations between agents that resulted in colonial distributors working with British publishers or distributors collaborating with authors to produce books that were suitable for the overseas market. For example, in 1873, Edward Petherick, on George Robertson's behalf, negotiated an agreement with Richard Bentley and Son for the firms to produce jointly colonial editions of Mrs Henry Wood's novels.[13] The direction of movement between agents runs counter to Darnton's model that suggests books circulated in a clockwise direction from publisher to distributor. In the case of the international book trade, colonial distributors wanted British publishers to provide regular shipments of books but the houses were initially uninterested in supplying books for the colonial or foreign markets outside North America and Europe: publishers believed the potential monetary return from the international sale of English-language books would be insufficient to cover the costs of shipping and distributing books overseas. George Robertson opened a London distributing and book-buying branch in 1857 in order to guarantee a regular supply of books and he took the initiative and approached British publishers to produce books for this emerging market.[14] By the 1870s when Petherick was manager of Robertson's London agency, he boasted to his father that he had made arrangements for Robertson to work directly with publishers not only in Britain but also in North America, Europe, and the colonies.[15]

Linear circuits of print production and distribution tend to assume the direction of the movement of the book is, if not the same, in a set direction; the author has contact only with the publisher and is largely isolated from other agents, such as booksellers, wholesalers, and printers.

In regards to the international book trade, interactions between agents are fluid and not necessarily predicated on set patterns of behaviour. Authors sometimes approached George Robertson or his London manager Edward Petherick directly and angered their London publishers in the process. For instance, popular British author Helen Mathers offered Robertson the Australian rights to her novel *Story of a Sin* without the apparent knowledge of her British publisher, Routledge. In July 1881, she wrote to Petherick that she had received a letter from her publisher that 'reduces me to despair!'[16] The letter informed her that her contract for the English rights of the book included the Australian rights. She expressed anger and bewilderment that she could arrange independently for the American and European sales of her novels but not the Australian sale: 'I had no idea of doing anything in any way dishonorable, and wish with all my heart I had not sold' the British rights. Mathers asked Petherick for advice because she did not 'know what to reply to W. Routledge'. Petherick's exact response to Mathers' request is unknown, but the following year Robertson's publication of *Story of a Sin* in Melbourne suggests that he made an arrangement with Routledge for the Australian rights to the novel.

The international book trade represented an opportunity and an 'ante-room' to which authors wanted to gain entry. Petherick's surviving correspondence with Mathers and other authors is a record of their determined attempts to connect to and participate in the social network of the international book trade and see their publications circulate outside traditional markets. Mathers ignored social niceties out of necessity as she wanted to negotiate the best terms possible and to secure a place for her publications in overseas and colonial markets. As the Australian colonies were the second largest market for popular fiction in the late nineteenth century, she was eager not only to work with Petherick and Robertson to produce colonial imprints of her books but also to offer to write manuscripts that would specifically appeal to Australian readers.[17] In 1883, Mathers wrote to Petherick that after *Story of a Sin* she would publish a book entitled *Sam's Sweetheart* that would be set in Australia.[18] Explaining that the setting should help her in the Australian market, she predicted that the book would 'perform' because she was specifically including Australian content to attract Australian readers. She also promised that the manuscript had been substantially edited because in the first draft 'I made a beautiful hash of the Australian Aborigines, but I believe my facts are correct now, & would not damage either me or my publisher.' Mathers did not want to chance offending Australian readers by writing a book that did not seem representative of Australian life. She was prepared to alter her manuscript in order to produce a book that was as 'authentic' as possible and to ensure Robertson's book order. While Darnton insists that his model examines a book's life cycle 'in all its variations over space and time', the communications circuit and other versions of this model are too linear to account for the international movement of books and interactions between book trade agents like Mathers and Petherick.[19]

A conceptual model needs to reflect the decentred networks of production and distribution of the international book trade, and this model is perhaps similar in nature to what John Jordan and Richard Patten argue book history in general needs – a hypertextual network. Jordan and Patten propose a comprehensive, multidirectional, and decentred system where the various stages of any form of a print text's 'life' are interdependent and all the mediating factors are considered.[20] They argue that academics need to adopt a hypertextual approach to book history that recognizes the interplay and interconnectivity between stages in a book's 'life history' that avoids a 'metanarrative of print history'.[21] This new model needs to allow for the 'polyvocal' nature of the discipline without negating the multitude of 'intangibles such as ideological and social formations' that affect the history of a print text.[22]

While I agree with Jordan and Patten that any model of a book's 'life history' needs to be decentred and 'polyvocal' in nature, I find hypertext a problematic starting point for a model of the international book trade. Jordan and Patten romanticize the possibilities of hypertext; for example, they argue that it is non-hierarchical and credit it with shifting agency to the spectator/reader. However, hypertext is hierarchical because a website only allows for a predetermined number of links or connections:

> hypertext, like any other written language, has its orthodoxies, which determine what its writers can do and what its readers can experience ... Although a measure of power is given to the reader, who may decide not to follow the link, most HTML writers 'encourage' readers to follow certain links rhetorically or by including image files which 'attract' readers.[23]

Hypertext is a language, or discourse, that is written and shaped by a person or persons, and therefore it is not that different in this regard from a printed text.

A model of the international book trade needs to be able to reflect the dynamic power relationships between actors within the international field. Hypertext conceptually offers a dead end for academics trying to develop a more fluid model of print production and circulation. Foucault argues that '[t]he frontiers of a book are never clear-cut: beyond the title, the first lines, and the last full stop, beyond its internal configuration and its autonomous form, it is caught up in a system of references to other books, other texts, other sentences: it is a node within a network'.[24] Similarly, the international book trade is a system of connections and 'ante-rooms' that is indefinite in shape and size because it is always developing and growing as agents connect and reconnect in the processes of producing, distributing, and selling books. Agents like Edward Petherick and George Robertson are nodes in an international book trade that cannot easily be modelled in terms of a circuit or hypertext; instead, it is perhaps best conceptualized, because of its complexity and indefinite nature, as an organic rhizomorphic network made up of a multitude of book trade agents.

Deleuze and Guattari use the concept of the rhizome to offer an image of capitalism's incessant urge to produce and consume within multiple decentred networks of distribution, production, and consumption. They define rhizome as an organic and decentred network in which agents continually engage and re-engage. While organic is a problematic designation, in this context it refers to the fact that a rhizome is not a set structure or system and that it is network based on rhizomes found in nature such as the potato. Conceptualizing the international book trade as a rhizome allows for the complexity of interactions between agents to play out without prescribing the nature of the relations between agents and predetermining the direction of a book's movement. A rhizomorphic or rhizomic network offers many of the same benefits of John Jordan and Richard Patten's hypertextual model – in that a rhizome is about connection and interconnectivity – but unlike hypertext it is non-hierarchal in nature.[25] A rhizome is also not a model in the traditional sense of Robert Darnton's communications circuit. One cannot draw a rhizome and predict a book will follow a set path; instead, a rhizome can only be traced after the fact and is best imagined as one of its organic counterparts such as grass or a potato plant. Once planted, a potato plant quickly grows 'by subterranean stems and flows' into a large network of nodes, roots, and shoots.[26] Moreover, a gardener can establish boundaries and an area where she or he wants the potato to grow but once planted the rhizome develops in a manner that can lead to tubers appearing throughout, and even outside, the vegetable patch.

Correspondingly, the international book trade expanded and ramified rapidly, like its organic counterpart, in the late nineteenth century once technical and other innovations made global trade possible. I am not arguing transnational trade did not exist before this period but that a number of catalysts occurred in the nineteenth century that precipitated the rapid expansion of the global economy in general and an international book trade specifically. An example of one catalyst was that out of necessity colonial and foreign firms developed the infrastructure needed to promote the growth of the global book trade and sought out established partners who could supply the international marketplace with publications. Edward Petherick on George Robertson's behalf pioneered new trade routes between Britain and the Australian colonies in the 1870s and repeatedly approached publishers about selling books overseas.[27] Petherick helped to convince British, American, and European publishers that there was a growing colonial demand for English-language books. As the print network developed, it involved many who had initially shied away from producing and distributing English-language books for emerging markets. New branches appeared and the print network soon included foreign markets such as Japan, which also demanded a supply of English-language books.[28]

While at first it might seem strange to compare the development of the international book trade to a potato plant or other rhizomorphic entity, conceptualizing the book trade as a rhizome helps to avoid some of the limitations inherent in earlier models of print production and circulation. Moreover, Deleuze and Guattari provide a vocabulary for clarifying the power dynamics of the international book trade. They theorize capitalist relations that challenge hierarchical or binary power dynamics, eschew a periphery–centre dynamic, and envision a positive image of capitalism's repetitive and constant urges to produce and consume because we are all agents or assemblages that continually connect and reconnect in processes of production and consumption. An agent is 'a node within a network', connecting with or referencing other nodes, and any object or subject of production and consumption is a possible agent.[29] Deleuze and Guattari define agent in the broadest possible sense; a book is as much an agent as a person. Consequently, this understanding of agency opens up a field of possibility in how one understands and defines social interactions within the network, but before developing this idea any further it is important to describe the physical nature of a rhizomic network.

Returning to my organic metaphor, a rhizome, like potato, grass, iris, or mint, is an underground, horizontal network of shoots that forms roots at the nodes in the root system to produce new plants. For example, an iris can be divided and the sections of the rhizome removed from the original iris clump and replanted. Deleuze and Guattari employ a rhizomic model to explain capitalist relations, describing a rhizome as 'an [organic] acentred, nonhierarchical, nonsignifying system',[30] where 'the fabric of the rhizome is the conjunction, "and ... and ... and ..."'.[31] A rhizome is a map or tracing that ceaselessly establishes connections: it is then a multiplicity of connections and interfaces between agents and structuring organizations. It stands in contrast to an arboreal model that fixes an order or hierarchy. Deleuze and Guattari argue that an arboreal model is not representative of nature even though it is influenced by it: 'Nature doesn't work that way ... [it is] a more multiple, lateral' network.[32] It is easy to view a book 'with its pivotal spine and surrounding leaves' in terms of an arboreal model made up of the key individuals who affect the shape and design of its spine and leaves; however, a tree inspires reductive models of a book's 'life history' and the workings of the book trade. The multiplicity of agents that participate in and social forces that influence the production and dissemination of a book cannot easily be replicated by an arboreal model that follows predetermined paths and is hierarchical in structure.

While I use Deleuze and Guattari's rhizome as an access point or inspiration for a social network model, it is important to acknowledge that I conceive of a social network as a particular type of rhizome. Deleuze and Guattari ascribe to the rhizome six key features: connection, heterogeneity, multiplicity, rupture, cartography, and decalcomania.[33] However, in developing a rhizomorphic model of print production and distribution, I find a social network has three primary components – connection, multiplicity, and rupture – where connection is the most important tenet: 'any point of a rhizome can be connected ... [The rhizome] is very different from the tree or root, which plots a point, fixes an order.'[34]

Connection is one of the principles that differentiate a rhizome from a fixed system and it is a fundamental component of a social network because a rhizomic model embraces a chaotic disorder where any book trade agent can potentially engage or 'meet' another agent. For instance, when Edward Petherick, on George Robertson's behalf, approached the London publisher Richard Bentley and Son with a proposal for a cheap colonial issue of Mrs Henry Wood's novels, he became friends with George Bentley who ran the family firm after his father's death. Bentley then recommended the Melbourne-based company, and Petherick specifically, to authors who wanted to distribute books overseas.[35] In 1879, popular Irish novelist May Laffan Hartley wrote to Petherick and offered the stereotype plates of *Flitters and Tatters and the Counsellor and other Sketches* – a collection of four stories about poverty and slum life in

Dublin and Glasgow – to Robertson so that an inexpensive Australian edition could be printed.[36] Hartley sought advice from Bentley, her British publisher, regarding whom to approach about producing the Australian edition. Not surprisingly, Bentley recommended Robertson, with whom the British firm had had a formal partnership since 1876 that allowed the Melbourne publisher to 'put [the Bentley] ... imprint on any work of good character' that he might issue in the colonies.[37] In 1887 when Petherick left Robertson to start his own distribution company, Bentley helped to finance the new firm. The network expanded as agents interacted and intersected as books were produced, distributed, and consumed.

In privileging connection and the conjunction 'and', a rhizome also eschews a simplistic understanding of both agency and agent, which better reflects the complex power dynamics of the international book trade. When British publishers first refused to produce and distribute publications for the emerging colonial and foreign markets in English-language books in the mid nineteenth century, their overseas counterparts took the initiative and developed transnational distribution routes and opened London branches in order to facilitate the circulation of books. When British publishers realized the potential value of these new markets, they found it necessary to work with firms such as George Robertson and Company that had knowledge of colonial and foreign markets and channels of distribution. Book trade agents did not necessarily network in terms of either an antagonistic model of dominated and dominant agents or a centre–periphery dichotomy; instead, agents, capitalizing on their individual advantage, fluidly moved between positions as they negotiated, collaborated, and competed with each other.

Agency is located in the connection or interplay between agents and with agents in the network. An agent is defined as 'a node within a network', connecting with or referencing other agents, and any subject or object of production and consumption is a possible agent.[38] Therefore, both Edward Petherick and a book are possible agents and an agent derives meaning and value in relation to what networks it belongs to, what connections an agent makes to other agents, and what functions an agent performs within networks. This approach defines agency broadly but avoids imprecision. Darnton's communications circuit limits the number of agents and types of interactions or moments of agency. While Adams and Barker expand agency to include books, in doing so they actually strip actors like authors, publishers, and distributors of some of their agency, leaving a certain ambiguity regarding who or what has agency in the circuit.[39] In a social network, when agent is more widely defined to include both books and people, the number and type of possible interactions between agents increase. Agents are not caught within a circuit of set events or possible responses. Moreover, an expansive understanding of agency moves beyond a binary model of dominated and dominant actors, which is a problem with Pierre Bourdieu's field of literary production. Still, Bourdieu's model has gained currency with academics as an innovative and contextualized framework that avoids the determinist problems of many traditional social science and arts methodologies.

In particular, academics like Lauren Benton argue that Bourdieu provides a template upon which literary and global histories can be mapped as the product of practices of fluid social networks and relationships.[40] Benton argues that Bourdieu offers a model for 'reimagining global structure by bringing into the light institutions that are constructed out of practice and do not exist at, or even merely bridge, separate "levels," but themselves constitute elements of global structure'.[41] In other words, Benton applies Bourdieu's methodology to the emergence and development of globalization, arguing that it cannot be separated into cultural and economic strands because the strands are interconnected and rooted in practice. She demands the 'identifying [of] key relationships that link cultural and local practice, and structural and economic forms, ... [and] understanding these aspects of social experience as congruent'.[42] Darnton acknowledges that Bourdieu's work also helps literary historians answer '[q]uestions about who reads what, in what conditions, at what time, and with what effect'.[43] Bourdieu conceives of books being produced and consumed within an interlaced network of circuits within a larger cultural field where '[t]he literary field is itself defined by its position in the hierarchy of the arts, which varies from one period and one country to another'.[44] His approach allows for a diachronic view of a complex process and emphasizes the intertwined and interconnected state of the economic, political, cultural, and other fields.

In terms of agency, Bourdieu considers all the different agents within the field as cultural intermediaries, each influencing the text as well as the field with his or her actions. Each field has its own rules and laws governing interactions between agents, and external pressures indirectly affect both the agents and the field. While this approach to agency values the impact of agents on a particular field and considers the different influences that affect an agent's actions, he privileges human agents and narrowly defines the relationships between agents in terms of 'oppositions between the antagonistic positions (dominant/dominated, consecrated/novice, old/young, etc)'.[45] Bourdieu argues that within the literary field agents involved in large-scale production, which categorizes the international book trade, compete for advantage and control of the market, and those agents who are richest in any form of capital are typically the first to capitalize and move into new positions within the field.[46]

He theorizes that established or dominant agents would be in an ideal position to capitalize on new opportunities in the field. However, British publishers refused to produce books for and distribute publications directly in overseas markets until their counterparts had demonstrated the economic value of selling books internationally. Robertson was the dominant figure in the Australian distribution market during Petherick's tenure as Robertson's London manager between 1870 and 1887. Once British publishers became interested in the Australian colonies, they curried Robertson's favour, offering him deep discounts so that he would distribute their publications and that their books would find an advantageous position on his bookstore shelves. Bourdieu does challenge some of the linear underlying assumptions of book history and offers a productive methodology for the study of economic change and globalization that accounts for the interconnections between culture and economics.[47] Still, his conception of agency lacks the necessary fluidity to capture the dynamics of the international book trade.

A social network offers more inclusive characterizations of agent and agency, as well as emphasizing interrelations and interactions between agents, and can more easily account for a colonial distributor and bookseller simultaneously occupying both dominant and dominated positions. On the one hand, Robertson struggled with his finances and the expense of a London agency. According to Petherick, British banks and publishers provided Robertson with a series of loans when transportation delays left the Melbourne-based distributor and bookseller short of funds.[48] No international financial system existed in the nineteenth century and Petherick sometimes could not pay the London agency's bills because money being sent from the Melbourne head office was delayed en route. On the other hand, during Petherick's tenure as London manager between 1870 and 1887, Robertson controlled what British publications he distributed and carried in his colonial shops, and his power over which British publishers he worked with and who could access his distribution network caused some of them to become resentful. In a letter to his father, Petherick notes that a number of established London publishers – never named – were in fact jealous of Robertson's success: 'I suppose success must always suffer from jealousy, envy and enmity … It is strange – there are large firms here who receive [a lot of money from Robertson] … who yet are not only dissatisfied but dislike

[George Robertson].'[49] Depending on point of view, agents can be seen to occupy concurrent, as well as ambiguous, positions within the social network. The international book trade is a network made up of a wide variety of interactions or social acts of meeting, reading, writing, talking, etc. that connect agents, and not all of these types of connections can be easily categorized. By not limiting the definition of agency or types of social acts, a social network avoids setting boundaries that can force both agents and history to fit particular moulds.

A social network's fluid understanding of connection and elastic interconnectivity also leads to a second principle of multiplicity, which refers to the fact that a rhizome can grow in any direction and is open to a diversity of connections. A tracing of a social network is distinctive because no rhizomic model develops like another, since there are no set 'points or positions in a rhizome' unlike Darnton's communications circuit.[50] Consequently, one can only trace or map a social network after the fact because of the innumerable connections between agents that are possible. Moreover, Deleuze and Guattari explain that the division of subject and object and other dichotomies do not exist within a rhizomic structure: what do exist are lines of multiplicities and assemblages. Both a book and a person are potential agents who can engage and connect, which further complicates the potential number of linkages in a rhizome. Mapping a social network is then an exercise in disentangling the individual lines and connections that make up the larger rhizomic entity. It is unlikely every connection and node can be traced, but an academic can start with one node and follow the flight of the line as connections multiply. Choices must be made regarding which connections to map and any disentangler needs to be self-aware of the influences affecting the shape of the network. While the social network is based on an organic model, it is an academic's construct.

The principle of multiplicity is both a strength and a weakness in a social network. On the one hand, a rhizomic model of the international book trade sets up no barriers to following the line of connections across a broad geographical field. For example, by the 1880s, the British publishing firm Macmillan had offices in London and New York and agents throughout Canada and the United States. In his letters to the London office, George E. Brett wrote about the firm's growing network of agents and their work developing new markets for Macmillan publications. In April 1885, Brett encouraged his employers to consider expanding into the Australian market.[51] Macmillan's business was not geographically confined to one country or region and tracing the connections between agents involves following the development of the firm's increasingly global interests, which is possible with a rhizomic model of the international book trade. On the other hand, the complexity of connections that are a part of any social network, in particular an international book trade that spans a large geographical and temporal space, almost defies mapping. This concern raises the issue as to whether a social network is perhaps more a conceptual model, or way of thinking about print production and circulation, rather than an actual physical model. Certainly, any attempt to draw a social network would run into the difficulty of too many connections and lines, leaving a scribbled mess on a page. However, a counter argument might be made that mapping is possible if academics follow and compare particular agents, such as Petherick, Robertson, Bentley, Macmillan, and the Bretts and their interactions and connections within the social network or networks. It almost goes without saying that multiplicity also refers to the idea that the social network is made up of a plurality of book trades, distribution networks, publishing organizations, etc.

Finally, a social network has a principle of rupture because it does not follow a predetermined path and eschews hierarchy. As it expands or changes, the social network, because it can both break and also start up again, creates new networks or re-establishes old ones. The social network as a rhizome horizontally spreads out, and as it does it ramifies and diversifies in often unpredictable and uncontrollable ways. For example, no one was prepared for the rupture in George Robertson's distribution network or the new distribution network that would develop as a consequence of Robertson's actions. In 1887, Robertson abruptly ceased distributing books for most of the British publishers his firm represented, including Macmillan and Bentley. Publishers were in a bind as they needed to secure the overseas distribution of their books, but there were no firms that could quickly replace Robertson.

If a potato is removed from the ground and planted somewhere else in the garden, a new network of shoots, roots, and tubers may result. Similarly, if you think of Robertson's business as part of one line of the social network, each node within the line is potentially capable of developing into its own network, which is what happened when the London publishers supported the launch of Petherick's Colonial Booksellers' Agency in 1887.[52] Deleuze and Guattari argue that agents, by repeatedly engaging each other – and in doing so influencing one another – spawn further interactions with each new interface leading to the potential multiplying, rupturing, or newly establishing of rhizomes.[53] A rhizomic network is a growth of infinite actions and reactions, where agents may borrow or use a 'part' of another agent or node in a way potentially unknown to the original agent.

Rupture as a type of borrowing within a rhizomic network can also be described as a type of cultural, social, and economic cross-fertilization. Deleuze and Guattari assert that books deterritorialize the world and the world reterritorializes books as they move through networks: 'from sign to sign, a movement from one territory to another, a circulation assuring a certain speed of deterritorialization'.[54] Deterritorialization and reterritorialization refer to the use of an idea, part, or image of an agent, such as a book, by another agent. In other words, as a book circulates internationally, it can develop new readings and new audiences, or it influences other writers and publishers. For example, George Bentley, at Petherick's urging, edited between 1887 and 1888 a series of books which Richard Bentley and Son had previously published. The books were marketed as being by Australians and about Australia, and Bentley presented them to the Australian public as 'new' Australian editions, where 'the vernacular and idiom are Australian'.[55] The Australian Library was part of Bentley's second colonial series and was marketed as a nascent 'national' collection, which defined Australian literature in terms of the books' subject matter and writing. Bentley did not let the fact that a number of the books were not written by Australians stop him from advertising both the authors and the books in the library as Australian. The Australian Library included British author Caroline Leakey's *The Broad Arrow*, which was edited for the series with an Australian readership in mind. The new edition of the novel emphasized the romantic elements in the book and de-emphasized a polemic against the convict system and colonial life.[56] Consequently, the novel, first published by Bentley in 1859 as a religious novel for a British public, became in 1888 a tragic national romance for Australian readers. In general, book serialization is a type of rhizome where deterritorialization and reterritorialization take place, as books are reshaped and grouped with other books into series, like the Australian Library, and can develop new readings and audiences.

Deleuze and Guattari's rhizome is itself reterritorialized in this chapter as I borrow the idea of a rhizome and develop a social network model. A social network with its principles of connection, multiplicity, and rupture is ideally suited to understanding and untangling the complex history of the international book trade at the end of the nineteenth century. In particular, a social network privileges 'conceptions of the activity of producing and consuming texts that decentre the principal elements and make them interactive and interdependent', without necessarily romanticizing or limiting the tangled web of interactions between book trade agents.[57] Also, a social network provides the opportunity to rethink how participants in print production and circulation are conceived. Expanding the possible field of agents to include both people, books, and other entities and providing a much more inclusive definition of agent leads to a realization that agency lies in the interactions and engagements between agents, which in turn enlarges the type and number of connections that impact and shape the network.

Petherick's surviving correspondence illustrates that he not only interacted with numerous authors and publishers but also with books, social policies, and even technology. For example, when Petherick wrote to his father that distance was no longer a problem, he made it clear in this and subsequent letters that his experiments with new technology were reshaping Robertson's business and enabling him to imagine the world as an interconnected series of rooms 'in which we dodge about before entering the next'.[58] Petherick employed the fastest ships, as well as developing new transportation routes. He extensively used the transpacific cable, after it was laid in 1872, to wire Robertson about book orders and shipments, and the firm was one of the first to use a telephone in both the London and Melbourne offices.[59] Developing more comprehensive understandings of agent and agency allows one to consider a wider array of interactions that influenced the development of the international book trade.

A social network model is not without its challenges; certainly, the fact that it cannot easily be drawn or described is problematic. Trying to draw a rhizome results in a mess of lines that can leave the paper more black than white. Is a digital mapping and visualization of a social network possible or is the model perhaps primarily a way of thinking about the production and circulation of print more so than the actual tracing of it? When I first read Petherick's letter that detailed his understanding of the connected nature of the Victorian world as a series of 'anterooms' I was struck by how he conceived of the late nineteenth century in terms that were not surprisingly that different from modern conceptions of the interconnected, electronic age in which we currently live. A social network offers a way of imagining and untangling the history of the international book trade that reminds one of the lines that connect modern globalization to this earlier period of transnational trade. Whether conceptual or corporeal, a social network offers a flexible and fluid model that potentially can map the density of interactions that make up the international book trade in the late nineteenth century, as well as that connect it to the modern global book economy.

2
Developing Distribution Channels and the Social Network[1]

> G. R[obertson] now makes use of the telegraph and orders larger supplies by cable, irrespective of cost. Two days ago I received a cable order for several books, not withstanding that other supplies had been recently shipped. The cost of the message would be about £20, and although the value of the whole order is under £500, the additional expense incurred will not be a reason for G. R. asking a high price than if they had been ordered in the usual way.[2]

In a letter published in *The Bookseller* in 1874, Edward Petherick boasted about Robertson's use of the telegraph to streamline the book ordering process and the fact that the cost of telegrams would not be passed onto consumers. Petherick's surviving letters to his father and colleagues in the book industry repeatedly emphasize his pride in working for an innovative firm that utilized advances in communication and transportation to gain a competitive edge. He not only praised Robertson's business practices but also eschewed modesty in favour of extolling his own virtues in publications like *The Bookseller* and in his correspondence. On 21 January 1874, Petherick half-jokingly wrote to his father: 'I like my work – only I may grow proud and conceited – think myself as important (and am I not in regard to my occupation equally as influential) as a Colonial Governor.'[3]

Petherick's correspondence between 1870 and 1887 provides an informative account of his adoption of and experimentation with new transportation and communication technologies and of his running of Robertson and Company's London agency. George Robertson started his bookselling business in Melbourne in 1852, and he opened a London distributing branch in 1857. While J. Walch & Sons was the first colonial bookseller and distributor to set up an office in Britain in 1854, Robertson's London agency soon eclipsed the sales of the Tasmanian firm and became the largest Australian colonial distributor of British books for the next two decades.[4] Petherick officially became manager of Robertson's London agency in December 1871. His correspondence from 1870, when he arrived in Britain, to 1887, when he started his own distribution agency, repeatedly highlights the importance of the London office to the success of Robertson's business and to British publishers who sought to maximize their profits by increasing book sales in foreign and colonial markets. The Petherick Collection at the National Library of Australia contains hundreds of letters and documents written by and to Petherick that reveal the frantic, productive pace of Robertson's London branch as the office struggled to keep up with the escalating demand from both colonial booksellers wanting to purchase books and British, European, and North American publishers who wanted to sell their publications overseas.[5] In particular, Petherick's letters to his father provide a candid account of his adoption of, as well as eagerness to use, new technology, and his belief that his efforts on behalf of Robertson convinced many publishers to distribute their books with the firm.

This chapter surveys Petherick's correspondence between 1870 and 1887, with an emphasis on letters written before 1878, examining how developments in transportation, communication, and book production both facilitated and obstructed the expansion of Robertson's business and the international book trade. While providing a history of Robertson's London agency in this chapter, I also analyse Petherick's letters regarding the growing interest of publishers in the Australian colonies and in other overseas markets for English-language books. Robertson and Petherick capitalized on the central location of the London agency and on the firm's existing Australian distributing networks in order to position themselves as important figures in the social network with whom larger British publishers needed to work in order to expedite the sale of their books overseas. Petherick boasted about his role in the emerging international book trade, calling himself as important as a 'Colonial Governor', and this claim, while exaggerated, was perhaps not completely incorrect. Petherick's correspondence attests to the fact that he personally knew many of the individuals and firms participating in the international book trade. As he made connections to other agents in the social network during his career, he convinced a lot of other people that books and texts could and should circulate internationally.

A recurring theme in Petherick's letters to his father and business colleagues is the shrinking of distance between London and Melbourne through improvements in transportation, communication, and book and text production. Nevertheless, the initial innovation that allowed Petherick to capitalize on changing technology was the creation of Robertson's London branch. In 1857, Robertson opened a London office, run by his brother William Robertson, at 11 Gough Square.[6] The London office not only purchased books for the firm but also acted as a shipping agent for other British and European businesses that wanted to distribute their books and stationery in the Australian market.[7] Having an agency located in London made communication easier for William Robertson and later Petherick, as the manager could meet face to face with publishers and be assured of quick delivery of and hopefully response to business letters. The London office raised George Robertson's profile in the city and the manager was able to lobby British publishers for a regular supply of publications. The office was an innovation that eased the firm's participation in the social network. There were cyclical economic depressions throughout the nineteenth century, and British and American publishers often sought out new markets and relied on innovation to get themselves out of the slump.[8] Petherick, in a number of letters to his father, also referred to a continuing depression in book sales in Australia that plagued the market throughout the 1860s and 1870s; he argued that the firm weathered the downturn in the economy because of Robertson's foresight in establishing a London office.

With Petherick's arrival in London, the branch also quickly recovered from William Robertson's mismanagement, which had negatively affected the firm's business. Petherick's letters to his father from 1870 to 1871 repeatedly note that William Robertson's erratic book ordering and shipping had imperilled the London office, if not the entire firm.[9] One of the advantages of having a London branch was that there was less of a delay in the firm paying bills for books and texts. Financial transfers between countries and over long distances were difficult, if not impossible in the nineteenth century; British publishers who directly sold books to the colonies often had to wait prolonged periods of time before they received payment from their distant customers. Robertson received favourable terms from British publishers because as long as the London office did not run out of funds, the manager could pay them without delay. However, William Robertson's excess stock purchases in 1870 left the London firm without the ability to pay all of its debts: Marie Cullen argues that 'only financial accommodation from the bank enabled G.R. to send the necessary remittances to London' to avoid financial disaster.[10] William Robertson's financial negligence resulted in his brother promoting Petherick, who had previously worked in his

Melbourne retail and wholesale business cataloguing and writing advertisements, and sending him to London to help with book ordering and shipping.

Petherick repeatedly stated in his letters to his father that there was tension in the London office between himself and William Robertson, who saw Petherick as an interloper.[11] He wrote that 'Mr. W^m is not [in] the best of tempers – he is irritable and complaining … ready to blame others for everything – and he seems pleased sometimes to find out the errors & faults of others.'[12] William Robertson complained to his brother about Petherick on a number of occasions, but George Robertson proclaimed that business had improved since Petherick had joined the London office.[13] Furthermore, in a letter dated 16 June 1871 to his father, Petherick quoted George Robertson that 'business [in Australia] continues in a very depressed state but I am happy to be able to report that in the finance department we already feel [since Petherick's arrival] the advantage of having a buyer in London'.[14]

Petherick's letters indicate that shortly after his arrival in London in 1870, George Robertson had him act as manager because of problems with William Robertson's running of the office.[15] However, John Holroyd argues that Petherick did not replace William Robertson as London manager until 1873.[16] Still, in a letter to his father dated 8 September 1871, Petherick mentioned that 'W.R. has declined the new conditions offered him (Joint Manager) and was going to leave [the branch].'[17] Moreover, in a letter from November of that year Petherick wrote to his father to report that George Robertson had ordered him to take over the firm at the end of December 1871.[18] Consequently, Petherick acted as the de facto manager shortly after his arrival in London in the summer of 1870, and he officially became manager in December 1871 after William Robertson left the agency.

Frequently in his letters to his father, Petherick acknowledged both Robertson's prescience in establishing an office in Britain and the importance of the firm being at the centre of the book trade: in 1874, he wrote to his father that he was 'satisfied to be in the [London] vortex'.[19] Within four years of arriving in the city, Petherick had successfully reorganized the branch, and the firm had moved to larger premises at 17 Warwick Square. While Robertson wrote to Petherick that he wanted him to consider his position permanent, he also warned Petherick that he would close the London branch 'if any other person is supported and assisted by the British publishers to rival' the firm.[20] Consequently, in 1874, when William Robertson, who had since leaving his brother's employment set up a book distribution business in Melbourne, wrote two circulars attacking his brother's retail and distribution business and insinuated that his Melbourne-based company could distribute British publishers' books in the Australian colonies better than Robertson's London and Australian branches, Petherick emerged as a vigorous defender of Robertson and his business. Most notably, Petherick wrote a letter to the British trade journal *The Bookseller* seeking to position Robertson as the primary distributor in the Australian colonies. Petherick defended the firm and stated that 'Mr. Robertson saw his opportunity, and while other booksellers seemingly looked after themselves, he began to import for them all.'[21] He wrote to his father that he did not want Robertson to feel threatened by William Robertson's scurrilous attacks and close a business that had in the past year 'opened up accounts with Paris Publishers. And ... opened up still larger and important accounts in New York, Boston, Philadelphia.'[22]

Petherick identified 'London [as] the centre of the publishing world'.[23] His employer's actions in opening an office in the city were an attempt to overcome the limitations of running a business that required British publishers to increase and improve the shipments of books to a neglected corner of the Empire. However, I would not describe the relationship between Robertson and British publishers in binary terms or Petherick's imagining of the relationship between the colonial and British book trades in terms of the power dynamics of periphery and centre. Petherick viewed both himself and Robertson as in an enviable position, as they were the middlemen who could improve British publishers' access to the Australian colonial market. While in one letter Petherick complained about the distances that separated him from his family, he also did not regard Australia as part of a distant colonial periphery.[24] On the contrary, he argued that the rising demand for books in the colonies was leading to colonial cities becoming important centres in the international book trade.[25] Moreover, these same developments were happening elsewhere in the world, though not necessarily at the same rate or speed of expansion. Cities like Melbourne, Sydney, New York, and Boston were new centres of the book trade. In a social network every node is potentially a centre; in other words, there is no periphery in a network. Connections between agents could be more straightforwardly made if an agent was in a certain place or position but firms needed agents to be located in the various centres of the international book trade, as well as to make use of communication technologies, in order to increase the chances and occurrences of connections. Petherick lobbied Robertson, asserting that the firm would eventually require correspondents and partners in many of these new centres, if the company wanted to continue expanding and improving its distribution channels. London was in pragmatic terms an important node in the network where Robertson needed to establish a presence but it was not the only node and Petherick was aware of this fact.

In the letter published in *The Bookseller*, Petherick boasted about both Melbourne and Sydney as increasingly important centres of the international book trade and the scale and scope of Robertson's enterprise. He characterized 'the sphere of operations' as massive: 'four or five travellers not only called daily upon booksellers in Melbourne and Sydney ... but also periodically visited booksellers throughout the other Colonies, including Tasmania and New Zealand'.[26] However, he also suggested that '[i]t must be remembered that the population of the whole of the Australian Colonies, including New Zealand, is only a little over two million, scattered over an extent greater than that of Europe; the principal towns and cities being quite as wide apart as the European capitals'. Petherick acknowledged in the letter that while '[t]ravelling and communication with each Colony, necessarily by water, is, notwithstanding distances, frequent, but very costly', advances in transportation, communication, and publishing were allowing the firm to overcome the distance between the colonies, and between Australia and Europe, as well as to improve its access to and position in the social network.[27]

Improvements in transportation enabled Robertson's firm to secure regular and more frequent shipments of books to the Australian colonies as well as other markets in the region. In an unpublished memoir, Petherick observed that 'when I came here nearly all goods were shipped to Australia in sailing vessels: we had the opportunity of shipping about once in three months by direct auxiliary steamer, and once a month limited supplies in small packages could be sent by the Overland Mail'.[28] Throughout his letters to his father and family, Petherick repeatedly wrote about how he was constantly trying new routes and ships in order to get parcels and letters home faster. For instance, in a letter dated 18 November 1870, Petherick told his father that he was sending this letter by the *Queen of the Thames* – a new steamer that promised to reach 'Melbourne in 45 days from Plymouth', whereas the fastest time previously had been 60 days.[29] In March 1871, Petherick cited another extract from a letter by George Robertson, in which Robertson congratulated him on arranging timely deliveries: '"<u>I am more than pleased about your Trade List ... It was well thought of & well done</u>" (then G. R. strikes out the short "and" between "of" & "well" and adds) "<u>and well come</u>."'[30]

In 1873, Petherick again tried to improve on the transportation of books and stationery between Britain and Australia by sending mail by way of the different routes, Plymouth, Southampton, and Brindisi, to see which was the quickest and most reliable method. Plymouth and Southampton ships sailed by way of Africa and typically took the slower passages, with differences only in the type of ships used: sailing, steam, or auxiliary steam ships. The third route saw packages sent by train to Brindisi and then shipped to Egypt where the goods would either go overland or via the Suez Canal, which opened in 1869, to Singapore and then Queensland where the mail would be couriered to Melbourne. Petherick repeatedly wrote to his father about testing 'the speed of the various routes now opening between Europe and the Australian Colonies'.[31] In a letter written in 1871, he told his father that 'your letter of the 5th Dec. came via Brindisi – yesterday 23rd. I am glad you sent via Brindisi – It is always desirable for me to have something by that, or whichever is the quickest, route.'[32] In the mid nineteenth century, the average length of time it took mail to reach Australia from Britain was 10 to 12 weeks; however, by the 1870s, steamers had cut the time in half.[33] In the 1890s the voyage via the Brindisi route was taking about a month, and English mail delivery to the Australian colonies had improved from monthly to weekly service. Petherick was constantly experimenting with the different routes and ships and was not satisfied with the status quo: in a fragment of a letter to Robertson written in the 1870s, he stated that 'my candid opinion is that the arrangements for the ordering, receiving and dispatch of goods, at present, are very imperfect'.[34] He continued to experiment with different distribution channels during his tenure as Robertson's London manager, writing in 1876 about sending mail to Melbourne by way of San Francisco.[35]

While advances in ship design and new shipping routes allowed Petherick to send 'by every monthly mail the newest and freshest issues from the leading publishing houses in London and Paris, and sometimes even, copies in advance of the home publication', the distribution of books and stationery was not without its problems.[36] He had to spend a great deal of time studying the shipping reports and experimenting with different routes and ships. Moreover, ships sometimes would be delayed or lost, and he would have to deal not only with the Melbourne office but also anxious authors wanting news of their books. For example, on 27 January 1876, George Manville Fenn, a prolific writer of adventure tales and serialized novels, wrote to Petherick about his regular monthly shipment to Melbourne of a serialized work and agreed with Petherick that the latest issue must 'have been delayed en route' or lost.[37] In another instance, Petherick told his father about 'the loss of the Rangoon [and] [i]t is possible that the mail may be recovered'.[38]

However, he lamented that the firm's cargo of books and stationery bound for Melbourne was probably lost: 'The loss may be about £250 to £300 for us besides the inconvenience.' Furthermore, shipments often had to be sent before books had been reviewed, and Petherick did not always judge correctly which books would be bestsellers:

> When the book arrives, it may be with a host of others more or less saleable; it may or may not be noticed (probably not) in the local press; may not have been noticed in the London literary organs, may have been praised highly or judged otherwise – because you order and ship generally before the reviews of a new book appears [*sic*]: a review of a book may not appear for several months – and then all the world asks for it.[39]

Consequently, books would be shipped in quantities that upon arrival would either not sell or would sell out. The sale of the books he bought and shipped to Australia was then influenced by the 'many things operating for months after the books are in the Market either to retard or help' sales.[40]

In his 1874 letter in *The Bookseller*, Petherick also reminded readers of the costs of importing books: 'Publishers are aware that we have to pack all books in zinc-lined cases, to pay freight, insurance, dock charges, cartage, commission agents, and other expenses incidental to shipping.'[41] Geoffrey Blainey argues that the quickest route between Britain and Australia, via the Suez Canal, was only used for the most valuable of cargoes, such as gold from the Australian goldfields, because the canal fees were too high for regular shipping traffic.[42] However, Petherick's letters indicate that books were considered a precious and time-sensitive cargo and that the firm regularly used the Suez Canal route for both mail and packages.[43] While the costs associated with transportation were high, Petherick also boasted in the letter in *The Bookseller* that 'it will, however, surprise many when I mention that, after paying these charges and expenses, Mr. Robertson supplies nearly all the books he imports to the Trade with sufficient allowances to enable them to retail at the *English published prices*'.[44] Regardless of the frustration caused by shipping cargo over vast distances, Petherick reminded the readers that not only was Robertson making a 'handsome profit' but also he could afford to sell the British books in the colonies at British prices.

Advances in nineteenth-century communications technology, such as the overseas telegraph lines, allowed Petherick to stay in regular contact with Robertson. On 16 May 1872, he wrote of receiving a telegram from

Robertson regarding his imminent arrival in London.[45] Petherick was shocked that the eight-word message cost five pounds, but added that Robertson was a proponent of the telegraph, having exchanged regular telegrams with Petherick since the completed cable between Britain and Australia started transmitting messages earlier in 1872. Blainey argues that the telegraph was far too expensive to be used on a regular basis until the 1890s: 'At first the cost of sending a message by telegraph from Australia to England was so dear that only about fifteen short messages were sent each way daily. A message of 20 words cost £10 – equal to five weeks' wages for a working man.'[46] Regardless of cost, Robertson and Petherick were early advocates of the telegraph, and my research indicates that the firm frequently used the telegraph to send book orders and communiqués between the offices in London and Melbourne, as well as between London and Robertson's other Australian branches. In September 1873, over a year after he first mentioned the firm's use of the telegraph, Petherick wrote to his father that he regularly sent cables 'in cipher' to protect the firm's orders and plans from prying eyes.[47] In a letter dated 16 April 1874, he asked his father to destroy any letters he had sent to the family that described the telegram cipher because 'it is so valuable to us'.[48]

Communicating over large distances became less of an issue with the advent of the overseas telegraph, and Petherick boasted to his father that because of his firm's modern distribution and communication practices 'people in Melbourne enjoy a greater privilege than Londoners in having such a varied stock to go to as George Robertson's – where they are yet able to purchase at English prices'.[49] Furthermore, in a letter dated 17 July 1880, Petherick informed London publishing firm Richard Bentley and Son that if the Australian bookstores found 'the supply of an English work [to] be small or insufficient', stock could be quickly ordered by telegraph: 'Using the Cable we now manage to get books occasionally in six or seven weeks.'[50]

Petherick's location in London also allowed him to take advantage of advances in printing technology that further facilitated both the distribution and production of books for the Australian market. For example, in a letter dated 18 February 1875, Petherick recounted meeting a Mr Clay in 'Kentish town' and enquiring about the purchase of 'a steam lithographic press' for the Melbourne office.[51] Petherick was able to purchase the latest presses and machinery for Robertson's printing facilities in Melbourne, which were opened in 1872.[52] Moreover, Petherick bought stereotype plates in order to create Australian editions of popular works such as Helen Mathers' *Story of a Sin*. In various letters to publishers and authors, Petherick inquired about the purchase of stereotype plates, which could be easily shipped to Melbourne where Robertson could print up copies especially for the colonial market.[53] For instance, Petherick proposed in 1876 that George Bentley sell the stereotype plates of 'the best and most sellable' of Richard Bentley and Son's novels to Robertson.[54] In an article in the Melbourne *Argus* published on 21 February 1874, Petherick already claimed that Robertson had deals with other British firms to produce colonial editions: 'A trade has sprung up in the department of local publication that promises to become in time something remarkable as an element in our social progress. By special arrangement with the leading publishers in London, Mr. Robertson acquires the right to issue special editions of popular works for which the demand is large, for Australian circulation exclusively.'[55] The next section of this chapter further details Petherick's negotiations on Robertson's behalf with British publishers, but the important point to note at this juncture is both Robertson's and Petherick's utilization of new technology in their business.

Whereas Petherick initially bemoaned the great distances that separated Britain from the Australian colonies, by 1875 he proudly claimed that he could get books from anywhere in the globe quickly sent to the Australian colonies and thought nothing of travelling in 1877 to Australia for a short visit home.[56] Moreover, when he mentioned to his father on 10 May 1877 that he planned a visit, he added that he would also make a business trip to the United States and Canada on his way back to London. In the letter he asked his father 'do these things startle you. I hope not. This is a wonderfully comprehensive business.'[57] While distance was a greater barrier to travel and business than it is today, the advances in the late nineteenth century in transportation and communications were as revolutionary as email is to this era. Petherick's attitude towards the distances between home and London undergo a 180-degree shift, as he thinks nothing of travelling to Melbourne then to North America before returning to London. Finally, as his letter suggests, by the late 1870s the business of books was increasingly becoming 'comprehensive'. This development necessitated that firms enter the international arena: if a bookseller, like Robertson, offered to get any book for a customer, he had to have contacts and business associates everywhere.

Over the course of Petherick's letters to his father and others, during his tenure as Robertson's London manager from 1870 to 1887, it becomes clear that improvements in transportation, communication, and production begin to affect positively not only Robertson's business but also other firms. As new, faster trade routes were established, quicker overseas communication became possible, and as the means of production became less centralized the international book trade flourished. Petherick could boast that 'if a book is not to be found on G. R.'s shelves he can soon obtain it if it is in existence at all – whether in Great Britain, on the Continent, in India, or America'.[58] His correspondence demonstrates how various advances and innovations facilitated, and sometimes frustrated, the expansion of Robertson and Company, which enabled the firm to have business affiliations with British, European, American, and colonial booksellers and publishers, as well as other agents in the social network. Letters from British publishers in particular illustrate Petherick's success in encouraging agents to take advantage of improving technology and make use of Robertson's London office to distribute their publications overseas.

While writing his memoir, Petherick noted that his correspondence with publishers 'anxious to get their books into the Colonies was of considerable amount and exceeding interest'.[59] His letters reveal British publishers' growing awareness of the importance of selling their publications in the Australian colonies, as well as other colonial and foreign markets, to their bottom line. Also, his letters indicate that colonial firms, such as Robertson and Company, were not in an unfavourable or unequal position in comparison to their British counterparts. Instead, Robertson situated his firm as a partner and competitor of more established European and British businesses. Publishers more often than not negotiated with Robertson in order to gain entrance into the increasingly lucrative Australian book market. The late nineteenth century was a period of both negotiation and competition as British publishing houses worked with their colonial counterparts to create a space for their publications outside Britain. An international book trade had existed for centuries, but the various developments in the second half of the nineteenth century enticed British and foreign publishers to begin regularly exporting large quantities of books to the colonies and elsewhere.

In the early nineteenth century, English publishers would at best send irregular shipments, often of remainders and excess stock, to be sold in the Australian colonies. While publishers, such as John Murray, recognized as early as the 1840s that large colonial reading publics were interested in a regular supply of inexpensive reading matter, the British trade generally ignored the Australian colonial market until the late nineteenth century.[60] However, a lack of interest in the colonies changed after Australians, such as George Robertson, lobbied the British book trade to produce inexpensive books for the Australian market, established London distributing offices, and pursued partnerships with London publishers in order to ensure the stable supply of books to the colonies. Between 1870 and 1887, the period when Petherick worked for Robertson as his London manager, London publishing firms witnessed the exponential increase of book exports to Australia and elsewhere. The Australian market in 1873 accounted for 20 to 30 per cent of British book exports, and by 1897 accounted for roughly 40 per cent of exports.[61] Consequently, Petherick claimed in his memoir that during his tenure as London manager publishers were increasingly anxious to get their books into the Australian colonial market and willing to work with him, as well as heed his advice about what publications would sell overseas: 'I arranged frequently for Special cheap editions of books likely to be in general demand and was the projector of the Colonial editions of which now nearly every publisher has a Series.'[62]

Persuaded by Petherick and Robertson that the burgeoning demand for books in Australia was an opportunity not to be missed, British publishers arranged with the firm to sell their books in the colonies. Included in Petherick's letters is correspondence from various publishers, including Chatto and Windus, George Adam Young, George Allen, and Richard Bentley and Son regarding the purchase, printing, and copyright of books for the Australian market. For example, in a letter dated 12 August 1879, George Adam Young offered Robertson the 'New Literal Translation of the Bible 2nd edition' that the religious publisher believed 'should sell largely in Australia'.[63] Young published Bibles and religious texts specifically for sale in Australia and was in regular contact with Petherick, who often purchased large enough quantities to merit a discount.[64] Young offered the Bible, to retail at 21 shillings, to Petherick at seven shillings and sixpence if he purchased more than a thousand copies for the Australian colonies. Publishers, like Young, wanted a share of the thriving Australian book trade; subsequently, firms offered their books at a deep discount to Petherick and Robertson in the hope that their publications would be purchased for the colonial market.

Another source of information regarding Petherick's business interactions and business relationships on Robertson's behalf are the archives of British publishers. For example, commission ledgers in the Longman archives indicate that between 1867 and 1908 Longman and Robertson had an arrangement for the marketing, and in some cases the reprinting, of William Edward Hearn's books in Britain.[65] Robertson first published Hearn's *Plutology* in 1863. Hearn was a political economist, politician, and university professor in Melbourne, who, with the British publication of *Plutology* in 1864, brought his work 'to the notice of scholars in

Europe and America'.[66] Macmillan, who also had a business relationship with Robertson, first published *Plutology* in Britain, and then Longman produced an edition of *Plutology* in 1864, although the Longman commission ledgers do not include any statements for this publication. However, the ledgers do indicate that by 1883 Longman was selling copies of *Plutology* and two of Hearn's later publications, *The Government of England: Its Structure and its Development* and *The Aryan Household*, in Britain and the United States.[67] A similar arrangement was also made for the distribution and reprinting of Henry Parkes' *Speeches on Various Occasions* in Britain after Robertson had first published the popular Australian politician's book in 1875.[68] An 1876 joint reprint of *Speeches* included Robertson's Melbourne imprint, followed by Longman's London imprint.[69] The Longman commission ledgers further reveal that Petherick, on Robertson's behalf, negotiated in 1875 for the right to produce, using Longman's stereotype plates, a Melbourne edition of Walter Richard Cassels' *Supernatural Religion*, which Longman had first published anonymously in 1874.[70] A note at the top of the ledger stated: 'Robertson to reprint the entire work from the 2nd Edition at his own cost and risk', with Longman's receiving 'one half the profits'. Throughout the 1870s, Robertson often had to accept the financial risk for Australian editions of British books first published by Longman, Macmillan, Bentley, and other houses.

Of all the publishers with whom Petherick exchanged letters, his correspondence with the house Richard Bentley and Son offers the greatest wealth of information regarding the evolving business relationship between Robertson's firm and London publishers.[71] While Robertson had published at least one Bentley publication before 1873, Petherick's letters to and from the London house between 1873 and 1887 mark a period of increased business dealings between the two firms. In 1873, Petherick, on George Robertson's behalf, approached the London publisher with a proposal for a cheap Australian issue of Mrs Henry Wood's novels.[72] Furthermore, Petherick tried to interest the London firm by noting that other British publishers were reprinting novels for the Australian market: 'a similar arrangement has been made with the publishers of "Ouidas" novels (for smaller quantities however) which ... is still a speculation of G.R.'s part'. Bentley favourably responded to Petherick's proposal; consequently, an agreement was struck to reprint Mrs Henry Wood's works for the Australian market and produce 'not less than 35000 to 50000 volumes in all'.[73]

On 25 November 1875, Petherick approached George Bentley about formalizing the British firm's business arrangement with Robertson.

The Australian bookseller wanted to give the publisher's imprints a prominent place in his Australian bookshops, to wholesale Bentley's publications to other Australian, New Zealand, and colonial booksellers, and to 'put [the Richard Bentley and Son] … imprint on any work of good character and in keeping with your own publications – which he might be issuing in Melbourne.'[74] George Bentley agreed to the proposal, and on 8 April 1876 Petherick passed along Robertson's 'great pleasure for the privilege of using your name, (i.e. Richard Bentley and Son) on the title page of any book he may issue, subject to conditions stipulated – that it shall be high class work, either Voyages or Travels or Works of Fiction, and desiring me to assure you that the privilege will not be used in any way that can passably be distasteful to you'.[75]

As part of their partnership, Robertson offered to protect Bentley's British copyright and protect against copyright infringement in the Australian colonies. In 1876, Bentley accused Robertson of an unauthorized reprinting of Annie Edwards' novel, *Leah: A Woman of Fashion*, for the Australian market, but Petherick insisted that his employer would not resort to piracy: 'Mr. Robertson has always defended the right of British publishers, frequently putting a stop to reprints in the local newspapers. I may add that he holds power of attorney for this purpose from some publishers – Notwithstanding the strong desire we have for cheap issues we like to get them legitimately.'[76] Bentley's accusation came during negotiations to permit Robertson to use the Bentley imprint and distribute Bentley's books in the colonies. Evidently, Bentley accepted Petherick's defence of Robertson, as less than a month later the British publisher agreed to the Melbourne firm using Bentley's imprint on some of Robertson's publications.[77]

Robertson's offer to defend the British firm's literary interests was put to the test in 1880 when Petherick informed the London publisher that one of Robertson's travellers had discovered American reprints of Bentley publications in a Christchurch, New Zealand bookshop.[78] Petherick also forwarded to Bentley Robertson's letter to the Collector of Customs in Christchurch, which protested the sale of New York publisher George Munro's Seaside Library in Richard Shannon's bookshop.[79] Munro's Seaside Library 'was a series of cheap quartos, often printed two or three columns to a page. Single volumes sold for ten cents.'[80] The series already 'dominated the [American] market' and Petherick, Robertson, and Bentley, as soon as he was informed of the incident, were concerned the cheap-priced series would leave Bentley and Robertson's more expensive Australian and colonial editions unsalable.

Robertson's letter to the Collector of Customs requested that Munro's reprints be confiscated:

> I need scarcely tell you that this is causing immense injury to honest traders as well as to publishers in England, who at considerable cost have secured the right of exclusive sale for their Editions in British Dominions, and whose right and interest in common with the Booksellers of New Zealand I respectfully ask you to protect by seizing the works complained of, or by taking other legal measures to prevent the said Richard Shannon, or any other person, from further infringing the law in this particular.[81]

The London publisher responded to Petherick's initial letter regarding the American pirated imprints by agreeing that Robertson would have to act for the British firm as 'whatever action is necessary will have to be taken on the spot'.[82] It was in Robertson's best interests to protect British copyright as he had exclusive agreements with British publishers, like Bentley, to distribute their editions in the Australian colonies. Therefore, Robertson's business would be undermined if illegal American reprints of British-copyrighted books were allowed free rein in the colonies. Moreover, Bentley had an agreement with Robertson to reprint up to 50,000 copies of Mrs Henry Wood's novels for the Australian market.[83] Consequently, once Robertson had agreements with British publishers to produce and distribute their books in the Australian colonies, there existed a '[m]utual commitment' between the British and Australian firms to protect the colonial market from interlopers.[84]

A further benefit of Robertson and Bentley's partnership was that when Robertson or another Australian firm published a work that interested the London house, but which Bentley did not want to take the risk of publishing in Britain, Robertson could have copies of the work shipped to Britain. For instance, when solicitor John McLeod informed Richard Bentley and Son about their author Marcus Clarke's death in 1881, he asked the publisher not only to 'furnish one ... with the fullest information in your power as to the business relations between the deceased and your firm' but also 'to ask if you will publish a memorial volume of extracts from the late M[arcus] C[larke]'s works'.[85] Bentley declined to publish a memorial edition of Clarke's essays, but agreed to accept between 80 and 100 copies of the books for the English market, which he asked McLeod to ship through Robertson.[86]

While Bentley had successfully produced inexpensive Australian editions of Mrs Henry Wood's novels, the firm generally believed the financial risk associated with producing colonial editions would not be offset by increased sales. In 1883, Clarke's literary executor, Hamilton Mackinnon, asked Richard Bentley and Son to produce an inexpensive Australian edition of *His Natural Life*, which Bentley had first published in 1875. In 1882, Bentley had printed 1000 copies of Clarke's novel, the first edition titled *For the Term of His Natural Life*, for sale at the regular price of six shillings. Mackinnon felt this price was a barrier to colonial sales and requested a cheaper edition be prepared for the colonies. However, the London publisher was opposed to the printing of an inexpensive edition of the novel.[87] Bentley preferred to produce jointly with Robertson one-volume Australian editions of books, such as *His Natural Life*, which were priced at six shillings. Also, if Bentley did not want to print the sheets of a book, he would offer the copyright and stereoplates of a book to Robertson, who could then print his own Australian editions of popular books. For example, in 1877, Bentley offered Robertson the stereotype plates and Australian copyright of Helen Mathers' *Cherry Ripe!* for 50 guineas. Added to the bottom of the letter was a note that stated, 'Bentley will not be making any two-shilling edition[s] of *Cherry Ripe!* – as you are aware we very seldom publish any works under 6/- in price.'[88] The London house did not want to run the risk of losing money if the colonial editions – which would often retail for around two shillings – did not sell in large enough quantities; the firm preferred to license the copyright of a book rather than publish their own cheap colonial edition.

George Bentley finally reconsidered the issue of an inexpensive colonial edition of the novel when Mackinnon and Clarke's widow threatened to ask an American publisher to reprint the novel for the Australian market.[89] On 24 June 1884, Bentley wrote:

> The matter of a cheap edition of 'His Natural Life' was carefully considered both with regards to Mrs. Clarke's interest and our own, and as there was, and still is a satisfactory sale of the more expensive form. It was not thought wise to jeopardize this by issuing the work in a less remunerative form ... Apart from this we have no bias in the matter, and in consequence of your letter [we] will consult Mr. Robertson on the subject, as his opinion, being on the spot would be of special value.[90]

In February 1885, Bentley further replied to Mackinnon that Robertson's advice had been that the sale of the low-priced edition would not be 'sufficiently great to compensate for the ... loss of "margin" involved in reducing a book from 6/- to 2/6'.[91] However, Robertson recognized that the threat of a cheap American edition flooding the Australian market must be countered and recommended the publication of an inexpensive edition of Clarke's novel. Bentley reluctantly agreed to produce jointly with Robertson a colonial edition of Clarke's novel.[92]

Bentley's concern about colonial editions being unnecessarily risky because of the slimmer profit/loss margin was allayed with the success of the cheap edition of *His Natural Life*. Moreover, Bentley's profitable partnership with Robertson eventually led to the British firm producing and Robertson distributing the low-priced Australian Library, which repackaged a number of books, including Clarke's novel, for which Bentley owned copyright. When American copies of Mrs Henry Wood's novels were found in a New Zealand bookshop in 1880, Petherick argued that the only way for their respective businesses to survive the scourge of piracy and stay competitive in an increasingly international marketplace was for the firms to produce, market, and distribute a cheap series of books for the colonies. Petherick complained about the lack of international copyright and that piracy damaged both the colonial and British book trades: 'For my part, I think the only cure for the present evil ... is in cheaper books. The so-called "Pirates" must be met upon their own ground.'[93] He asked: '[w]hat is there to forbid a 2/- or 2/6 edition of ... [a] popular work issued in heavy size and readable type?' The British publisher's own aversion to inexpensive editions and the failure of the firm's first colonial series, the Empire Library, published between 1878 and 1881, hindered the development of the Australian Library.[94] Only after repeated requests from Petherick, Robertson, and others and the successful sale of the cheap edition of Clarke's novel was Bentley willing to produce another colonial series.

The Australian Library was part of Bentley's second colonial series, 'entitled Special Editions for Colonial Circulation Only'. In contrast to the Empire Library, Bentley's colonial library series was expanded and reissued between the series' inception in 1885 and 1898. The series included national libraries created for and marketed to colonial readers. Further research is warranted to develop a list of all the books and individual national libraries that formed part of the series. However, research completed so far suggests that Bentley constructed a national library for Australians, going so far as to edit some of the books in the series to emphasize their Australian qualities. He also sold libraries in Canada, South Africa, and India that included colonial content, but the books in these collections were not edited. The initial Australian Library included Clarke's novel plus four other works: Caroline Leakey's *The Broad Arrow*; Arthur Nicols' *Wild Life and Adventure in the Australian*

Bush; Frederick Edward Maning's *Old New Zealand: A Tale of the Good Old Times, and a History of the War in the North against the Chief Heke*; and William Delisle Hay's *Brighter Britain: or Settler and Maori in Northern New Zealand*. The Australian Library, first referred to in a draft of a new publication catalogue for booksellers, was a list of 'Australian Books and Especial Australian Editions' to be offered for sale in 1887 and that Robertson would distribute in the Australian colonies.[95] Bentley accounts ledgers indicate that each of the Australian Library books had initial print runs of a minimum of 2000 copies, were reprinted in 1888 and 1892, and generally sold quite well in the Australian colonies.

The Australian Library was the last major venture Bentley collaborated on with Robertson. The first year the Library was published, Robertson downsized his London agency and his colonial distribution network, concentrating on his Australian bookselling operation. While Robertson continued as an Australian distributor for a few of Bentley's publications, Edward Petherick's Colonial Booksellers' Agency, which he established in 1887, acquired the volume of Bentley's Australian business.[96] In 1887, Petherick advertised the Australian Library in the *Circular*, a quarterly periodical issued in connection with the Colonial Booksellers' Agency, as Bentley's Series of 'Australian books by Australian writers' that were available at all bookstores, and, by 1888, Robertson's imprint had disappeared from Australian Library editions.[97]

While Robertson had Petherick primarily focused on establishing business transactions with British publishers between 1870 and 1887, Robertson also asked him to make arrangements with European publishers in order to streamline the export of books from Europe. In a letter to his father dated 24 January 1872, Petherick wrote: 'G.R. suggests the advisability of my taking a runner to Paris in order to open a few accounts with French publishers. So I hope before next writing to have had that pleasure trip.'[98] In a draft of his memoir Petherick referred to this business trip to Paris and other European cities to make arrangements with publishers, such as the French firm Hachette et Cie and the German company Tauchnitz: 'my travels include two or three short trips to Paris, and once upon a time I wandered through Belgium to Germany, as far as Berlin, Dresden and Leipzig, returning by the Rhine to Cologne'.[99] Four months after Petherick's initial trip to Paris, Robertson wrote to Petherick that the Australian 'trade are now beginning to understand that our supplies are more reasonable than of old and in consequence to buy more freely'.[100]

Moreover, Petherick expanded the sphere of operations of the London office to include accounts with American publishers. In a letter dated 11 June 1874, Petherick reported to his father that he had 'last year ... opened up ... important accounts [with publishers] in New York, Boston, and Philadelphia'.[101] By 1878, the firm was regularly importing books from the United States, though shipments would go through the London office and not directly to the colonies. Because of all the changes Petherick made when he took over the reins of the London office from William Robertson, and new contracts with British, European, and American publishers, Robertson had a regular supply of books for sale in his bookstores and that he distributed to other booksellers and book buyers throughout the Australasian region, which included Australia, New Zealand, Tasmania, and Fiji.

While Robertson was the principal Australian wholesaler between 1870 and 1887, Petherick feared that if the firm did not continue to develop its international contacts it would lose business to other firms. By the late 1880s some London publishers had 'agents resident in Australia' and British representatives took 'frequent trips' to the colonies.[102] The need for an independent colonial wholesale firm like Robertson's was diminishing, unless the firm could offer a wider array of texts at better prices than anyone else. In a letter to his father, dated 10 May 1877, Petherick forecast the increasing competition in the industry, and he argued that existing trade agreements with various European, British, and North American publishers were insufficient.[103] He wrote that on his return journey from his visit to his family that he was planning, he would travel via San Francisco and arrange to meet publishers and booksellers in the United States and Canada before returning to London:

> I might effect that on my way back, I shall have to go to America shortly and it will be convenient to return that way via San Francisco. Do these things startle you. I hope not. This is a wonderfully comprehensive business and a vast amount of trouble. Outsiders might say I wouldn't have anything to do with N. Z. or I would leave the American book alone – Well, we must do it. If we didn't get the American books direct, we should have to purchase them in London at 20% advance in cost price and then we couldn't compete with others – besides which we shall have to secure representation of American publishers who are now looking sharply toward Australia and sending supplies direct to Australian ports, as we shall have to do.

North America was, in Petherick's opinion, rapidly becoming an important book centre and the firm needed to take advantage of the possibilities in the fledgling trade between North America and Australia via the port of San Francisco, and the growing interest American publishers had in the Australian market. Petherick argued in the letter that it was imperative that the firm expand operations by establishing further agreements with the leading North American publishers. Moreover, Petherick explained to his father that 'the Americans are ahead of England in the production of books on the Industrial and Mechanical Arts and probably works on Manufacturing and Agriculture, and for a new country they are likely to be more suitable and practical than English books on similar subjects'. He acknowledged that United States publishers were producing non-fiction books more suitable to Australian consumers' tastes, and he argued that it was a bookseller's duty to provide the best possible books to the reading public. In order for the firm to both retain control of the Australian wholesale business and compete with the established publishing houses, like Macmillan, which were also 'looking sharply toward' colonial markets, Petherick believed Robertson had to continue expanding. He advised Robertson to import directly American books that could not claim British copyright and that were legal to sell in the colonies.

After visiting Melbourne in March 1878, Petherick crossed the Pacific to Honolulu and then to San Francisco, from where he travelled by 'rail to Chicago, Toronto, Boston to New York, Philadelphia and Washington', briefly visiting publishers in each city before returning to London in May of that year.[104] Unfortunately, no records have been found that detail which firms and individuals Petherick visited on his trip; the most revealing letters of Petherick's correspondence are those he wrote to his father before his trip, which describe his business relationship with George Robertson, his opinions on the state of the overseas book trade, and his belief that he was a central figure in the trade between Australia and the rest of the world. On 21 January 1874, after receiving a pay rise from Robertson, Petherick wrote to his father that 'Australians have seconded my efforts – they buy my books well, and seem to grow in confidence – Am I not conceited? Never under value yourself – nor think no one else can fill your place.'[105]

Petherick's father died shortly after Petherick first told him, in 1877, that a trip to North America would be necessary. Petherick did not mention the North American trip in any of his other surviving letters. However, it is clear that his business trip, in 1878, to the United States and Canada concerned gaining some measure of control over the anticipated flood of American imprints into the colonial market and directly exporting to Australia American books that had previously had to be ordered through London. However, Robertson failed to heed

Petherick's advice that the company needed to continue innovating, building on past successes, and expanding to include new markets.

In September 1876, Petherick learned from a mutual friend that Robertson wanted Petherick to partner with the Melbourne manager, Mr Bunney, and buy the company so that he could retire. Petherick was shocked and wrote to his father in January 1877 that his initial 'answer was I did not desire it … I was perfectly content to remain as I am, his humble servant.'[106] However, he added in the letter that he 'was not afraid of work: my capacity being almost unlimited, at least, I acknowledge no limit to my abilities'. Petherick asked his father to negotiate with Robertson and Bunney, reminding his father that 'this may be my opportunity'.[107] In 1878, Robertson withdrew his offer of partnership, because he had changed his mind about retiring and possibly because he did not agree with Petherick that the firm needed to continue developing and to be positioned as a transnational, rather than colonial, distributor in order to stay competitive. Petherick returned to Britain as manager of the London office, but he bitterly complained in his memoir that during his second term as manager, between 1878 and 1887, Robertson slowly wound down the distributing business, offering him a weak explanation that he 'could invest his money to better purpose'.[108] Finally, upon leaving the firm in 1887, Petherick established the Colonial Booksellers' Agency, which was financially backed by Bentley, Longman, Macmillan, and other London publishers who recognized, even if Robertson did not, the value of having a knowledgeable, ambitious distributing agent directing the overseas sales of their publications in the Australian colonies and elsewhere.

Increasingly, Petherick realized that this 'wonderfully comprehensive business' meant that those involved in the book trade needed to cooperate, as well as compete, on an international stage.[109] Even though Robertson was not the only wholesale supplier of British and European books, his company controlled a large proportion of the Australian wholesale business, and failure of publishers and authors to place their work with Robertson meant limited access to the Australian market, whereas a successful business arrangement with Robertson meant their book would find a place in bookshops throughout the Australian colonies. Consequently, by the late 1880s, British publishers, desiring a larger share of the booming Australian market, were offering their books, often deeply discounted, to the firm. In a January 1887 letter to Robertson, Swan Sonnenschein indicated: '[w]e should be very pleased if we could do more business with you during this new year. Would an offer on our part for 1000 juveniles … at our lowest possible quotation, meet with your probable acceptance?'[110]

As well, authors felt that their financial success depended upon their direct engagement of foreign and colonial wholesalers and distributors regarding the international sales of their books. Mary Francis Cusack, a nun who founded the Irish order Sisters of Peace and wrote both novels and histories of Ireland, expressed in 1880 her hopes that her new book that would be distributed by Robertson would 'have a <u>very</u> <u>large</u> sale in Australia'.[111]

Petherick's correspondence discloses that both publishers and authors were acutely aware of the advantage of placing their publications before Australian and international audiences and the role innovation and technology played in facilitating the expansion of the social network. Improvements in transportation and communication enabled new connections to be made and improved the speed of interconnectivity between agents in the network. John Holroyd observes: 'George Robertson was one of the earliest subscribers to the telephone exchange, which was then a private company. The number, 135, was used by the firm for many years after the telephone was installed in 1882.'[112] Robertson used the telephone and the telegraph to improve his ability to correspond with his employees and other agents, as well as to streamline book ordering and distribution processes. Phone calls could be made between Robertson's office and his printing factory, which were both in Melbourne. Robertson could send telegrams to Petherick in London ordering books, adjusting book orders, and setting the terms for negotiation regarding contracts with publishers and authors. However, technology was not a panacea and sometimes caused disruptions in the network as telegrams went missing, phone calls were dropped, and shipments were lost at sea.

Still, while Petherick admitted to his father that the business of books could be 'a vast amount of trouble', his correspondence suggests that he, along with other publishers and authors, felt that the financial benefits compensated for the frustration and problems that came with selling books internationally.[113] In a letter to the British Secretary of the General Post Office, dated 21 March 1882, Petherick noted the steady growth of Robertson's use of the Brindisi shipping route to send mail and parcels to the colonies between 1877 and 1881 and disclosed the considerable number of packages the firm had shipped during this period using this route, which did not account for the parcels sent by other means. Petherick reported that in 1877 he shipped 5871 packages, in 1878 the total number of packages exported rose to 6331, and by 1881 the number of packages sent out was 7087.[114] Petherick wrote that in total, between 1877 and 1881, the London office shipped to Australia and New Zealand by way of the Brindisi route approximately

32,000 parcels, '100 to 150 weekly', assessed at £15,000 'inclusive of postage £4000'. He was proud of the role he played in improving Robertson's business and he encouraged others to produce books for the potentially lucrative colonial and foreign markets. Moreover, in Petherick's personal and business correspondence he argued that the trade would be more inclined to enter international markets if they no longer considered the world as a vast geographical expanse but instead as a negotiable social network in which agents could exchange ideas and commodities.[115] However, he also stressed in his writing, even with the shrinking of distance, the need for the trade to continue working with Robertson and himself because of their depth of knowledge and experience in distributing books overseas.

3
Piracy, Copyright, and the International Book Trade

The fear of piracy was pervasive in the nineteenth century as publishers, authors, printers, and others felt that book piracy, or the reprinting of books without the consent of either the author or the publisher, was increasingly an acute problem. The rapid spread of this fear had a symbiotic and rhizomic relationship with the development of transnational copyright legislation, as well as with the growth of the international book trade in the nineteenth century. As the fear of book piracy spread, individuals and firms involved in the social network engaged with, discussed, and debated the effects of and solutions to this problem, and these interactions eventually resulted in the growth of the social network and the development of both professional associations and international copyright treaties, which further propelled the growth of a global print economy. However, diverging perspectives and opinions initially led to a period of competing practices between individuals, firms, and different sectors of the book trade. While certain individuals and firms fought book piracy, others within the book trade embraced the reprint industry and accepted it.

The term 'piracy' is problematic given that few international laws existed before the ratification of the Berne Convention (1886), and while a British publisher might describe an American imprint as illegal, '[t]here was, in law, no reason why any American publisher should seek permission to reprint a British book' before the ratification of the Chase Act in 1891.[1] Nevertheless, while the term 'book piracy' may be somewhat inaccurate, it is a useful heuristic term that characterizes how individuals felt about the practice of reprinting books without the permission of the author or publisher. John Feather argues that three factors stimulated the growth of book piracy of English-language books in the nineteenth century: 'First, the English language came to be more widely known on the continent, and more English people travelled there. This created a demand for English books in Germany, Italy and France, which was largely met by local printers reprinting fashionable English works.'[2] Secondly, the growing demand in the American market for British literature was large enough to validate reprinting British publications in the United States, and there was a rapid proliferation of unauthorized imprints in the 1830s 'as the American book trade tried to survive a depression which ravaged it as much as it did other parts of the American economy'.[3] Thirdly, while countries developed copyright laws that protected 'their own citizens' in the first half of the nineteenth century, not until much later in the century did a few countries enact laws that protected the rights of foreign authors in local markets.

While the pirates were predominantly described as American, piracy was not solely an American occupation. On the contrary, British, Australian, Canadian, Dutch, and many other publishers and printers of diverse nationalities also pirated books. For example, British publishers George Routledge and Richard Bentley were both 'equally unscrupulous in reprinting American books without permission'.[4] Still, in the British and colonial press, and in the business letters of British and Australian publishers, the pirates were typically described as Americans. In the American press, and in the business letters of American publishers, the culprits were portrayed more often than not as Canadian publishers and printers. A lack of any international laws and regulations governing the publication and distribution of books created a legal vacuum that allowed the reprinters, regardless of nationality, to operate with impunity, and common throughout the book trade was a fear that these usurpers would siphon off business and profits.

As publishers, authors, booksellers, and others in the book trade either confronted actual book piracy or worried about the spectre of foreign companies potentially flooding local markets with reprints, debate raged regarding the solution to this problem. While book trade agents devised different responses to book piracy, the overriding reaction was that the industry needed to cooperate at local, regional, and international levels in order to neutralize the threat. Moreover, reprinters also collaborated with others in the trade, and with politicians who supported the reprint industry, initially to hinder the development of an international copyright treaty, but eventually to secure concessions in national and international laws that would legalize reprinting, while compensating the owners of copyright. Thus, the various debates and divergent perspectives concerning book piracy and international copyright law generally led to increased cooperation among participants in the industry, and this increased collaboration within the social network supported the development of social, political, and economic associations that in turn propelled the growth of the international book trade.

This chapter examines three different branches of the social network and how the anxiety regarding book piracy and the lack of international copyright fostered cooperation among publishers, wholesalers, authors, booksellers, and others involved in the production and distribution of books. In 1855, William and George Robertson attempted to use the widespread fear of book piracy to pressure British publishers into developing the trade between Britain and the Australian colonies and into working with their colonial counterparts. In the 1870s, Canadian William Kirby tried to interest British, Canadian, and American publishers in his novel, *The Chien d'Or*, but issues surrounding book piracy and international copyright stymied Kirby's initial plans. The publishing history of Kirby's novel illustrates a different response to the fear of book piracy but another branch of the social network that also debated the effects of and cures for unauthorized reprinting. Finally, articles and letters from the American book trade periodical *The Publishers' Weekly*, from 1879, provide insight into another line of the social network and how book trade agents thought they could solve the problem, in the case of the American market, of Canadian book piracy. The correspondence of George E. Brett, who managed the New York office of Macmillan from 1869 to 1890, and his son George P. Brett, who replaced his father in 1890 as manager, provides an interesting counterpoint to the discussions in *The Publishers' Weekly* regarding copyright law and book piracy. Father and son struggled to carve out a space in the American market for Macmillan and devised ways to defeat both Canadian and American book pirates. Common to all three branches of the social network is both a fear of book piracy and a belief that cooperation between book trade agents, though the nature of the cooperation initially varied, was the only way for the industry to quash the threat. By the 1880s, agents increasingly defined cooperation in terms of transnational literary and industry associations that lobbied for international copyright law.

Before Britain ratified the Berne Convention in 1886, a patchwork of Imperial and Continental copyright laws existed that weakly protected British authors' and publishers' rights in Britain, the colonies, and some European nations. For example, the 1842 Imperial Copyright Act 'gave protection throughout the Empire to works first published in London or Edinburgh, and made provision for prohibiting unauthorized foreign reprints of British copyrights into British territory'.[5] While the

Act directed Customs officials to seize unauthorized reprints, Customs'
enforcement of the law was uneven, and American reprints of British
books continued to flow into British North America and other colonies.
Colonial booksellers lobbied British publishers to produce inexpensive
colonial editions that could compete against the American reprints, but
the only publisher who heeded their request was John Murray. Murray
produced his short-lived Colonial and Home Library, which consisted of
49 titles published between 1843 and 1849, as a substitute for the often
shoddily produced unauthorized reprints.[6] Still, the series was an unsuc-
cessful venture for Murray partially because of the competition the series
faced from the cheaper reprints that continued to flow into the British
colonies. Furthermore, British North American booksellers and politicians continually lobbied the British government to repeal the Imperial
Copyright Act until it was finally amended in 1847. Titled the Foreign
Reprints Act, the amendment to the Imperial Copyright Act legalized the
sale of unauthorized reprints in the colonies; this legalization negatively
affected sales of titles in Murray's Colonial and Home Library.[7]

The Foreign Reprints Act was principally influenced by the doctrine of
free trade. The Act allowed British colonies to pass laws that permitted
the relatively free circulation of reprints in the colonies and placed an
onus on the colonies to collect duties in order to compensate British publishers and authors for the violation of copyright. While British North
America quickly took advantage of the Act, other colonies, including
the Australian colonies, opted to remain under the auspices of the 1842
Imperial Copyright Act. The Australian colonies' distance from Britain
kept the flow of both authorized and unauthorized books to an irregular
trickle. While Wallace Kirsop cautions academics that '[w]hat is essential
is not remoteness from some metropolitan centre ... but sharing the
same language and cultural heritage', he acknowledges that the effect
of distance on the development of the Australian book trade cannot
be completely ignored.[8] In the 1840s and 1850s, book piracy was not a
problem in the Australian colonies because the colonies were too remote
for reprinters to easily sell their wares. Steep transportation and distribution costs quickly turned inexpensive reprints into expensive reprints
that were no cheaper than the authorized books. However, distance did
not isolate the Australian book trade from the fear of book piracy.

The British colonies found it impossible both to prevent the flow
of unauthorized reprints into the colonial markets, such as Africa and
India, that had not taken advantage of the 1847 Foreign Reprints Act
and to collect the revenue owed to British and colonial copyright
holders in the markets, such as British North America, that had taken

advantage of the Act. Reflecting these failures, reports indicated that the fear of book piracy was pervasive throughout the international book trade, especially in the British Empire in the mid nineteenth century. Moreover, this fear spread like a contagion and infected the social network. Still, both Wallace Kirsop and Brian Hubber argue, in their respective studies of book piracy in the nineteenth-century Australian market, that there were few documented accounts of American or foreign unauthorized reprints circulating in the colonies.[9] While it is possible that a few cases of book piracy might have gone undocumented in Australia in the period between 1850 and 1880, the interest of local and British media and the book trades in the issue suggests that any incidents of book piracy would surely have been documented. Consequently, Kirsop and Hubber contend that book piracy was not a problem in the Australian colonies.

If the actual threat of book piracy in the Australian colonies was negligible in the nineteenth century, especially when compared to the problem in the book trades in North America and in other parts of the British Empire, why were the few reported accounts of book piracy in colonies so heavily publicized? Enterprising booksellers and wholesalers purposely spread the fear of book piracy to mobilize both their industry and the British book trade into developing the trade between Britain and the colonies. Beginning in the mid nineteenth century, agents in the Australian book trade capitalized on the widespread fear of piracy in order to plant the seeds of panic in the British–Australian book trade. The danger of a foreign 'invasion' of the local colonial markets was inflated in order to cultivate the fear that the Australian market 'will be closed, and perhaps closed for ever, against English editions of many works'.[10] In particular, both William Robertson and George Robertson exaggerated the quantity of American and foreign unauthorized reprints circulating in Australia, and they tried to pressure British publishers into sending regular and inexpensive shipments of books and stationery to the colonies. Also, they positioned George Robertson's Melbourne firm as a business partner that would protect British publishers' interests in the Australian colonies and facilitate the sale of British books in the Australian market.

In a letter printed in the 27 January 1855 issue of *The Athenaeum*, William Robertson responded to a letter previously published in the literary journal by British author William Howitt, who had visited Australia and believed the market to be saturated with unauthorized foreign imprints of British books. William Robertson was the brother of Melbourne bookseller, publisher, and wholesaler George Robertson, and he agreed with Howitt that there was a problem with book piracy in the colonies. He also observed that if the circulation of unauthorized, inexpensive American imprints was allowed to go unchecked, British publishers, with their more expensive books, would be shut out of the growing Australian market: 'it is not to be expected that booksellers in Australia will continue to order English editions, if American editions are allowed to be imported for sale at half the price of the English editions. It is, doubtless, the fact that these American reprints have been introduced into Australia and advertised in the Australian papers; but it does not follow that this should continue.'[11] However, Robertson disagreed with Howitt's assertion that fighting the American literary pirates was pointless, and he argued that Australian Customs officials were ready 'to enforce the Copyright law'. Moreover, Robertson reported that a leading Melbourne bookseller, his brother, had 'advocated the rights of English publishers' in a published rebuttal to an editorial in a Melbourne newspaper that supported the sale of American reprints in the Australian colonies.

William Robertson's letter in *The Athenaeum* took advantage of Howitt's observations and attempted to propagate the contagious fear of book piracy, to affirm George Robertson's support of the British book trade, and to suggest that there was a market in the Australian colonies for inexpensive literature. William Robertson's letter not only portrayed his brother as the Australian defender of British copyright, but also warned the British book trade not to ignore the colonial market: 'if no remedy can be applied, and no law can prohibit, then will the Colonial bookseller, however reluctant, be forced to go into the sale of American reprints, and thus narrow his sale of English books'.[12] By drawing upon the British and colonial fear of the American reprint industry, William Robertson sought to deterritorialize and reterritorialize the discourse of book piracy in order to develop the network of book production and distribution between Britain and the Australian colonies.

In the 3 February 1855 issue of *The Athenaeum*, William Howitt responded to William Robertson's letter: 'It would be a very false security into which authors and publishers here would be lulled, if they received the impression which Mr. Robertson's letter is calculated to convey.'[13] Howitt implied that George Robertson was the Melbourne bookseller who sold unauthorized imprints: 'If then the very advocates of the law daily infringe it, – if the very champion of it against the newspaper press was, at the identical moment of his championship, selling such reprints, – how can we expect the Custom-House officers to be more consistent or rigorous?' Howitt argued that there was a large and growing population in Melbourne 'who will read, and who will have their reading cheap'. Howitt's letter did not damage William Robertson's argument; in fact, it confirmed that there was an influx of inexpensive American reprints into the colonial market that Australian readers were happy to purchase. Nonetheless, Howitt disagreed with Robertson's opinion that the Australian booksellers and Customs officials could stop the flow of pirated books into the colonies. Howitt believed that the Imperial Copyright Act was ineffective; Australian bookstores would persist in stocking unauthorized, cheap reprints of British books. Regardless, William Robertson argued that Australians were willing to abide by the copyright law and stop the reprints, if the British trade was willing to meet their demand for a regular supply of inexpensive literature.

In the 24 February 1855 issue, *The Athenaeum* published a sequence of letters between George Robertson and the Collector of Customs for the colony of Victoria. William Robertson submitted the correspondence to the British periodical as further proof that vigilance could stem the tide of foreign reprints of copyrighted works: 'The success which has attended the efforts made, both at Sydney and at Melbourne, to diminish and stop the evil complained of, will encourage the holders of copyright, and others having an interest in the subject, to carry out similar efforts in all our Colonies, either individually or in an organized capacity.'[14] In the first letter, dated 27 April 1854, Robertson wrote to the Melbourne-based Collector of Customs 'that American and German reprints of English copyright books are allowed to pass the Customs, and so obtain circulation in the Colony, although strictly prohibited by the Copyright law'. In a response dated 8 June 1854, a Customs official, Hugh C. E. Childers, promised to inform his officials of the law but argued that it was impractical to think that the existing Customs agents could entirely prevent the influx of unauthorized reprints. This series of letters left British readers with the impression that book piracy in the Australian colonies was a serious and growing problem that could not be entirely stopped by Customs, yet that the British book trade had a strong advocate in George Robertson.

However, the dire warning in *The Athenaeum* of an American invasion of the Australian market did not substantially increase the flow of books from Britain to the colonies. In the late 1850s, colonial booksellers stopped relying on British publishers' irregular shipments to the colonies, and they established London buying offices to buy books directly from British publishers. In 1857, George Robertson opened a London office, run by his brother William, that he hoped would facilitate the export of books to the Australian colonies. Between 1860 and 1887, Robertson also entered into business arrangements with various London firms in order to publish colonial editions for the Australian market; as part of these arrangements, Robertson offered to safeguard British copyright and protect against copyright infringement in the Australian colonies. In 1876, George Bentley accused Robertson of illegally reprinting Annie Edwards' novel, *Leah: A Woman of Fashion*, but Edward Petherick insisted his employer would not resort to piracy. He even offered to send Bentley copies of Robertson's published correspondence in the 1855 *Athenaeum* as proof that 'Mr. Robertson has always defended the right of British publishers'.[15] Bentley's accusation came during negotiations to permit Robertson to use the Bentley imprint and distribute Bentley's books in the colonies. Evidently, Bentley accepted Petherick's defence of Robertson, as less than a month later the British publisher agreed to work with the Melbourne firm.

Through his arrangement with Bentley, Robertson also offered to 'protect' the British firm's literary interests in the colonies against the 'breaches of British copyright by pirate American publishers'.[16] This offer was put to the test when, in a letter dated 12 July 1880, Petherick wrote to George Bentley that one of Robertson's travellers had discovered American reprints of Bentley publications, including a number of Mrs Henry Wood's novels, in a bookshop in Christchurch, New Zealand.[17] On 16 July 1880, Richard Bentley responded to Petherick's initial letter by agreeing that Robertson would have to act for the British firm as 'whatever action is necessary will have to be taken on the spot' to stop the sale of George Munro's Seaside Library series.[18] It was in Robertson's best interests to defend British copyright, as in turn his defence protected the firm's exclusive agreements with British publishers that he and his brother had fought to secure in 1855 with the publication of the letters in *The Athenaeum*.

Petherick wrote to Bentley in reply to the British publisher's query regarding the status of the New Zealand piracy case that 'I believe that the only course is to seize the books just in the same manner as it would be done in this country. No one can legally sell them, and anyone offering them for sale in New Zealand or any British Colony – Canada excepted – is liable to the same penalties as any London or Provincial bookseller.'[19] Canada could legally sell reprints because it had under the 1847 Foreign Reprints Act enacted legislation that allowed for the legal importation of reprints. Petherick complained about the lack of international copyright and argued that piracy damaged both the Australian and British book trades. He suggested that 'the only cure for the present evil' was for book trade agents to work together to produce legitimate inexpensive editions for the colonies and he suggested Bentley think about producing a colonial series of new books.[20]

Throughout the nineteenth century, British North American readers had access to American 'cheap pirated reprints of British books'.[21] While John Murray attempted to compete against the pirates with his Colonial and Home Library, British publishers could not match American prices; consequently, the British North American market was largely closed to British firms. The proximity of British North America to the United States meant any attempt on the colonial book trade's part to mount an effective campaign for inexpensive colonial editions of popular British books failed before it even started because 'aggressive [American] publishers turned out cheap pirated reprints of British books and periodicals, and these found thousands of ready buyers north of the border'.[22] However, Australia's distance from the United States insulated the Antipodes from the onslaught of illegal reprints circulating in British North America and other British colonies in the mid nineteenth century.

While distance initially protected the Australian book trade from book piracy – though the Robertson brothers and Howitt disagreed with this assertion – distance also left the colonial book trade without a regular supply of books to meet the growing demands of book-starved colonials. In the mid nineteenth century, Australian booksellers complained that when British publishers did irregularly dispatch consignments of books to the colonies, the shipments were made up of 'excess stock' of dubious quality.[23] Distance left British publishers unsure of and uninterested in the exact conditions of the Australian book trade. George and William Robertson capitalized on both the British book trade's lack of knowledge regarding the Australian book market and their fear of book piracy; in their letters in *The Athenaeum*, they made it seem as though the British book trade was about to lose another colonial market to the pirates, while simultaneously informing British publishers about the buoyant and book-starved colonies. As a result, their campaign for British publishers to increase shipments and to produce inexpensive colonial editions for the Australian market was somewhat successful. While British publishers did not start producing editions for the colonial market until the 1860s, and the irregularity of their shipments to the Australian colonies only moderately improved, the British book trade was willing to supply books when Australian booksellers and distributors, such as George Robertson, opened London offices in the late 1850s.

Once British and Australian firms began to cooperate in order to distribute British publications in Australia and to produce books especially for the colonial market, they needed to continue collaborating in order to protect their share of the Australian book trade. Therefore, when Robertson's traveller found American reprints of Bentley publications in New Zealand, Robertson had to protest the infringement of the British publisher's copyright as his arrangement with Bentley was at risk – as were his profits from the sale of the Bentley imprints – if American reprinters gained a foothold in the Australian market as they had in Canada. In 1880, the piracy of Bentley publications strengthened the bond between the colonial and British firms, as distance meant Bentley had to rely on his colonial counterpart to defend and protect his copyright.

The 1842 Imperial Copyright Act impeded the flow of illegal reprints into British North America, but it did not stop colonial readers who could not afford expensive British books from getting 'American reprints one way or another'.[24] British publishers, except for John Murray, were generally uninterested in issuing 'competitive cheap editions for colonial circulation' because of British North America's proximity to the United States: British publishers believed that colonial editions would fail to compete with the cheaper American reprints of British publications. The failure of John Murray's Colonial and Home Library bore out British publishers' suspicions that the small Canadian market was largely closed to them and that the Imperial Copyright Act had done little to stop the flow of American imprints into British North America. However, colonial readers and booksellers were threatened with a possible loss of their cheap editions if the British and colonial governments improved their capacity to detect American reprints crossing the Canadian border. Colonial politicians, booksellers, and the public lobbied the British government to repeal the Imperial Copyright Act. In 1846, the British government announced it would implement free trade policies, and this change in policy opened the way for an amendment of the 1842 Act. The 1847 Foreign Reprints Act allowed for the legal circulation of American reprints only in those British colonies that enacted legislation to administer a duty, 'which would then be paid to the copyright owner'.[25]

However, the Foreign Reprints Act was a failure in that 'no serious attempt was made to enforce it. British publishers received almost nothing, and cheap American reprints of British books were on sale throughout the British territories in North America'.[26] Moreover, the British House of Lords decided in 1868

> that where the 1842 Act had been suspended by an Order-in-Council under the 1847 Foreign Reprints Act, the copyright acquired by publication in that territory did not extend to the rest of the Empire ... the

effect of all of this was [that] American reprints of British books could be sold in Canada, and that British publishers could not even protect themselves by authorizing Canadian reprints of their own because that could undermine their rights elsewhere in the Empire.[27]

While colonial readers and booksellers benefited from the Foreign Reprints Act and from the influx of inexpensive American books, Canadian authors, publishers, and printers had difficulty surviving in a market where they could not easily compete against the cheaper American imprints. The structure for large-scale publishing and production did not exist in Canada until after Confederation in 1867, and even then a writer like William Kirby struggled throughout the 1870s and 1880s to find a Canadian, American, or British firm willing to publish his novel.[28] William Kirby wrote the novel *The Chien d'Or: A Legend of Quebec* or *The Golden Dog*, which was a historical romance set in eighteenth-century Quebec, while living in Niagara-on-the-Lake, where he was the editor of *The Niagara Mail*. Between January 1873 and May 1876, Kirby received a series of rejection letters from publishers that attest to his difficulty in getting the novel published not only because of its 678-page length and subject matter but also because of the problems created by the Foreign Reprints Act and a lack of international copyright law.

In a letter dated 8 July 1873, the Toronto firm of Adam, Stevenson, and Company offered to publish *The Chien d'Or*, which 'Professor Goldwyn Smith and Mr. A[dam] have been reading'.[29] However, the firm delayed the Canadian publication of the novel. Partners Graeme Mercer Adam and John Horace Stevenson believed that they needed to publish the novel jointly with a British house in order both to limit the Canadian firm's risk and to protect Kirby's copyright in Canada and in the rest of the British Empire. Despite Adam and Stevenson's actions to secure a British publisher for Kirby's novel, the manuscript did not receive a favourable response in Britain.[30] Kirby's own attempts to place the novel with a British or American publisher also ended in failure because 'works relating to Canada meet with such an unfavourable reception'.[31] A repeated complaint regarding Kirby's manuscript was that it would not interest a wider audience because it was 'peculiar to Canada'.[32] Even though Adam and Stevenson's believed the novel would find an audience within Canada, the firm 'was caught by the 1873 depression and went bankrupt in 1874', which left Kirby's novel without any publisher.[33]

Still, Adam personally believed *The Chien d'Or* deserved to be published and attempted to find either a Canadian or an American firm that would accept the novel. In a letter dated 12 July 1875, Adam wrote to Kirby that Canadian publisher George Maclean Rose had expressed interest in jointly publishing the novel with Adam.[34] However, Rose added that his firm would not take such a risk 'while trade is so paralysed' and asked Kirby to pay the production costs, if he wanted the novel published: 'The cost would be $1800.00 for an Edition of 2500, printing & binding.' Finally, in 1876 the American firm of Lovell, Adam, Wesson, and Company agreed to publish *The Chien d'Or*. However, the company's subsequent bankruptcy shortly after the publication of Kirby's novel would result in the stereotype plates of *The Chien d'Or* being sold as part of Lovell, Adam, Wesson, and Company's bankruptcy proceedings to an American reprinter. Still, before I examine the publication of *The Chien d'Or* by Lovell, Adam, Wesson, and Company, it is important to analyse the connection between the New York firm and Canadian publisher John Lovell.

Enterprising publishers like John Lovell challenged the American domination of the Canadian market in the 1870s by promoting a local reprint industry. A Montreal publisher, Lovell wanted to develop a reprint industry 'either by copying the American pirates or by arranging contracts with British authors and publishers'.[35] In 1872, Lovell built a printing plant at Rouse's Point, New York, and his son John W. Lovell was responsible for the day-to-day operations of the factory. Printing plates were made in Montreal and then shipped to Rouse's Point, which was 'about fifty miles south of Montreal'.[36] The unbound sheets would then be sent back to Canada for binding and eventual sale – with John Lovell paying the Foreign Reprints tariff, which 'was far less than the British copyright owners would have received had they contracted for a Canadian edition'.[37] Lovell planned to expand his business into the United States eventually, but his initial focus was simply aimed at demonstrating the injustice of the Foreign Reprints Act.

While John Lovell never officially expanded his firm to include selling his publications in the United States, he provided the initial financial backing for his son's New York reprint firm, Lovell, Adam, and Company. Moreover, the Montreal-based John Lovell Printing and Publishing Company continued to have a close business relationship with his son's reprint companies throughout the 1870s and 1880s.[38] John W. Lovell was a notorious New York reprint publisher: 'a business magnate, a "Svengali" in commerce, who was accused from time to time of piracy and sharp practice'.[39] In 1876, John W. Lovell started with friend Graeme Mercer Adam the New York publishing firm of Lovell, Adam, and Company, and the subsequent year Francis Wesson joined the firm. Lovell, Adam, Wesson, and Company specialized in inexpensive authorized and unauthorized editions of British books for the American market that were produced at the Rouse's Point printing facilities.

In a letter dated 5 October 1875, Adam suggested that John W. Lovell's firm might publish Kirby's novel, but he was waiting for news from 'Rouse's Point with reference to your project & hope to get away to see [John] W. Lovell at an early day'.[40] After an eight-month delay, Adam – who did not at first indicate he was one of Lovell's partners – wrote to Kirby that he had submitted the manuscript to 'a Montreal Gentleman of some literary competence who is to satisfy Mr. L[ovell] of the character of the work & who will also put the MS in some better shape than it now is in'.[41] The 'Montreal Gentleman', possibly Lovell's father, favourably received the novel and Lovell, Adam, Wesson, and Company published it in 1877.

In a letter dated 29 January 1877, Adam warned Kirby that '[n]ow comes the crisis – How will it sell, & how vigorously & successfully can it be pushed'.[42] Three months later, Robert Lovell, John W. Lovell's brother, noted the slow sales of the novel with 'small orders in Ontario'.[43] Also, he wrote to Kirby that the Dawson Brothers had sold only '50 copies in all so that I am afraid that your Quebec friends over-estimate the sale it is having there'. The Dawson Brothers were a Montreal publishing and bookselling firm that supplied the book trades in Quebec and the Maritimes; Robert Lovell's letter suggested the firm had not sold as many books in Quebec as Kirby had anticipated. While the novel initially had meagre sales, the actual crisis that occurred was that Kirby's novel had neither American nor Canadian copyright.

Kirby lost control of the novel's printing plates, which were owned by Lovell, Adam, Wesson, and Company, when the firm failed in November 1877: 'In the United States the work was protected inasmuch as the proprietor of the plates could control its distribution in both countries.'[44] Under the terms of the Canadian Copyright Act of 1875, 'the work of a person domiciled in Canada had to be registered here within a month of its publication in the United States', yet no one had registered *The Chien d'Or*. Meanwhile, John Lovell wrote to Kirby, on 2 April 1878, belatedly informing him that his son's firm was bankrupt and that Kirby's plates had fallen 'into the hands of the creditors. They are now offered for sale, and it is possible the holder would take $100 cash for them. I write to know if you would like to become the purchaser, even up to $200, if that amount be demanded. Should they fall into the hands of a Canadian you will, I believe, lose all right of royalty.'[45]

After receiving John Lovell's letter about his son's bankruptcy, Kirby had only a matter of days in April 1878 to make arrangements to buy his novel's printing plates. On 11 April 1878, John W. Lovell responded to Kirby's inquiry of 6 April about the stereotype plates by writing that one of the firm's creditors, Wesson's father, had already sold the plates to Richard Worthington.[46] Lovell informed Kirby that Worthington was a well-known New York reprint publisher of British and colonial books, and '[t]his publisher speaks of selling them to some one in Canada ... or if he publishes the book himself he will not pay any royalty nor will the parties he sells to'. Yet, because he still thought that 'the book will have a good sale', Lovell argued that Kirby should try to purchase the plates from the American reprinter. However, Kirby was unable to buy the plates from Worthington, who quickly reissued the novel with a new title page in 1878, and later in 1884 either sold or lent the printing plates to John W. Lovell so that Lovell could reissue the novel as part of his Library series.

In 1884, Graeme Mercer Adam recommended to Kirby that an inexpensive edition of *The Chien d'Or* be issued as part of a proposed Canadian Library.[47] However, Adam's continuing financial difficulties prevented the publication of the series. Still, Adam believed that an inexpensive edition of Kirby's novel was warranted, and he asked Lovell to reprint the novel. Lovell agreed and used Worthington's plates to produce a cheap edition under his new company's imprint, John W. Lovell Company, though he later wrote to Kirby that he would only pay him if the book made a profit.[48]

Kirby received no remuneration from the reprints issued by Worthington, Lovell, and other unauthorized persons.[49] However, in a letter dated 7 May 1885, his friend the Reverend William Withrow congratulated him on being pirated by Lovell: 'It is only a book that is worth stealing that is so stolen.'[50] Withrow contended that the unauthorized publication of Kirby's novel might not increase Kirby's monetary worth, but it would make his novel, and him, well known. Other Victorian authors also recognized that increased fame was a possible benefit of having a book pirated: the inexpensive issue might be distributed in new markets and lead to increased sales of authorized editions of future works. Withrow took an optimistic view of piracy, arguing that the upside of this scourge was that Kirby's novel might enjoy transnational circulation.

Still, in a letter to Richard Worthington, Kirby argued that the fundamental problem with pirated editions was a loss of authorial control of the text: 'It is useless for me to find fault with you for publishing my book nor can I prevent it ... What I want to say is that if you are going to continue the issue of it, I should like it for my own sake to be corrected. The work was got out ... in a hurry and was stereotyped without being revised and contains many ... errors.'[51] Moreover, the existence of pirated editions of *The Chien d'Or* made publishers leery of printing a new authorized version, as the more expensive publication would have to compete with the cheaper Lovell and Worthington imprints. In 1885, Alexander Macmillan politely refused to publish the book: 'Your publication in Canada & in the States has blurred these markets for us.'[52] The North American market was saturated with the inexpensive editions of *The Chien d'Or*. Piracy may have introduced Kirby to a larger audience, but weak and ineffectual copyright laws, as well as publisher misfortune and mismanagement, left him without control of his own novel.

In 1887, Canadian publisher Samuel Dawson lamented to William Kirby about 'the absence of international copyright. The best books are stolen' and the Canadian industry injured by the pirates.[53] While the Canadian reprinters managed to survive, and sometimes thrive, others in the Canadian book trade, especially authors, suffered. Moreover, the reprinters were viewed by Americans as threatening their industry and their right to export to Canada; consequently, editorials in the American newspapers and periodicals in the 1870s described a 'Canadian Invasion', and publishers such as J. W. Harper raised the possibility of retaliation.[54] In addition, British publishers often refused to sell to Canadian firms the rights to colonial editions because they did not want to antagonize the American firms 'by agreeing to Canadian reprints that would undoubtedly circulate (illegally) in the United States and probably find their way into the United Kingdom'.[55] Also, British authors declined to authorize Canadian reprints for fear that the Canadian editions would enter the American market. In a letter to Hunter Rose in 1872, Wilkie Collins reported '[a]s to your new [proposed] copyright act, we are furious about it here', and, in another letter dated 4 February 1875 and sent after the compromise Canadian Copyright Act was reached, he stated that he would be still 'compelled to abandon my Canadian rights' if they threatened the American sale of his novels.[56]

In 1872, the British government sought legal opinions on both Montreal publisher John Lovell's plan to ship unbound sheets from the Rouse's Point factory back into Canada, and the proposed revisions to the Canadian Copyright Act. While Lovell's actions were found to neither infringe on nor contravene the existing copyright laws, the legal opinion of the revised 1872 Canadian Copyright Act stated that it would negatively affect the British book trade: the Act would have reduced the existing 20 per cent duty to 12.5 per cent and licensed

Canadian publishers to reprint all British copyright works.[57] The law failed to receive Royal Assent, and even when a compromise Copyright Act was given Royal Assent in 1875, the new Act did not stop the flourishing American and Canadian reprint trades.

Between 1870 and 1890, when the reprinting industry in Canada and the United States expanded, various individuals and groups increasingly demanded the Canadian, American, and British governments to negotiate an international copyright treaty that would replace the Foreign Reprints Act and make book piracy illegal. However, Adam wrote to Kirby that he believed Canadians were 'indifferent to these [copyright] questions'.[58] While opinions varied widely on the potential effect of an international copyright law on the Canadian book trade, the flurry of letters and articles in Canadian journals suggested the trade was not 'indifferent' to the issue of copyright. For example, in a letter published in the November 1884 issue of *Books and Notions: Organ of The Book, Stationery and Fancy Goods Trades of Canada*, George Maclean Rose agreed with Graeme Mercer Adam's 'remarks in your last issue' that the existing copyright laws were unfair to the colonial book trade: 'After many years experience in the publishing business, I have come to the conclusion that it is almost useless to attempt building up a large and profitable publishing trade in our country ... As the British Copyright Act is at present understood and worked it is all one sided, that is, it gives the United States author and publisher entire possession of our markets.'[59] Rose expressed a sentiment, felt by a number of Canadian publishers, that the Foreign Reprints Act discriminated against the colonial book trade. Rose called for a renewed Imperial Copyright Act and a repeal of the Foreign Reprints Act of 1847, and he advocated for a protectionist policy that gave precedence to British and colonial literary products in the British and colonial markets.

The editorialist writing in the September 1880 issue of Goldwyn Smith's *The Bystander* agreed with Rose that 'Canada suffers with regard to the Copyright Question by the inability of the English trade to recognize her position in a country adjoining the United States and exposed to American competition, while her hands are tied by the English law.'[60] Nevertheless, the editorial welcomed free trade and also noted that change was inevitable in the North American book trades, particularly since 'the book question' or international copyright was perpetually before Congress in the United States: 'Unquestionably, the revolution will be great: ... we may be sure it will prove beneficent; it is the intellectual complement of political democracy: the invention of printing was the first great step, the cheap library is the second.'

Correspondence among the British Colonial Office, the British Board of Trade, and the government of Canada indicated that British publishers and authors also advocated the repeal of the Foreign Reprints Act and demanded international protection of British copyrighted works. London publishers Thomas Longman and John Murray suggested that the British government needed to secure the colonial markets for the British book trade: 'foreign reprints have been made in the United States, and the British Colonies in question have been flooded with them, to the serious damage of British authors and publishers, and the various trades'.[61] The British book trade was not necessarily protectionist; Longman and Murray wanted the British government – a proponent of free trade – to promote an international copyright agreement. However, they also wanted the British government to repeal the 1847 Foreign Reprints Act, and re-enact the 1842 Imperial Copyright Act, until such time as the United States agreed to a reciprocal copyright treaty. Fear of book piracy and the damage it was doing to the various trades fuelled the debate and interest in international copyright legislation.

When the International Literary Congress met in Vienna in 1881, members from Britain and other European countries, as well as observers from the United States, agreed that 'the most formidable obstacles in the way of a practical [copyright] result were the conflicting views and antagonistic interests of British and American publishers'.[62] Even though Britain lost its productive advantage towards the end of the nineteenth century, it was still committed to the policy of free trade '[yet] Germany and the United States which ... [were] becoming more advanced in production remain[ed] protectionist rather than embracing free trade'.[63] Traditionally, the American book trade was opposed to extending domestic copyright to foreign nationals; in particular, the manufacturing sector argued that extending copyright would destroy the local print, paper, and ink-making industries.[64] Nevertheless, the fear of piracy made typically protectionist industries, like the German and American book trades, more receptive to the development of international copyright law. For example, the *New York Times* reported that the German delegation at the Congress supported an international copyright treaty as 'they [currently] suffered on account of the unauthorized reproduction of German books in the United States'.[65] Also, the article noted that '[h]appily, public opinion in America now showed a marked improvement' towards the need for the United States to take part in an international copyright convention. One reason for this 'marked improvement' was the mounting anxiety of American publishers who 'were horror-stricken at the enormity of Canadian wickedness'.[66]

In the 1870s and 1880s a number of anti-Canadian articles were published in the American book trade periodical *The Publishers' Weekly* that denounced the Canadian reprint industry. For example, American publisher George Putnam argued in the 22 March 1879 issue of *The Publishers' Weekly* that '[a] very considerable business in cheap reprints has also sprung up in Toronto, from which point are circulated throughout the Western States cheap editions of English works for the "advance sheets" and "American market" of which Eastern publishers have paid liberal prices'.[67] According to Putnam, 'enterprising Canadian dealers' were also sending reprints to American customers through the mail. The United States and Canada ratified the Universal Postal Union (UPU) treaty in 1878, and, under the terms of the UPU, books mailed across the US–Canada border could be taxed but 'could not be prohibited'.[68] The American book trade was uncertain about the ratification of the UPU; letters in *The Publishers' Weekly* indicated some within the trade thought the law would end the 'smuggling through the mails' of books, while others thought it would have little effect in stopping the Canadian pirates.[69] The United States imposed a 25 per cent duty on imported books, but as Putnam noted in his article Canadian booksellers and publishers circumvented this duty, before and after the UPU, by sending books to the United States through the mail service. While the United States government levied duties on parcels in 1879, the government found the suppression of book imports difficult. As a result, Putnam and others in the American book trade believed that their market was being permeated with Canadian reprints and that they were the aggrieved victims of book piracy.

Both the threat of Canadian imprints on the American market and the problem of copyright were also issues repeatedly discussed in Macmillan's New York manager George E. Brett's correspondence. In a letter in 1885 to Frederick Macmillan, Brett wrote about the British office shipping a new work recently published in Britain directly to Canada in order to avoid paying 'the New York Duties and Charges'.[70] However, he observed that the problem with Macmillan supplying the Canadian market 'is that the book will be reprinted in Canada in that 10% understanding which, it is understood, neither Publisher nor Author ever gets. In the meantime our object must be to render a Reprint needless.' While some Canadian publishers circumvented the law by printing books in the United States, shipping them back to Canada to be bound, and paying the Foreign Reprints tariff, other Canadian publishers flouted copyright law and issued unauthorized editions of British books within Canada. Brett was concerned that a Canadian publisher might reissue Macmillan's publications and promise to pay a tariff that Brett noted rarely reached the owners of copyright. His solution to the problem was to make the pirating of Macmillan publications a futile endeavour. Consequently, Brett sought to secure Canadian and Imperial Copyright on works published by Macmillan. For example, he registered two works by Tennyson in 1885 with the help of the Dawson Brothers in Canada.[71] Brett made use of the 1875 Canadian Copyright Act, which 'extended Canadian copyright protection to works registered, printed, and published in Canada, even though the plates could be made elsewhere'.[72] He reported to Frederick Macmillan that he had secured the help of the Dawson Brothers and planned to warn the 'Canadian trade that we [Macmillan] shall take whatever steps are necessary to protect our interests'.[73] Despite Brett's actions to secure Canadian copyright of Macmillan's publications, existing copyright laws did not entirely protect the firm's works. In 1888, Brett wrote to Frederick Macmillan that 'Canadians have a notion of not being left out in the cold as regards cheap literature.'[74] His comment came in reference to the reprinting of one of their publications, W. E. Norris' *Chris*, by the National Publishing Company of Toronto. Brett could not believe that the Toronto firm could make a profit, considering the cost of producing the book, if they sold it for only 30 cents: 'one does not quite see how they can manufacture and sell 30 cent books at a profit unless indeed they can print without regard to copyright'.[75]

In its 12 April 1879 issue, *The Publishers' Weekly* noted that the Canadian trade was 'engaged in making the most of their opportunity in the United States market'.[76] According to the journal, Canadian publishers and printers 'put themselves outside the pale of the courtesy of the trade', which was the informal practice of paying token amounts to reprint books. Moreover, the article warned that 'whatever is to be said of ordinary "cut-throat" competition, American dealers cannot afford and ought not to give encouragement to publishers who seek by questionable practices to break down the business of houses on this side who are known to do business squarely and fairly'. In 1879, a number of articles critical of Canadian book piracy and of American firms buying unauthorized Canadian reprints appeared in *The Publishers' Weekly* at the same time as George Putnam's four-part series in support of an international copyright treaty. While the existence of a Canadian reprint industry was not the only reason why an increasing number of American publishers and authors supported international copyright, the uproar over Canadian pirates invading the American market with reprints of British and American books strengthened Putnam's argument that the

United States needed a reciprocal copyright agreement in order to protect both the American market and American authors.

In a letter to the editor in the 19 April 1879 issue of *The Publishers' Weekly*, John W. Lovell responded to the 12 April article. He regarded it as a thinly disguised attack on his publishing practices: 'I must presume that I am the person alluded to, and that your remarks upon Canadian publishers are intended to apply to me also.'[77] While he agreed that the comments levelled at the Canadian reprint industry 'may be just', he added: 'I think American publishers are fully able to meet any such competition without the necessity of attacking the personal character of their opponents.' Moreover, he wrote that he felt it 'almost criminal negligence to attack the character of any one in the manner you have done in my case when, by very little inquiry, you could have so easily ascertained the true particulars'. Lovell identified himself '[a]s an American publisher and an American manufacturer' – distancing himself from his Canadian origins – who employed a large number of Americans in his current reprint publishing firm, the John W. Lovell Company.

Lovell was one of the more prominent reprint publishers. He was infamous for not paying foreign authors for American imprints of their books. He was also accused of pirating American-copyrighted books, and participating – along with other publishers of inexpensive reprints – in a race to provide the cheapest literature possible. For example, in their advertisement in the 18 December 1880 issue of *The Publishers' Weekly*, Boston publishers Estes and Lauriat included a caution to the public and the trade against buying Lovell's unauthorized imprint of the *Chatterbox* series of books, which was 'a close imitation of the original, and well calculated to deceive'.[78] The series was originally published in Britain by James Johnston, who had authorized the Estes and Lauriat's American reprint. The *Chatterbox* case eventually wound up in the United States Circuit Court, where, in 1884, Lovell won the case because British authors could not transfer their copyright to an American firm.[79] Lovell's actions were not that unusual, as more established American publishers also printed rival editions of books that British authors and publishers had previously authorized other American firms to produce. For example, in a letter dated 16 May 1881, George Bentley wrote to Harper Brothers, objecting to the New York company's reprinting of a Bentley publication that the British firm had contracted Scribner to publish in the United States: 'I am not foolish enough to expect you to consider me beyond the bare possibility that you may desire pleasant relations with a house with which you may someday wish to do business.'[80]

George Brett and others in the book trade viewed Lovell and the entire American reprint industry as another constraint on the growth of the American and international book trades, and – to a certain degree – a larger problem than the Canadian reprint industry. The race to supply the cheapest books meant that a number of American reprinters were selling books for less than the cost of publication; the only way to recoup their initial expenses and realize any profit was sales by reprinters of substantial quantities of their publications. As a result, the North American market was awash with inexpensive books, and the overabundance of cheap reprints curtailed the sales of other American, British, and Canadian publishers' titles. For example, in 1885, Brett wrote to Macmillan that he must be 'as much mortified as myself' at Richard Worthington's 'pirated editions of "Alice" and "Looking Glass"'.[81] Brett could not understand how Worthington could publish Lewis Carroll's novels so inexpensively. He devoted much of his correspondence to Macmillan outlining plans and schemes to defeat the pirates, including buying up and securing the stereotype plates; consequently, he suggested that the firm must quickly 'get possession of ... [Lewis Carroll's] Plates at a low price'.[82] Unauthorized, cheap reprints enraged authors and publishers on both sides of the Atlantic, and Brett was not alone in his protestations against book piracy.

In February 1879, *The Publishers' Weekly* asked its readers five questions in relation to George Putnam's four-part series on international copyright:

1. Do you favor International Copyright?
2. What plan seems to you most practical in view of all interests concerned?
3. What method of accomplishing this plan seems most feasible?
4. Can you (if author) estimate sales of your works abroad, and your loss for want of International Copyright?
5. Can you suggest any desirable changes in the domestic copyright law?[83]

Over the course of the year, responses of authors, booksellers, and publishers were printed in the journal. Generally, the majority of respondents supported some type of international copyright; however, there was little consensus concerning the form of the law, the definition of copyright, and the method of implementing international copyright. For example, in February 1879, J. B. Lippincott wrote that he supported international copyright 'providing there be introduced therein the all-important condition that all copies sold here of works protected by such a law be manufactured entirely in this country'.[84] In contrast to the Philadelphian publisher's opinion, New York publisher G. W. Carleton argued in the same issue that an international copyright law should include '[a] universal, absolute right and control, through the world, to eternity, of the author's brain-work to the author, his heirs, executors, and assigns'.[85]

Also, a number of authors wrote about how an international copyright law would help protect their intellectual property from piracy. In answer to question four, in the 22 February 1879 issue of *The Publishers' Weekly*, Joseph Cooke observed that '[s]ome 40,000 or 50,000 copies of two editions of the "Boston Monday Lectures" have been sold abroad'.[86] Other authors wrote about 'courtesy of the trade' and how the foreign reprinting of their books earned them token payments that did not compensate them fairly for their books. In the 19 March 1879 issue of *The Publishers' Weekly*, John Habberton wrote that '[a]t least nine different firms in England and Scotland [have] reprinted my "Helen's Babies," and between them sold more than a quarter of a million copies of the shilling editions before 1878 ... The book was translated into German, French, and Italian ... Two Australian houses reprinted the book, and two in Canada, but without any remuneration to the author.'[87] The *New York Herald* drama critic, Habberton noted that while a couple of foreign firms offered token or 'courtesy' payments, of the 'twenty foreign editions of which I know ... have sold at least half a million copies, and I have received for all of them rather less than $200'. Authors agreed that 'courtesy of the trade' was only sporadically practised and that an international copyright law was essential if they were to get their monetary due in terms of the foreign sales of their works.

John W. Lovell argued that only established and well-off firms could afford 'courtesy of the trade', and in his own experience '[g]o in heartily for the "courtesy of the trade" and – starve'.[88] Even Lovell believed the United States needed to take part in an international copyright treaty, though he contended that the American print manufacturing industry must be protected at all costs. Lovell promoted a royalty scheme – similar in nature to the Imperial Reprints Act – that allowed firms to reprint any books, as long as the holder of copyright received a royalty for that publication. However, Lovell's royalty scheme was generally dismissed by the trade.[89]

The 'Canadian incursion' into the American market and the American reprint industry incited many within a trade that previously had been very protectionist to reconsider the issue of international copyright.

In 1886, Britain, France, Germany, Belgium, Spain, Italy, Switzerland, Liberia, Tunis, and Haiti signed the Berne Convention, which was a reciprocal copyright treaty that guaranteed signatories of the Convention would abide by each other's copyright Acts. However, the American delegation refused to sign the treaty, and '[t]he exclusion of the United States from the Berne Convention ... [further] provoked some American authors and publishers into action'.[90] For example, George Putnam helped to found the American Copyright League in 1883 and the American Publishers' Copyright League in 1887; both organizations lobbied the American government for copyright reform. In particular, Putnam was interested in a reciprocal copyright agreement between the United States and Britain, as well as other nations.

George Brett's correspondence documented the repeated attempts in the 1880s to get a new American copyright law passed, and the negative consequences for British firms when the United States failed to sign the Berne Convention. In a letter dated 23 October 1885, Brett wrote to Macmillan that he feared the firm's American business would not expand until the 'Copyright question is settled and that seems as far off as ever'.[91] However, he was somewhat more optimistic in February 1888 when he mentioned a conference in Philadelphia that was reconsidering the issue of international copyright.[92] Despite Brett's confidence that the United States would eventually sign the Berne Convention, he developed various coping strategies to deal with the Canadian and American reprint publishers, and a lack of international copyright, during his tenure as Macmillan's New York manager. For example, he utilized new technologies, including developments in transportation, to outwit the reprinters. In 1870, he asked the firm to send printing plates by the fastest ships so they could keep 'the field to ourselves'.[93]

Brett died in 1890 and his son George P. Brett took over as manager of the New York agency and became a resident partner in Macmillan.[94] He continued his father's actions in battling the reprinters. George E. Brett, George P. Brett, and Frederick Macmillan frequently used the telegraph to transmit book orders and communicate with each other.[95] However, reprinters also used the telegraph to ascertain what books were popular and merited reprinting. When technology did not give the firm an edge over the pirates, George P. Brett devised other schemes to outwit the pirates. For example, in 1890, he wrote to Frederick Macmillan about the possibility of Rudyard Kipling co-authoring a book with an American writer: 'I suppose Mr. Kipling would not like to publish this book with an American Author as Collaborator, who might indeed be only a hack writer, and whose name would be of use simply on account of it carrying the copyright. There will be so many reprints of the book that it would be a source of great satisfaction to me, if not to the author, to out do the "pirates".'[96] The book in question was Kipling's *The Naulahka: A Story of West and East*, which he co-authored with American Wolcott Balestier.[97] Brett's plan was for Balestier to register for American copyright and Kipling to register for British copyright; thereby Macmillan's publication would be protected in both the British and colonial markets, and in the United States. However, Balestier was John W. Lovell's London agent and friend; consequently, Macmillan worried that Lovell might get an advance copy of *Naulahka*. In April 1892, Frederick Macmillan wrote to George P. Brett reminding him that if 'Lovell does anything in the way of piracy' the firm would need to exercise their legal rights.[98]

In 1890, George P. Brett wrote to Macmillan that '[t]he Secretary of the copyright league tells me that a majority can be counted in both houses in favour of the international copyright bill'.[99] The Chase Act (1891) protected the work of non-resident authors; however, in order 'to claim copyright protection in the United States, a book had to [be] published there no later than it was published in its country of origin. Secondly, it had to be printed in the United States, or printed from type set in the United States or from plates made from type set in the United States.'[100] While Brett's letters to Macmillan expressed pleasure that the new law existed, he also expressed frustration that the publication of a book now needed to be synchronized in Britain and the United States.[101]

In the late nineteenth century, anxiety and fear of book piracy were common emotions expressed both in American trade periodicals, and in George E. Brett's and George P. Brett's correspondence. Reflecting the growth of a social network, the escalation of this fear initially stimulated the debate surrounding American copyright laws and made publishers apprehensive about their firms' survival. Eventually, the growing concern with book piracy and the reprint trade coalesced into organized movements and organizations such as the American Copyright League and the American Publishers' Copyright League. Further reflecting this concern with piracy, the United States passed the Chase Act in 1891 and finally joined the Berne Convention in 1896. Also in that year, at a meeting of different national publishers' associations and publishers discussing international copyright in Paris, the International Publishers Association was established to defend existing national and international copyright laws and to lobby on the international stage for further copyright laws and treaties, which in turn supported the growth of the international book trade.

Throughout the second half of the nineteenth century, British, American, Canadian, colonial, and other book trades struggled with the problem of book piracy. In September 1890, an article in the journal of the Society of Authors, *The Author*, suggested that book piracy was still a problem in the British colonies even after Britain's adoption of the Berne Convention in 1886.[102] The anonymous article in *The Author* reviewed the responses to a Society of Authors' survey of 'prominent book-sellers in our various Colonies', regarding 'how much the author is at present injured by these reprints, which are mostly American, and how far anything could be done to prevent injury'. The survey of booksellers revealed that unauthorized editions of British and colonial books were imported freely into Penang, Singapore, Africa, 'India, and into British Guiana ... In some colonies, what legal protection the law affords, is enforced, and in some it is not.'[103] However, the article claimed that book piracy did not threaten 'to any extent ... Australia or New Zealand', as both international and imperial copyright law was particularly enforced in the Australian colonial market.

Still, book piracy continued to be a problem in other colonial markets. For example, in South Africa unauthorized reprints were 'openly exposed for sale: it was not so very long ago there was a book-seller in Cape Town who had his windows simply swamped with these pirated American books'.[104] Moreover, according to the article in *The Author*, colonial booksellers agreed with Edward Petherick 'that the most certain remedy imaginable would be to issue cheap authorized editions for the Colonial market'. The article recommended that the British government and Colonial office take steps to prevent such widespread robbery by enforcing existing copyright laws and by negotiating further copyright treaties with countries like the United States. The Society of Authors believed that the British book trade, in particular 'English authors[,] ought to secure a better hold on this enormous market'.[105]

Authors, publishers, wholesalers, booksellers, and others involved in the international book trade were anxious about the effect of piracy on the book industry. This pervasive fear was common to all the major developed and developing nineteenth-century book trades. Moreover, as the panic surrounding book piracy circulated and grew, the fear of book piracy was deterritorialized and reterritorialized. Importing this fear into a market historically unaffected by the scourge of book piracy, William Robertson and George Robertson drew on the experiences of other colonial and foreign book trades, used the discourse surrounding the issue, and overestimated the few cases of book piracy in order to create the perception that piracy was a serious problem in the Australian colonies.

In 1855, William Robertson's and George Robertson's public protest against book piracy in *The Athenaeum* drew attention to the increasing demand for literature in the Australian market that outstripped the existing supply of books from Britain. Consequently, William Robertson warned British publishers that if they did not increase the supply of books, the Australian trade would have to find books elsewhere. The brothers manipulated the fears of British publishers – who were already largely shut out of the Canadian market because of piracy – that they would once again lose access to a potentially lucrative market.

The international trade in English-language books developed in tandem with the growth of book piracy in the nineteenth century. On the one hand, the reprinters had a dampening effect on the growth of the international book trade as some publishers gave up on markets such as Canada that they felt were awash in unauthorized editions. On the other hand, book piracy stimulated the development of a global book economy by bringing cheap literature to the masses and leading to debate regarding potential inoculations or cures for this illness, including international copyright law. In Canada, the proximity of the American reprinters to the Canadian market, and of the Canadian reprinters to the American market, also led to fierce transnational competition in the nineteenth century between reprint publishers to produce inexpensive books for the North American market. The destructive actions of reprint firms caused a number of individuals on both sides of the border to reassess their trade's protectionist stance. Like-minded individuals in both the Canadian and American book trades cooperated and lobbied for an international copyright agreement and for the reformation of the Canadian and American domestic copyright laws. However, other individuals welcomed the reprinters and fought against any further attempts to regulate the book trade. Regardless, the increasing anxiety regarding book piracy in the North American market had a transformative effect on the entire industry.

While piracy caused some firms to entrench and focus on protecting their established markets, other firms expanded their business networks in an effort to combat decreasing sales by entering new markets and entering into new partnerships and business arrangements. Thus, as the reprinters sought out new markets and the fear of book piracy spread around the world – both aided by developments in communication and transportation – the reprint industry's actions in turn also spurred the growth of the social network. The fear of reprinters destroying local, developing book trades further encouraged cooperation among individuals, who in turn supported both the development of international copyright law and the growth of the international book trade. Moreover, publishers, authors, booksellers, and others lobbied the different levels of government for protection against what many felt was a scourge that would, if unchecked, destroy the existing book trades. Eventually, informal networks developed into formal national organizations like the American Publishers' Copyright League and the Society of Authors. These organizations lobbied for copyright reform on both the local and international stages. By the late nineteenth century, national organizations united to form international associations like the International Publishers Association that encouraged both countries to join the Berne Convention and the development of new international copyright treaties, which in turn supported the expansion of the international book trade.

4
The International Book Trade

In 1855, William Robertson's and George Robertson's respective letters in *The Athenaeum* drew attention to the increasing colonial and foreign demand for English-language books that exceeded the sporadic supply from British publishers. George Robertson and others in the Australian and colonial book trades wanted publishers to send regular and inexpensive shipments of books and texts to the colonies. When the brothers' correspondence did not produce the desired results, George Robertson sent William to London to open a distribution office in 1857. Twenty-four years after the launch of the branch, which would help to pioneer transnational distribution routes between Britain and the Australian colonies, Robertson's *Book Circular* would report the ready availability of British books at British prices for the colonial reading public, as well as colonial editions and Australian publications. Moreover, the *Book Circular*'s 'Literary Notes' would allude to the development of the international trade beyond the colonial sphere with the recent publication and translation of Augustus Mongredien's essay on 'Free Trade and English Commerce' for Japanese readers interested in trade with Britain and its colonies: '[it] is now on sale throughout Japan at a very low price'.[1] By 1881, publishers, including Cassell who published Mongredien's essay, were supplying colonial and foreign markets like Japan with English-language and translated works.

Edward Petherick credited his employer's efforts in 1855 and the opening of the London distribution agency for galvanizing publishers into supplying Australia's growing demand for books and spurring on the expansion of the international book trade.[2] Petherick implied that Robertson's actions had a domino effect on the book trade as publishers by the 1880s realized that large profits could be made supplying not only colonial but also foreign book buyers. While the increase in trade between Britain and the Australian colonies certainly led to the further development of the transnational print economy, Petherick's boast must be viewed in the context of a loyal employee who was very much aware that Robertson was not the first colonial bookseller to demand a regular supply of books and that other markets, particularly in India and the United States, had attracted the attention of British and European publishers in the first half of the nineteenth century. The Australian colonies, India, and the United States were all markets that were part of the larger international book trade. Robertson and Petherick contributed to the formation of the social network but so did other agents, who distributed and sold books in India and the United States long before the book boom in the Australian colonies.

The Indian market for British books developed in the late eighteenth and early nineteenth centuries as a consequence of literacy and reading being seen as tools that could be used by the British to prompt Indians to support the East India Company.[3] English-language books were used to teach Indians to value and crave British manufactured goods and to respect British culture. As a result, throughout the nineteenth century there was an escalating demand for textbooks, as well as general fiction and non-fiction, for use in Indian schools and homes. By the 1840s 'enterprising publishers' like John Murray 'awoke to the realisation that there was a lucrative market waiting to be developed among generations of English-educated Indian readers who clamoured after new fiction titles'.[4] Even then, Murray's Colonial and Home Library was a dismal failure for the publisher who stopped adding to the series in 1849. While Macmillan and other British publishers enjoyed a 'brisk trade' supplying Indian booksellers like Thacker, and Macmillan would in the preceding decades lay 'the ground work for ... a successful business enterprise in India', it was not until the 1870s and 1880s that the British houses would once again turn their attention to developing series for the Indian and colonial markets.[5] Generally, London publishers believed that the potential monetary return from the international sale of English-language books would be insufficient to cover the costs of shipping and distributing books overseas and there was little profit to be had in publishing books specifically for colonial and foreign markets.

While British firms were reticent to produce books for overseas markets, there was a vibrant transatlantic book trade in the nineteenth century that Michael Winship contends underwent 'tremendous, even exponential, growth ... [in] exports from Britain and imports into the United States'.[6] However, the related problems of book piracy and the lack of international copyright law stymied the growth of this transatlantic trade. Still, the common irritant of book piracy did not stop commerce; instead, it led to British and American firms working together to protect their interests in both markets. For example, Macmillan and Bentley allied with their American counterparts to quash reprinters, such as Canadian John Lovell and later his New York-based son John W. Lovell, who offered inexpensive unauthorized versions of their British and American competitors' publications.[7] While British publishers established partnerships with American firms to combat book piracy and to reprint British books and texts for the American market, supplied the Indian market, and pursued opportunities in Europe, British houses still showed little interest in other international markets until enterprising booksellers like Robertson demonstrated the viability and profitability in supplying overseas book buyers not in a piecemeal fashion but as an important segment of the books trade overall.

Frustrated by the inconsistent supply of books, George Robertson opened a London agency to facilitate the regular shipment of books between Britain and the Australian colonies in 1857. During the 1870s and 1880s when Edward Petherick was Robertson's London manager, the firm made a 'handsome profit' as the business was buoyed by a rapidly expanding Australian reading public who demanded a regular supply of inexpensive English-language fiction and non-fiction.[8] In the nineteenth century, reading was central to both English and colonial culture and society 'as a process of communication and as a social and leisure activity. As an activity, accomplishment or ambition, the reading and possession of books were seen to reflect literary taste, respectability and social rank.'[9] Australian colonists regarded the practice of reading particularly as 'central to [an] ... objective of cultural advancement'. The introduction of universal education programmes in the colonies also increased the demand for books and the pressure on Robertson to supply both the Australian public and the Australian school system.[10] Petherick recounted in a letter to the British Secretary of the General Post Office the hundreds of packages the London office would ship to the colonies weekly in order to try and meet this escalating demand for books.[11] As the firm increased its book orders, British publishers awoke to the potential of this market and the importance of working with Robertson who 'was probably the single most important influence in determining what books were supplied to Australian readers'.[12]

Moreover, by the 1880s Petherick and Robertson had taken advantage of improvements in communication and transportation technology to develop their distribution network that disbursed books throughout the Australasian region. The firm also occasionally shipped colonial publications to British and European book buyers. Furthermore, Petherick wanted to develop Robertson's company from primarily a colonial bookseller and distributor that irregularly supplied other markets into a transnational company that regularly supplied the international marketplace. A publisher's successful business arrangement with Petherick and Robertson meant their books could be distributed throughout the Australasian region and possibly further afield. As a result of Robertson's success with his London agency and the rapid growth of his colonial business, British publishers like Bentley and Macmillan became more interested in supplying the Australian colonies and other underserviced markets. However, it is important to stress that Robertson and Petherick were not alone and their actions were representative of other agents in the social network; as the British–Indian and the transatlantic book trades developed, agents active in these markets also promoted distributing and selling books internationally.

While publishers had supplied the American, Indian, and now Australian markets before the 1880s, when Robertson's *Book Circular* included the notice of the Japanese translation and publication of Mongredien's essay on 'Free Trade and English Commerce' in 1881, it marked a new stage in the expansion of the international book trade. British publishers had grasped the financial benefits of not only supplying books to meet the growing transnational demand but also producing books specifically for American, Indian, and Australian readers, as well as looking to establish trade with other markets that had once been thought to be too distant and too small to bother with. British houses had provided stock to Robertson and other distributors and booksellers for distribution in colonial markets before the 1880s and a few firms had established branches and agents in the United States. Still, British publishers were generally at a disadvantage from their earlier ignorance of most overseas markets, which arose from the inclination to leave the transnational distribution of books largely to colonial and foreign firms like George Robertson and Company. As a result, many publishers found it necessary to work with colonial and foreign agents who could expedite their plans to seek a more active role in the international book trade.

British houses found it expedient to work with local firms who could act as distributing and publishing, as well as retail, agents. For example, Thacker sold Macmillan's books in Calcutta and generally 'were important intermediaries in the conduit of British texts to Indian shores'.[13] In North America, the October 1872 edition of *The Canadian Bookseller* announced that Graeme Mercer Adam represented over one hundred important American and British houses, including Scribners, Longman, and Murray.[14] Before opening a New York agency in 1869, Macmillan had 'distribution arrangements with J. B. Lippincott & Co., Scribner's and Pott & Amery' in the United States.[15] In the 1860s and 1870s, Richard Bentley also worked with Lippincott, as well as Henry Holt, to produce American editions of Bentley publications and to distribute books that the British firm shipped to the United States. Bentley and Robertson collaborated in developing special editions for the Australian colonies, and the two firms signed an agreement in 1876 to use Bentley's imprint on colonial editions of the London firm's popular novels that Robertson printed in Melbourne.[16] While British houses had the material and the capital to produce English-language books for the North American, Asian, Australian, and other overseas markets, publishers often found it beneficial to work with their colonial and foreign counterparts who had knowledge of the markets and experience developing and using the transnational, as well as regional, distribution networks.

This chapter surveys Bentley's and Macmillan's forays into the American, Indian, and Australian markets, and how cooperating with local agents was initially necessary to further an individual publisher's goals. Bentley cautiously and slowly expanded business to include over-seas trade and throughout the nineteenth century worked with local booksellers, publishers, and distributors to meliorate the house's risk. The British publisher needed assistance in navigating and making con-nections in the social network. For example, Bentley's association with Henry Holt facilitated and led to the British house working with other American publishers. One connection led to another and the interna-tional book trade developed.

Macmillan offers a case study of a firm that aggressively sought out opportunities to expand overseas. While Macmillan also cooperated with local counterparts, by the late nineteenth century the publisher was directly competing in a number of overseas markets for a share of the international book trade. In particular, I focus on George P. Brett's trip, in 1887, to Australia and New Zealand as it illustrates the firm's desire both to work with others, particularly seeking their advice about the textbooks and publications that would sell in colonies and the gen-eral market conditions, and to explore the possibility of establishing distribution offices in Australia and New Zealand. The trip also provided an occasion for Brett to tackle some of the continuing problems that impeded the development of the international book trade. By the late 1880s, British publishers' eagerness to collaborate with and support colonial and foreign agents' enterprises waned as the houses gained experience and knowledge of transnational distribution routes and overseas markets. Still, when Macmillan, Bentley, and other publishers learned George Robertson was failing to distribute their books in Australia, the firms preferred to provide loans and stock so that Edward Petherick could launch the Colonial Booksellers' Agency rather than distribute their own publications in the colonies.

Richard Bentley's forays into colonial and foreign markets can be summed up as a cautious gamble. Bentley recognized that publishing 'was a speculation and a very uncertain one', but if one was careful one could profit by it.[17] Bentley, his son George, and later his grandson Richard also learned as they worked with colonial and foreign companies that part of the gamble was figuring out who to work with to distribute and sell Bentley publications overseas. Richard Bentley and Henry Colburn started the London-based publishing house in 1829, but after an acrimonious split, the partnership dissolved and in 1832 Richard Bentley became an independent publisher. In the 1860s, Bentley made arrangements with the American firms Lippincott and Henry Holt to sell Bentley publications in the United States, which he identified as a lucrative market for the British house. Mutual trust and reciprocal benefits led to a sustained association between Bentley and the two American publishers. Bentley viewed with more suspicion other American partners like John W. Lovell, who was a notorious reprinter. In the 1870s, the London house further gambled that expanding their trade to include Australia and other colonial and foreign markets would also financially benefit the firm. Relying solely on the British market limited the quantity of books the London publisher could sell in an already crowded and competitive business, but, as Bentley would find, certain markets in the international realm were also increasingly crowded and competitive.

Readership in Britain grew rapidly in the 1830s, partially because of 'the various educational movements initiated early in the century that expanded literacy among children, women and men of different classes'.[18] Many publishing firms, including Bentley, focused on producing works for the growing reading public: bestsellers that 'would flood the bookstores for three to six months and then disappear from the shelves'.[19] Similarly, popular genres such as fiction, travel narrative, and history also found an appreciative audience in the United States, where a parallel expansion in the reading pubic occurred in the nineteenth century. Richard Bentley sold his publications in small irregular shipments to North American booksellers throughout the first half of the nineteenth century. By the 1860s, he regularly shipped larger quantities of his books to the United States, as well as occasionally imported American works. For example, in a letter dated 14 February 1868, Richard Bentley wrote to Lippincott about the prospect of the Philadelphian publishing firm's purchasing a discounted quantity of Lady Mary E. Herbert's *The Mission of St. Francis of Sales* and Frederick Boyle's *A Ride Across a Continent: A Personal Narrative of Wandering Through Nicaragua and Costa Rica*: 'In regards to Lady Herbert's *St Francis of Sales* we should be happy to let you have 250 copies at half-price ... and 100 copies of Mr. Boyle's *Ride Across a Continent* also at half-price.'[20] Bentley not only sold British publications to Lippincott but also offered to purchase copies of the Philadelphian firm's publications. In a letter dated 8 February 1870, Bentley wrote to Lippincott that '[i]n regard to any works which you may publish henceforth, likely any way to interest the English public, I would suggest that where they were of a popular nature you would find it more to your interest to negotiate with me'.[21]

By 1879, the London firm was regularly working with Lippincott and other American publishers to protect each other's market share in the respective countries. Lippincott wrote to Bentley in August 1879 confirming the details of a contract that was under negotiation to publish Louisa Parr's novel *Adam and Eve*. The Philadelphia-based publisher wanted to serialize Parr's novel in *Lippincott's Magazine* and the letter to Bentley outlined the conditions the firm would abide by in order to control the circulation and sale of the magazine in each other's market:

1) To confine ourselves to a sale in this country [Britain] of 50 copies monthly during the run of that story (Adam & Eve).
2) To abstain from sending any copies for review to any English newspaper or periodical during the same period.
3) To abstain from mentioning the title in any Advertisement or Catalogue that we may issue in this country during the same period.
4) To abstain from issuing Lippincott's Magazine in this country until the 5th of each month so as to allow a clear week's priority to Temple Bar.[22]

Bentley was preparing to publish Parr's novel in London and was leery about agreeing to a contract with a firm whose magazine sold in both the United States and Britain and competed with Bentley's *Temple Bar*. However, Lippincott readily agreed to 'limitations to our circulation in England'. While the lack of international copyright law was a problem, publishers could not simply refuse to deal with their counterparts and hope material from one market would not flow into the other. Bentley and Lippincott were aware that their respective primary markets were linked and the circulation of books between Britain and the United States could not be stopped; instead, the firms tried to come to a mutually beneficial agreement that acknowledged, but tried to control, the transnational movement of books. The details of Lippincott's letter to Bentley demonstrate a pragmatic acceptance that the two markets were connected and imply both publishers understood they were part of a larger network and that the goal was for both firms to benefit from the international growth of the book trade.

Throughout the 1870s and 1880s, Bentley's business dealings with American firms increased and the London publisher collaborated with not only Lippincott but also Henry Holt and other publishers to produce American editions of British novels and books. In 1878, George Bentley, who had taken over the firm after his father had died in 1871, and his son Richard Bentley II, who was in charge of the Foreign and Colonial Department from 1877 to 1879, offered to sell to Henry Holt the moulds for an unnamed multi-volume work that the British firm had found expensive to have set and readied for printing: 'As the initial expenses of the work are heavy we would be willing to supply you with the moulds at cost price.'[23] Bentley suggested that the American firm reprint the book in the United States, and 'should the work answer satisfactorily you would no doubt permit us to participate in the profit'. The London publisher regarded the business deal as potentially beneficial for both parties and promised Holt that if the New York firm should 'expect the sale to be a limited one we could furnish you with 100 copies (or perhaps 200 copies) in sheets at a reduced rate' that the American house could then bind in the United States.

Bentley also asked that if Holt was not interested in a book, the firm find a publisher who would be willing to purchase the sheets and/or the plates in order to produce an American edition. In a letter dated 12 November 1880, Frederick William Jordan, who succeeded Richard Bentley as head of the Foreign and Colonial Department, proposed that Holt produce an American edition of Lady Florence Dixie's *Across Patagonia*.[24] Jordan wrote that he would send Holt the illustration electroplates 'on the chance merely of their use'. However, he accepted that Holt might not want to reprint *Across Patagonia* and asked the American firm to pass on the plates to Harper Brothers who might be interested in producing an American edition: 'should you not use the book please shew [*sic*] to Harpers – & let them have the sheets and Electros for £25 or any sum above £25 that you can get – but not for less certainly than twenty guineas'.

Once an agreement was reached between the London publisher and Holt or another American firm, Bentley would arrange for the simultaneous publication of the books in both the United States and Britain. George Bentley insisted that the publication dates of the British and American editions of a book like *Across Patagonia* be synchronized in order to combat book piracy. Unscrupulous American publishers would have their London agents acquire recently published books and send the books to the United States where the reprinters would quickly produce copies for the American market. Bentley's strategy was simple: if the British and American publication dates were coordinated in advance, and the American publisher could release the book on the same day, or shortly thereafter, as the British publication, then the reprinters would not be able to publish their cheaply made editions before the authorized American edition appeared.

Bentley, his son, and Jordan often wrote to their American partners cautioning them about letting anyone know about upcoming publications. For example, in a letter dated 10 March 1880, Jordan warned Appleton against telling anyone the title of Rhoda Broughton's new novel *Second Thoughts*.[25] Also, he reminded Appleton that the New York firm would receive 'from time to time (by different steamers) proofs of Miss Broughton's new story ... We will write to you at the close of this month stating time of publications, as it is of course necessary that the work should not appear in the United States before it does in England.' While Appleton would receive the proofs as they were readied, Bentley did not want to run the risk of the American firm's accidentally publishing the book before the British edition was ready for publication; consequently, he reminded the New York firm that they should only publish after he had confirmed the British release date.

While Richard Bentley and Son had arrangements with a number of different American publishers, including Lippincott, Appleton, and Putnam, the firm the British publishing house did the most business with was Henry Holt. Bentley sold books and stereotype plates to Holt and purchased the New York firm's publications for the British market. For example, Bentley ordered 750 copies of Henry Adam's novel *Esther* in 1885.[26] Holt also often acted on the British publisher's behalf and sold the rights to Bentley publications in the United States. For instance, on 3 February 1885, George Bentley wrote to Holt asking the New York firm to receive electroplates intended for Funk and Wagnall and to collect the money owed to the British firm: 'Messers Funk and Wagnall of New York applied to us in November last for a set of Stereotype plates of LETTERS FROM HELL through their London agent and agreed to pay £40 down in cash for them ... Their London Manager ... became ill or went out of town and no settlement could be effected with him.'[27] George Bentley in the meantime republished Valdemar Adolph Thisted's *Letters from Hell* in London, which the house had first published in 1866, and he requested that Holt approach Funk and Wagnall to settle the matter.[28] He added that if Funk and Wagnall 'will not pay for the stereos will you kindly give effect to some other arrangements in other quarters for the American issue of the book'. However, Holt did not need to find another publisher as Funk and Wagnall settled their account with Bentley and published the novel in 1886.

In 1891, Bentley also asked Holt to assist the London publisher in securing American copyright for their works. While the Chase Act protected Bentley's copyright in the United States, the same logistical problems, which had inconvenienced the London firm's American sales and publications before the Anglo-American treaty of 1891, continued. The treaty required that '[f]irst, to claim copyright protection in the United States, a book had to [be] published there no later than it was published in its country of origin. Secondly, it had to be printed in the United States.'[29] George Bentley worried about satisfying the treaty's requirements for acquiring copyright in the United States. For instance, he negotiated with Holt to print copies of Augustus W. Dubourg's *Angelica: A Romantic Drama in Four Acts* in the United States so he could fulfil the second requirement of the treaty. In addition, the novel had to have coordinated release dates in both the United States and Britain to fulfil the first requirement: 'We will also advise you of the date of issue. If it does not cause inconvenience, the New York edition should appear about the end of March.'[30] In 1892, Bentley wrote to Holt that the London firm was not interested in selling the novel in the United States; Bentley only wanted to secure his copyright and to prevent the reprinters from printing the novel: 'the publication which takes place in America is for protective purposes only'.[31] As a result, Bentley had only 100 copies of *Angelica* printed in the United States and told Holt that 'sale beyond one or two copies is quite immaterial, and it is not necessary to send to the Press. The copies to the Librarian of Congress are most important.' Under the Chase Act, copyrighted books needed to be deposited at the Library of Congress. Also, Bentley offered to return the favour to Holt, if the New York firm ever needed to copyright one of their works in Britain: 'Before concluding, please accept our best thanks for your kind assistance in the matter. If we can at any time perform a similar service for you we shall have pleasure in doing so.'

While Bentley relied on Holt to act as their proxy in the United States, other American publishers the British house worked with were not granted the same degree of trust. For example, Bentley had a number of business transactions with John W. Lovell, who was notorious for his unauthorized printing of British fiction. In sharp contrast to his earlier activities, Lovell opened a London office in 1888, and through his London agent, Wolcott Balestier, bought the American, and occasionally Canadian, rights to British novels. Lovell arranged to pay 'English authors substantial payments for the use of advance sheets of their forthcoming books. In that manner Lovell could anticipate the pirates at the same time that he salved his conscience and lined the purses of the English literati.'[32] In 1890, Bentley offered Balestier Matilda Betham-Edwards' *The Parting of the Ways* for £28, and the firm inquired if Lovell would also be interested in a Rhoda Broughton novel.[33] Lovell did not want Betham-Edwards' book, but was interested in Broughton's *Alas!* However, he required the advance sheets for Broughton's novel to be shipped as soon as possible as well as an assurance that he could publish the work by a specified date. However, the London publisher could not guarantee that the firm would be able either to send all the advance sheets for Broughton's novel at once or to avoid delaying the date of British publication (a delay would affect the date when Lovell could publish the American edition of the novel).[34] Nevertheless, Bentley promised that the firm 'should endeavour to study [at] your convenience as far as possible by sending on (as was done with Miss Carey's book) instalments of the work in good time'.[35] On 11 April 1890, the British firm signed an agreement with Lovell to sell the Canadian and American rights to Broughton's *Alas!*, which Macmillan had previously published in 1889 and Bentley had published in 1890.[36] Lovell paid Bentley £100 'as an advance or guarantee upon royalties', which represented 10 per cent of the retail price. Five months later, Bentley wrote to Balestier providing him with the British publication dates for *Alas!* and three other Bentley publications for which Lovell had purchased reprint rights:

> 1890   August 21 – '<u>Name and Fame</u>' (Sheets from Miss Sergeant)
> September 10. <u>Lover or Friend</u> (sheets from Miss Carey)
> September 25. <u>House of Halliwell</u> (sheets from W. Wood)
> October 7. <u>Alas!</u> (Sheets from ourselves)[37]

Bentley required Lovell not to publish the American editions of the four novels 'earlier than the dates named' and the letter implies a degree of concern that Lovell might not comply and print American editions before the British ones, which could potentially siphon Bentley's sales if the American imprint crossed the Atlantic. While Lovell bought a number of Bentley publications, George Bentley never trusted Lovell as much as other American publishers or asked Lovell to act as his proxy as he had with Henry Holt.

Initially in the 1870s, Richard Bentley and Son's American trade was handled by the Town Department, which dealt with foreign business transactions and the London branches of colonial booksellers and publishers.[38] However, the publisher created the Foreign and Colonial Department 'in 1877 to meet {cope with} the growing claims of the Colonies'.[39] In a review of the Foreign and Colonial Department, produced in 1889, the writer suggested that before the establishment of the new department 'the most noticeable previous activity of the Foreign section of the Town Department was shown in the United States and West Indies but the ultimate results of the large masses of shipments recorded in the Consignment Book were of an unsatisfactory nature and delayed the development of the Foreign and Colonial Department'. Moreover, the review indicated that '[a] considerable loss is annually experienced at the present time by the lax administration of the Customs on the Canadian Frontier'. However, Richard Bentley and Son's increasing business with Australia made up for the firm's losses in North America. In 1877, the volume of Bentley's business had shifted to Australian and South African booksellers: 'The increase of trade with Australia stimulated by the more rapid means of transit and increasing population of Australia, and with South Africa owing to the sudden influx of capital into the English colonies there contributed largely to swell the returns of exports about this period.'

Further contributing to the rapid increase in and profitability of Richard Bentley and Son's book exports was the British publisher's association with Melbourne-based George Robertson and Company and with Robertson's London manager Edward Petherick. In 1876, Bentley and Robertson signed an agreement that allowed Robertson to use the Bentley imprint in Australia on 'any work of good character and in keeping with your own publications'.[40] Robertson also became Bentley's proxy in the Australian colonies in regards to certain business transactions. The partnership followed the firms successfully working together on at least two separate occasions. In 1873, Robertson reprinted a Bentley publication, *South Sea Bubbles* by the Earl of Pembroke and Doctor Kingsley regarding visits to Tahiti, the Cook Islands, and Samoa, which had first been published in Britain in 1872. The title page of the Australian edition stated that the book had been 'printed for R. Bentley and Son, London, By George Robertson' and, according to a sticker on the back cover, bound by Robertson in Melbourne.[41] The title page included a warning at the bottom of the page: 'This edition being printed for circulation in the Australian Colonies only.' The partnership also followed in the wake of Robertson's and Bentley's successful agreement in 1873 for Robertson to produce between 35,000 and 50,000 copies of Mrs Henry Wood's novels for sale in the Australian colonies.[42] Between 1876 and 1887, the majority of Bentley's Australian exports were shipped and distributed by Robertson's company. Moreover, in 1887, Bentley produced and Robertson distributed the Australian Library as part of Bentley's second colonial series. The London publisher tried to limit the firm's risk by working with knowledgeable and trustworthy partners, like Henry Holt and George Robertson, who could distribute Bentley publications overseas.

While the British firm continued to use Robertson as an Australian distributor into the 1890s, the creation of the Australian Library was the final major project that Bentley and Robertson worked on together. After 1887, Robertson downsized his London office, including discharging 14 men, and focused on his Australian bookselling operation.[43] According to Petherick, Robertson's actions displeased George Bentley and other London publishers 'who had helped him with unlimited credit when he most required it'.[44] Bentley, Macmillan, Longman, and other prominent London firms financially supported and helped to launch Petherick's Colonial Booksellers' Agency, a firm that specialized in advertising and distributing British books in Australia and other colonial and overseas markets. Between 1888 and 1893, the Colonial Booksellers' Agency would ship the majority of Bentley's exports to the Australian colonies.

While Robertson and Petherick were the two primary distributors of Bentley's books in the Antipodes, the London firm also occasionally sent their own publications to other booksellers in the colonies as well as directly negotiated with Australian authors like Rosa Campbell Praed for British publication rights. In 1886, Praed telegraphed the firm offering Bentley the opportunity to buy *Miss Jacobson's Chance*, which was currently being serialized in the *Melbourne Age* and the *Sydney Telegraph*: 'She will sell the Library right for £150 or entire copyright ... for £250.'[45] The official advice form included a notation acknowledging receipt of Praed's telegram and recorded the firm's recommendation, which was '[s]ubject to approval of plot' to purchase the rights to produce a colonial edition: 'one hundred Guineas for the Library Rights might be risked'. While Bentley was willing to risk a certain amount of money by purchasing the rights to the novel, which was set in Australia, it is important to note that the London house was generally cautious about producing books by colonial authors or for the colonies. George Bentley repeatedly refused to print inexpensive editions of books like Marcus Clarke's *His Natural Life* for the colonial market that were under six shillings in price.[46] Rather, Bentley preferred to share the risk and produce jointly with Robertson or another firm one-volume editions of books that would still not be sold for less than six shillings. Also, if Bentley did not want to print the sheets of a book, he would offer the copyright and stereotype plates of a book to a local publisher or sell the serial rights to a journal or newspaper.[47]

George Robertson distributed the majority of Bentley's publications in the Australian colonies until 1887, but even before this date, the London publisher pursued other avenues of circulation in the colonies, including offering the firm's books for serialization in Australian newspapers and periodicals. In 1884, Bentley received a reply from the office of Melbourne-based *The Argus* and *The Australian* in regards as to when Bentley needed to send books for serialization in *The Australian*, which was a weekly newspaper distributed throughout the Australian colonies.[48] While the letter was about a specific unnamed book under consideration for serialization, the writer (name obscured) also explained that he was waiting for a telegram to confirm the precise date when new novels would need to arrive for serialization in *The Australian*. Thus, the letter implies that Bentley was inquiring not only about a specific book but also about the newspaper's publication schedule and when the paper would need to receive future Bentley publications in order to make publication deadlines. While the firm only sporadically sold editions overseas before 1860, by the 1880s George and Richard Bentley were directly selling books in the United States and Australian colonies, though it was still more common for the British publisher to work with local agents in both markets to reprint, distribute, and/or retail the house's publications.

Bentley was also looking to branch out into other colonial and foreign markets. The publisher's accounts ledgers for 1888 and 1889 indicate business dealings with firms based in the United States, Australia, Germany, France, Italy, and Turkey.[49] Moreover, the 1889 review of Bentley's Foreign and Colonial Department also included a list of British post mailing times between London and various overseas locales in Africa, Asia, Australia, North America, and Central and South America. The review estimated letters would be in transit from London to Shanghai for 42 days, London to Rio de Janeiro for 21 days, London to Bombay for

18 days, and London to Constantinople for 4 days.[50] While not conclusive, the mailing list and the Foreign and Colonial Department review disclose Bentley's growing interest in supplying overseas markets. The firm wanted to be able to gage accurately how long it would take to mail a reply to a request for books regardless of whether the letter or parcel had to be posted to Asia, Africa, or somewhere else. There is a shift from a firm initially reluctant to risk capital to manufacture books for colonial and foreign markets, particularly books under six shillings in price, to a company not only willing to produce a cheap series specifically for colonial markets but also generally eager to compete for a share of the booming international trade in English-language books by 1889.

In particular, Bentley was interested in improving the firm's existing portion of the Indian book market and capitalizing on the growing demand for books in the colonies. The Foreign and Colonial Department review noted that India 'has considerably increased its import of books in the last two or three years'.[51] The 1889 review stated that the growing demand for English-language books in India was recent; however, Bentley's reticence to enter new markets had perhaps led the firm initially to overlook India, while other publishers, particularly Macmillan, had been supplying the Indian market for decades and were already producing texts and series for book buyers there. In 1886, Macmillan launched the Colonial Library series, which targeted an audience of Indian and European expatriate book buyers. The inexpensive series of new and popular fiction drew on the firm's experience providing texts for the colonial education market and Maurice Macmillan's visit to India in 1884 and 1885 to produce a collection that met colonial requirements.[52] Macmillan's lucrative business supplying the colonies, particularly India, with education texts to a degree subsidized the Colonial Library. Still, Priya Joshi notes that 'the logic of profit' motivated Macmillan in launching the series, and the publisher's success would lead other firms, including Kegan Paul and Longman, to develop their own colonial series.[53]

Bentley's first series, the Empire Library, produced between 1878 and 1881, was a dismal failure. The series repackaged Bentley publications for the colonial market but, like John Murray's earlier Colonial and Home Library, did not take into account colonial readers' needs. Also, the series was not specifically for the colonies as it was 'intended for purchase at home and throughout the Empire'.[54] The Empire Library books were 'devoid of colonial content' and priced at six shillings, which Petherick had told the publisher was too much for a colonial edition.[55] Bentley's second series, 'entitled Special Editions for Colonial

Circulation Only', was more successful. The books in the series were priced at two shillings and sixpence for cloth binding. In comparison, Macmillan's Colonial Library books were priced at one shilling, though if you wanted cloth binding the books would then cost one shilling and sixpence.[56] However, even though Bentley's second series was more expensive than Macmillan's Colonial Library, it was still profitable for Bentley and expanded repeatedly between the series' inception in 1885 and the firm's sale to Macmillan in 1898.

Bentley's second series included national libraries or book lists produced for and marketed to colonial readers in Canada, India, South Africa, and Australia. While Bentley provided a library or list of books specifically for the Indian market that included colonial content, India was secondary to the Australian market for the publisher; as a result, Bentley did not tailor the series to meet colonial requirements as the firm had done with the Australian Library or as Macmillan had done with the competing Colonial Library. Macmillan, Kegan Paul, and other London houses had developed their Indian trade networks in the 1860s and 1870s and generally viewed India as their principal colonial market. Bentley, perhaps because of the firm's partnership with Robertson, considered Australia as the firm's primary colonial market and did not have the Indian contacts like other publishers. Consequently, while the Foreign and Colonial Department review revealed the publisher's interest in gaining Indian market share and the house had produced the second series a year before Macmillan had started its Colonial Library, Bentley was not in an advantageous position and did not have the leverage other firms enjoyed in this increasingly competitive colonial book trade.

In 1886, George Bentley complained to Alexander Macmillan about his company's actions in asking authors – with agreements with Bentley – to sell their 'Indian & Colonial' copyrights to Macmillan: 'Twice this month have I received letters from Authors for who I am publishing, advising me that they have received offers from your house to publish Indian & Colonial Editions of work which I am publishing.'[57] Macmillan exploited loopholes in copyright agreements between authors and their British publishers. If the publishers did not specify in the contracts that they were purchasing British *and* colonial copyright, Macmillan capitalized on this omission and tried to buy the colonial copyright from the authors. In 1886, Macmillan either rescinded the house's offer to authors under contract to Bentley or proposed to compensate Bentley for Indian copyright. However, in 1894, Frederick Macmillan once again approached an author under contract to Bentley and made an overture to purchase the colonial and Indian rights of his works; the author, J. M. W. Poorten-Schwartz, reported the overture to George Bentley who angrily wrote to Macmillan in protest, accusing the firm of another 'unfriendly act'.[58] Poorten-Schwartz, who wrote under the name Maarten Maartens, was a popular novelist, and in 1895 Bentley published *The Greater Glory: A Story of High Life*. Macmillan may have been interested in *The Greater Glory* or one of the author's earlier novels. Certainly, after Macmillan took over Bentley, the firm reissued *The Greater Glory* in 1902, plus four other novels by Poorten-Schwartz. While George Bentley complained about Macmillan's repeated actions, his objection was at best perfunctory as he soon agreed to work with the other British publisher when Macmillan proposed the two firms try and find a mutually agreeable solution.

While Bentley wanted to compete for a share of the Indian and colonial markets and the firm's second colonial library proved popular, he was pragmatic and realized Macmillan had a larger colonial and overseas trade network, particularly with regards to India and North America. Moreover, Macmillan had sent George P. Brett in 1887 to investigate opportunities for expansion in Australia and New Zealand and to meet individuals involved with the book trade. In the intervening years, Macmillan had continued to improve the firm's Australian distribution network, lessening any advantage Bentley may have had in this particular market. Also, between 1887 and 1893, Bentley and Macmillan had distributed their publications bound for the Australian colonies through Edward Petherick's Colonial Booksellers' Agency, which granted both publishers similar access to the market. When Petherick started to run out of funds and his debts mounted preventing him from distributing books after December 1893, Bentley returned to distributing the majority of the house's Australian-bound books with George Robertson. Whereas Bentley was left working with a company now run by Robertson's son that had a reduced distribution capacity than during its heyday in the early 1880s, Macmillan had not only an extensive colonial but also an international network in place to distribute its own books overseas.

Consequently, when Frederick Macmillan amended his proposal and asked George Bentley either to cooperate with his firm to produce colonial editions or to sell Macmillan his colonial copyright of Poorten-Schwartz's novel and other authors' publications, Bentley agreed, depending on the situation, to either sell copyright or partner with the other publisher.[59] Macmillan had a demonstrable advantage over the other British publisher in terms of transnational distribution capacity and knowledge of overseas markets and it was in Bentley's best interest to work with the house. Still, Bentley was not particularly gracious in his acceptance of

Macmillan's offer: 'Should not your proposition have been made to us in the first instance?' He even went so far as to brag about his colonial successes: 'Any controversy with your house is so distasteful to me, that … I shall content myself, as on a former occasion, by observing that our series of … Novels has in the Colonies through Messrs George Robertson & others and in India, through Messrs Thacker & others, a very large sale.' While he boasted about the 'very large sale', George Bentley recognized that both his firm and Macmillan could benefit from the growing colonial book trade, and allying with the London and New York branches of Macmillan was better than losing market share to the rival publisher.

A year later, the two firms were cooperating, with Bentley sometimes supplying sheets or stereotype plates to Macmillan for American or colonial editions. In 1895, Bentley offered Macmillan copies of *The Life of David Henry Thoreau*, which was first published by Bentley in 1890, for the American market: 'Provided that the copies are sold in the United States and that your American House would be willing to pay the Author a royalty of ten per cent (10%), we could spare from our stock here two or three hundred copies, which would at all events enable you in the first instance to test the feeling of the American market.'[60] Two years later, Bentley serialized Agnes Castle's memoir *The Pride of Jennico* in the *Temple Bar* and also submitted the manuscript to Macmillan for American publication.[61] George Bentley bragged about his success with his second colonial series but while not a completely empty boast it was one that referenced past successes not future ones. Richard Bentley succeeded his father, who died in 1895, and after this date and until the firm's sale to Macmillan in 1898, Bentley increasingly entrusted the international sale and publication of the house's books to Macmillan, a publisher who had more aggressively pursued expansion into overseas markets and developed a transnational distribution network.

Frederick Macmillan, Maurice Macmillan, and the firm's New York manager George E. Brett generally agreed that the future of the company, which had started in 1843, lay in expansion into the international sphere and hesitation to do so would only lead to the publisher's eventual failure. In 1885, Brett proposed to send his son, George, P. Brett, on a fact-finding mission to the Australian colonies.[62] Brett believed that the American agency could take advantage of the Pacific shipping route to the colonies to expand Macmillan's exports to this thriving market. He suggested that the arrangements for his son's trip the subsequent year could be made through the firm's Indian department, which was managed by Maurice Macmillan who had visited Australia earlier in 1884 and 1885 and could provide letters of introduction to booksellers and other agents in the colonies.[63] Both father and son were aware that Macmillan was in an excellent position to develop the firm's colonial and overseas distribution network. The company had branches in London and New York and an extensive network of colonial and foreign contacts. However, George P. Brett argued in a letter to Frederick Macmillan that the firm could not depend on the continuing success of the American and British offices, and he concurred with his father that the firm needed to open distribution branches and expand the firm's international business to include not only the Australian colonies but also Asia.[64] Frederick Macmillan, who 'look[ed] after the firm's interest in America', readily agreed that George P. Brett should follow up on his brother's initial visit to Australia and examine the possibility of increasing the exportation of books to these markets and opening distribution agencies in the Australian colonies.[65]

Even a publisher like Macmillan, which had invested in the international book trade, found it necessary to work with foreign and colonial booksellers, publishers, and distributors who were familiar with the local markets. For example, George E. Brett worked with the Montreal publisher Dawson to register Macmillan publications for copyright in Canada.[66] Also, upon arrival in Australia, George P. Brett sought out the advice of colonial booksellers like Samuel Mullen and George Robertson who could educate Brett about the colonial trade and recommend what Macmillan publications would sell in the colonies, as well as what books the publication could produce specifically for this market. What sets Macmillan apart from Bentley is that the house did not wait for colonial and foreign firms to establish the infrastructure needed to promote the growth of the international book trade. Macmillan expanded into a number of overseas markets in the second half of the nineteenth century and developed its own line of the social network, while simultaneously cooperating with Robertson, Petherick, and other colonial and foreign agents. Macmillan not only utilized the connections made and distribution system developed by Robertson and others, it also forged its own international shipping routes and directly competed in overseas markets with local branches in the United States, agents in markets like the Australian colonies, and divisions of the business devoted to the production and sale of books in colonial markets like India.

In 1867, Alexander Macmillan visited the United States and found that other British firms were opening American distribution agencies: 'Routledge, Nelson, and Strahan were amongst a dozen houses already well-established in New York.'[67] Macmillan believed that the company needed a presence in the United States in order to compete with the other British publishers who had opened American branches, as well as to market and sell books in the United States. The firm decided to open an American branch in New York two years later. Previous to this date, Macmillan had, like Bentley, collaborated with American publishers like Lippincott to distribute the London house's publications. However, this practice still did not protect the firm from book piracy. The decision to open a New York agency was about both establishing a presence 'in the face of severe competition' and trying to gain some measure of control over the reprinters and Macmillan's publications in the North American market.[68] In 1869, George E. Brett opened the New York branch of Macmillan: 'initially he only distributed consignments of Macmillan publications from London, but soon he began to publish books on his own'.[69] While Brett bemoaned the loss of profits to the American and Canadian reprinters flooding the market with unauthorized editions of Macmillan books, the New York office was a profitable branch for Macmillan and Brett was granted a degree of autonomy, which allowed him to implement his plans developing Macmillan's distribution network throughout North America and farther afield.

It is important to acknowledge at this point that not all British publishers were cautious like Bentley and many firms were active in the United States and other overseas markets. Besides Routledge, Nelson, and Strahan, John Cassell was also established in New York and had opened an agency there in 1860. By the 1880s, Cassell's New York branch was independent of the British parent publisher and represented 'T. Fisher Unwin, Heinemann, and Chatto and Windus' in the American market.[70] In May 1884, Cassell also opened a branch in Melbourne and two months later Ward Lock sent out a 'resident representative' to Australia.[71] Two years previously, Ward Lock had opened a New York branch.[72] Other publishers employed agents to visit the colonies on their behalf. Beginning in 1890, Oxford University Press, Hodder and Stoughton, John Murray, A & C Black, and Chapman Hall employed E. R. Bartholomew to make biennial trips to the Australian colonies.[73] Brett's trip to Australia was then to a certain degree about not being left behind and making sure Macmillan remained a competitive presence in this particular market.

Besides the United States and Australia, the other overseas market that British publishers competed for market share of was India. By the 1860s, 'Macmillan, Blackie, Nelson, Longmans, and Chambers' were working with local booksellers and distributors and developing their connections in India in order to supply the growing demand for books.[74] After visiting India and Australia in 1884 and 1885, Maurice Macmillan returned to London to run the India department for the publisher and help to launch the Colonial Library that targeted readers in India. By 1892, Macmillan 'had an exclusive agent working for them [in India] ... and in 1901, began opening book depots first in Bombay, then Calcutta (1907), then Madras (1913)'.[75] Other publishers, including Kegan Paul, Cassell, Longman, Bell, and Bentley, also launched Indian and colonial series. Oxford University Press developed the 'more school-bookish than scholarly' historical series Rulers of India specifically for Indian readers.[76] Still, Priya Joshi argues that Macmillan was in a particularly good position 'to become ... a successful enterprise in India'.[77] While Macmillan was not the only publisher working to develop overseas holdings, the firm is an illustrative case study of a British publisher operating in the international field that made the most of its advantages and sought to improve its position in the social network as it competed in the three main markets of the international book trade and looked to expand into other areas that were not as well serviced.

As father and son planned the trip to Australia, George P. Brett advocated that the firm consider expanding the scope of his travels to include Japan. In a letter dated 22 June 1886, he wrote to Frederick Macmillan that he had spoken to a representative of the firm 'Iveson AJM ... and I learn[ed] from him that their Japanese trade is growing larger year by year and I obtained from him the promise of a list of their customers there, without intimating however that we purposed making a visit to the country'.[78] Cassell was already publishing Japanese translations of works like Augustus Mongredien's essay on 'Free Trade and English Commerce' and Macmillan was interested in selling both translated works and English-language books in Japan and throughout Asia.

Examining in more detail George P. Brett's trip to Australia offers the opportunity to demonstrate Macmillan's awareness of the importance of the firm increasing its presence in the Australian colonies, as well as other markets, in order to stay competitive. In a letter dated 1 March 1894, George P. Brett wrote to Frederick Macmillan about the company's advantage in being able to offer prospective authors access to multiple markets with the Macmillan imprint.[79] After George E. Brett's death in 1890, his son continued to enlarge the New York operations and in the following decades would open 'branch offices in Atlanta, Boston, Chicago, Dallas, and San Francisco', as well as help to establish agencies in Canada, Australia, India, Japan, China, and the Philippines after he became a partner in the firm and Macmillan New York became a separate business from the parent publisher.[80] By the end of the nineteenth century Macmillan had international publication and distribution capabilities. The Australian trip came at a crucial time in the history of the house as it underscored Macmillan's commitment to selling books globally and developing its international advantage, as well as prefigured the transformation of the firm from a British publisher into a transnational concern. Brett's correspondence with his father, Frederick Macmillan, and Maurice Macmillan in planning the trip and in reporting his findings also illustrates some of the specific issues and problems publishers and distributors faced when expanding their business to include international book circulation.

Frederick Macmillan approved enlarging the scope of Brett's travels to include Japan, but in October 1886, Brett informed him that 'I regret to find that the time during which I can be spared from the house here [New York] is insufficient to accomplish the trip entire, and I write to ask if you will allow me to give up, for next year, the Japanese portion, and devote the time at my disposal to Australia and New Zealand only, leaving Japan and possibly some of the Chinese Posts to the following year if you so desire.'[81] Brett proposed that he leave at the end of February 1887 and spend three months in Australia and New Zealand.[82] He promised that curtailing his trip would allow him 'to give the cities of the Australian Colonies the attention and time they deserve'. He would also still be able to test the viability of Macmillan developing a Pacific distribution route. While Brett intended to visit Asian markets, including Japan, the following year, he most likely did not go because of his father's illness, which left Brett taking over most of his father's duties in New York upon his return from the colonies.

As he planned his Australian trip, Brett wrote to Frederick Macmillan about what he regarded as the largest stumbling block to the publisher increasing its business in the colonies. The problem was not the lack of a quick distribution route; instead, he felt Macmillan's difficulties in arranging for transferring payments between countries and overseas hindered the expansion of the firm into new territories. Brett argued in his letters to Macmillan that his trip afforded the firm the opportunity to find a solution to the problem of international financial transfers. In a letter dated June 1886, he reported to Macmillan that the firm could securely send bank drafts overseas by using a certain Scottish bank with ties to an Australian financial institution.[83] Brett described how the Scottish and Australian banks had reciprocal arrangements where each bank honoured the other bank's drafts: 'the charges made by the Scottish banks for collecting Australian drafts are 10% per cent; of which 5% per cent goes to the Scottish bank and the other 5% to the Australian bank collecting the draft'. Brett noted that the firm could make use of these 'reciprocal arrangements' in paying outstanding bills in the colonies, and in accepting colonial drafts against payments of book orders. Brett's plan was similar to the arrangement the American publisher Ticknor and Fields had developed to pay for British book orders: 'the firm purchased a bill of exchange with cash from the Boston bankers Brown Brothers and deposited it with Baring Brothers ... Ticknor and Fields could then pay the London trade for purchases with promissory notes drawn on Baring Brothers'.[84]

Brett admitted that there was still a problem in that the drafts would take time to travel between Britain and the colonies, with the delay resulting in higher interest expenses: 'the money is remitted by a draft at sixty days ... which taken with the time lost in transit is a loss of 140 days interest on the money'.[85] While Macmillan was willing to pay the extra interest on a draft, colonial customers did not always have the financial ability to pay the additional interest. Therefore, Brett proposed that Macmillan discount their publications for sale in the colonies, thereby making the entire transaction less expensive for the Australian book trade.[86] In December 1886, Macmillan agreed and sent him specially priced catalogues. Still, Brett argued that the firm needed to do more and suggested that they offer 'purchasers of bills of £100 and upward especially in the cases of firms of acknowledged good credit ... bills in the Australian and New Zealand markets at 3 and four months, and occasionally in exceptional cases even six mo[nth]s' to pay for their book orders.[87] When a colonial bookseller bought books from Macmillan, the firm would write up a bill of sale that would specify the amount owed and the deadline for delivery of the books. Typically, the bills became due between a month and a month and a half after purchasing the books. Brett pointed out that Macmillan's 'strict adherence to ... 30 & 50 days will in some cases prevent me from effecting sales to customers perfectly worthy of credit'. He believed that the firm could offer colonial customers a bill of sale with a longer due date, and thereby take into account the distance and protracted transportation times between the Australian colonies and Britain.

George E. Brett added a note to his son's letter, supporting his son's proposal: 'will you permit me the suggestion that a special journey like this would afford an excellent opportunity to breaking up the objectionable system'.[88] Brett argued that the firm could use the occasion to change policy and extend the usual due date of bills of sale: 'instead of 60 and 90 days I would suggest 3 and 7 months. Of course such time will only be allowed to solid men.' While Brett noted that 'the ideal system of business is of course ... cash', he contended that it was not a practical means of doing business in the Australian colonies. The firm had to make allowances in their financial policies if they wanted to sell books in Australia. Also, he discerned that offering longer due dates on bills of sale would support his son's trip: 'his visit should be regarded by the Colonial trade as an event so important in itself as to be deserving of their every encouragement'. Both father and son suggested that lengthening the due date on bills of sale was a way by which Macmillan could ensure that the trip would succeed in meeting its aims.

Frederick Macmillan decided against extending the due dates of the bills of sale to six months or for a shorter duration for colonial booksellers. However, Brett broached the subject of liberalizing due dates again while in Australia. In a letter to Maurice Macmillan dated 10 May 1887, Brett wrote that in the course of a conversation with Samuel Mullen the Melbourne bookseller argued that 'I sent £300 last month, making £700 since the first of the year and I will again remit by the end of the month or beginning of next. I never have less than £1000 of your stock in store or in transit and often much more, my business is nearly all credit many bills to my customers running six months or more.'[89] Brett added: '[i]t seems to be necessary in some cases to be lenient as regards time with customers of Mr Mullens [*sic*] ... it seems natural to him that the firm should give him all accommodation ... perhaps you will allow me to suggest that you might make an exception in this case'. If Macmillan would not consider changing the policy, Brett wanted the firm at least to consider an exception to that policy for a good customer like Mullen.

On 12 February 1887, Brett sailed from San Francisco and arrived a month later in Sydney, New South Wales. As soon as he arrived in March, he used the developing railway network in New South Wales to visit the surrounding towns of Bathurst, Newcastle, and Maitland.[90] Brett would spend three months in Australia and Tasmania and one month in New Zealand visiting a total of 27 cities, towns, and hamlets. In a letter dated 9 April 1887 to Maurice Macmillan, he described the amount of travelling he was doing:

> Since last writing I have been to Newcastle and Maitland [in New South Wales] and the Railway not having been opened to Brisbane, returned to Sydney taking Steamer for this place [Brisbane] where I arrived yesterday. The next three days being holidays, I leave tonight for Rochhampton returning here via Maryborough [in Queensland] in about a week; Townsville is I fear out of the question, as it would take another week, and although still growing ... I doubt very much whether the future city of N. Queensland is as yet decided on.[91]

Moreover, later that month, Brett complained to Maurice Macmillan, who supervised Brett's Australian trip, that travelling was taking up all his time: 'The Easter holidays delayed my trip up the coast [of South Australia] considerably, the Steamer lying up for the best part of two days at small towns on the way.'[92] In a later letter written while Brett was in Hobart, Tasmania, he expressed to Macmillan his irritation that '[a]s usual the Steamer is late, the Steamers always are late I think, in this part of the world, a good deal of time has been lost in this way on this trip'.[93]

While Brett felt he wasted time travelling, he managed to visit every major city and town in Queensland, New South Wales, Victoria, South Australia, Tasmania, and New Zealand. In fact, his letters to Maurice Macmillan afford a snapshot of the Australian book trade in 1887; Brett described the places and economic prospects of each city and town he visited, and provided detailed lists of the newspapers, booksellers, and schools in the colonies. For example, he portrayed the trade in Marybourough, Queensland as consisting of four booksellers:

J. Miller. good house. Small order enclosed. not very enterprising.
   W. Dawson. Good but hard to sell to ... sayd [*sic*] he will send an order later which I think is doubtful.
   The other two booksellers are Mr. Caldwell and W. Mitchell, both in a small way. & W. M. is not good I hear.[94]

Additionally, Brett ranked the booksellers regarding their ability to pay Macmillan. For example, he wrote that fellow booksellers advised him that 'J & J Black of Toowoomba [Queensland], while rated as perfectly good and able to meet their bills, are said to dishonor drafts and money can only be collected from them by threat of suit ... If you send Blacks [*sic*] order I feel sure that the money could be collected, but at that distance considerable trouble and sour experience might occur.'[95] He also described the prominent newspapers in each town and what sort of literature Macmillan could place with each paper. For example, he observed that the *Newcastle Herald and Advocate* was an eight-page newspaper: 'the only one of importance [in Newcastle, New South Wales], it might be useful for receiving light literature'.[96]

Brett also listed in his letters to Maurice Macmillan all the school and university officials and teachers in the colonies who he thought might purchase the firm's publications and more importantly had influence over book acquisitions. While in Newcastle, he determined that J. McCormack, who bought textbooks for the Newcastle school district, was 'very well thought of and of some influence in the Dept., he did not like the Collins readers and would be glad to look over ours'.[97] Brett brought a number of sample books on his trip to give to booksellers, schoolteachers, school officials, and university professors in Sydney and Melbourne. Brett found that officials and teachers in smaller towns were also potential customers, and he wanted to supply them with sample texts. At one point he asked Maurice Macmillan to clarify the firm's instructions regarding who could have sample books.[98]

As soon as Brett arrived in Sydney, he met with local primary, secondary, and post-secondary school officials and vigorously promoted the sale of Macmillan's line of textbooks. Brett 'found the Professors [at Sydney University] very busy, it being just at the opening of the term' but he still met with a Professor Scott who 'expressed himself as very grateful to you for the many books received which are proving of great help to him in his work [and] ... he is using many of our books and intended to adopt more of them finding them very satisfactory'.[99] In the 1870s, the firm diversified its catalogue by adding school texts for use 'both at home and abroad'.[100] Since then, Macmillan had developed its Indian trade, sending regular shipments of textbooks to India, and Brett was tasked with promoting the publisher's textbooks in the Australian colonies and finding out what kind of textbooks colonial school officials wanted Macmillan to produce. While Brett's visit included meeting with local booksellers, publishers, and wholesalers, the majority of his letters document the education system in each city and town and whom the firm should approach about acquiring their textbooks. When Brett wrote about Sydney University, he also encouraged Maurice Macmillan to provide 'Mr. W' with copies of Macmillan textbooks: 'it might be worth while to keep him supplied with sample copies of the books suitable for secondary and higher branches, as I gather that his influence very largely determines the books required for the ... examinations'.[101] Brett added that he wished he 'had more time ... so that I might visit the more provincial private schools, which would I think be of service; to do this thoroughly a year could be spent in the Colonies'.[102] Moreover, he wrote that booksellers, school officials, and teachers repeatedly invited the firm to expand their sales of textbooks in the colonies. For instance, Samuel Mullen encouraged Macmillan to display their educational texts at the Centennial Exhibition in Melbourne in 1888.[103]

However, Brett informed Maurice Macmillan that the firm's existing textbook trade in the colonies was at risk because of the negligent distribution practices of their principal Australian distributor, George

Robertson. In a letter dated 24 March 1887, Brett wrote that in Sydney 'the local bookseller is very much afraid of ordering a full supply of a book on a teacher's estimate of the number required, and much annoyance results, a short time since G.R.s [George Robertson's] branch here attempted to make a teacher pay for a number of copies of an expensive book which had been introduced and the class had not come up to the teacher's estimate'.[104] George Robertson was Macmillan's primary distributor of educational textbooks in the colonies, but Brett feared that Robertson was not fulfilling his duties in promptly distributing textbooks. In addition, Robertson, in charging an instructor for unsold copies of a book, effected a practice that Macmillan did not condone. Brett added that in Rockhampton, Queensland, J. Wheatcroft of the Grammar School 'complains that the local dealers are unable to get the books he wants in Sydney from Robertson and he is often compelled to substitute something he can get'.[105] Also, Brett wrote that 'the Sample copies of School books sent to the trade' were poorly displayed in Robertson's shops: 'G.R.'s are upstairs and without any order or arrangement of any kind.'[106] In another letter written to Macmillan dated 28 May 1887, Brett angrily declared:

> [t]he school samples sent to G. Robertson for ... Ballarat [in Victoria] have been wasted I fear, instead of sending them to the best house ... they have been divided among all the booksellers large and small ... I made no attempt to collect them [books] ... not quite knowing how far I was at liberty to interfere with G R's arrangements; his traveller was in Ballarat during my visit and seemed to think I was taking the trade out of his hands.[107]

Finally, Brett reported that a Sydney school official 'complains that [George] Robertson does not keep stock of the books which he requires, even after lists have been furnished him, and I hear the same complaint from other sources indeed. Eventually the house will I think be obliged to establish a stock branch in the Colonies, in order to protect their school book interests which are already large.'[108]

In 1887, Robertson's business was in disarray, and he closed branches in the colonies and scaled down the London office's operations. Robertson 'gradually from 1886 drew out all his working capital' from his wholesale and publishing business.[109] Brett reported to Maurice Macmillan that Robertson was trying to sell his business: 'In answer to your letter of Feb 18th, I hear that G. Robertson's Adelaide branch has not [closed] ... and there is no likelihood of it within a short time. They still have an agent in Brisbane who however has no stock, but simply samples of new goods to take orders from. I gather from rumours in the trade however that G.R. would be glad to sell out the whole business if a purchaser could be found.'[110] In Adelaide, Brett described Robertson's manager as complaining about the lack of stock.[111] When Brett finally met Robertson in Melbourne on 10 May 1887, he confirmed that Robertson was dissatisfied with the depressed state of the book trade and 'was curtailing his business'.[112]

Brett could only agree with Robertson that 'business was very dead ... all over the colonies'.[113] While both he and his father characterized the book trade in the colonies as buoyant before the trip, in his letters to Maurice Macmillan Brett repeatedly described the Australian trade as depressed: 'Most of the Queensland booksellers in the small towns are in very small way indeed, their stock consists of ... novels chiefly and usually £200 would buy out their entire book stock, they all sell other lines as well ... very few of them have direct a/co [account] with any London publishers, buying chiefly of Cassell, Ward Lock, and the Sydney wholesale houses.'[114] He added that '[b]usiness in Queensland according to all accounts is most fearfully bad'.[115] Moreover, Brett con-fided to Macmillan that business in 'Melbourne is not coming up to my expectations at all'.[116] Even book orders from the larger booksellers, like Samuel Mullen, were quite small: 'S. Mullen's order is not as large as I had hoped it would be.'[117] In one of his last letters to Macmillan while in the colonies, dated 28 June 1887, Brett wrote that 'Invercargill and indeed the whole of New Zealand is suffering great business depression at this time, and many failures are taking place, so that great caution must be exercised in doing business here.'[118]

Despite Brett's and Robertson's observations that the Australian book trade was depressed, Brett was still excited about the potential of both the educational textbook market and the colonial book trade in gen-eral. He mentioned in one letter that textbook sales 'are already large and will continue to grow'.[119] Moreover, he suggested that Macmillan could support the emerging colonial market and solve the distribution problems caused by Robertson 'curtailing' his business by opening a stock agency in Australia. He argued that many local booksellers told him they could not buy books directly from Macmillan unless the firm could guarantee the chain of distribution and lower costs. In a letter dated 19 April 1887, Brett wrote that bookseller G. S. Young and Co. of Bundaburg complained about the high cost of freight from Sydney.[120] Brett added in another letter that 'I think it but right to tell you that I am frequently asked to [convey] ... upon the house the necessity of establishing an Australian stock agency.'[121] Another reason why, in the face of an economic depression, Brett felt the firm needed to invest in the colonies was the fact that other British firms were directly entering the Australian market. He reported that in Melbourne 'Mr Gould, traveling for Nelsons is here at present, also Mr Trench … Ward Locks traveller has just left here for New South Wales and Queensland. W.L. & Co travel all the small towns throughout the Colonies regularly, as do also Cassells, Griffith and Fassen, Routledge & some others.'[122] Also, he observed 'several long advertisements of Bentley's Publications in the papers here'.[123]

While new shipping routes and faster steamers had, by 1887, seemingly minimized the distance between the Australian colonies and the countries in the Western hemisphere and improved British–Australian book distribution channels, distance within the colonies was still a problem. In addition, the flow of both capital and books was further impeded by both the distances that separated cities and towns in the colonies and the 'curtailing' of George Robertson's wholesale business. In suggesting an expansion that mirrored the firm's actions in 1869, when they opened their agency in New York, Brett advised Macmillan to open an Australian agency immediately in order to fill the breach caused by Robertson's lack of interest in distributing books. However, perhaps because of Brett's letters describing a depressed trade, Macmillan did not employ a dedicated Australian traveller or representative until 1895, and did not open an Australian agency until 1905.[124] Nevertheless, the firm understood that something had to be done regarding the breakdown in the chain of distribution: 'pencilled annotations' in Brett's reports to Maurice Macmillan demonstrate that Brett's suggestions 'did not go unnoticed'.[125] Still, Macmillan was not ready to compete directly in this market and preferred to collaborate with a knowledgeable individual to secure the distribution network. Shortly after Brett's return from the Australian colonies, Macmillan, along with other British publishers, financed the establishment of Edward Petherick's Colonial Booksellers' Agency.

Pierre Bourdieu contends that agents compete for control of the market within the literary field, and the agents who are richest in 'economic, cultural and social capital' will be able to exploit new positions and opportunities.[126] However, in the international book trade in the late nineteenth century, the British firms with the funds and the production facilities necessary to increase the supply to meet the growing global demand for books did not have knowledge of the local colonial and foreign markets. Also, whether British publishers were interested in the international book trade or reluctant to enter certain colonial and overseas markets, the firms found it necessary to work with their foreign and colonial counterparts who were familiar with local markets and who had also, with the larger firms' earlier disinterest and absence, developed transnational distribution networks. As a result, the power dynamics within the social network cannot simply be explained in terms of a binary of dominant and dominated positions. The relationship between British publishers and colonial and foreign counterparts was more fluid and dynamic as agents jockeyed to make the most of their individual advantages.

Edward Petherick had established himself as an experienced distributor when he worked for George Robertson between 1870 and 1887, who could help British publishers' works circulate in the colonies and in other overseas markets. Petherick made the most of his advantages and when Macmillan and other British publishers realized that Robertson was failing to distribute their publications in the colonies they turned to Petherick to solve their problem. George Brett's Australian trip was about Macmillan gaining knowledge of the colonial market so that the firm could eventually distribute their own publications and compete with other British firms attempting to gain market share. Upon learning about Robertson's problems, Brett wanted the firm to take the risk and open a depot in Australia but Macmillan was not quite ready to do so. While the knowledge gap that had first led to British publishers cooperating and collaborating with their colonial and foreign counterparts had narrowed and Macmillan and other firms were now operating in a number of different markets, the British houses had not yet acquired enough connections to navigate the social network and directly vie for market share in all areas of the international book trade. Macmillan, Bentley, and other publishers preferred to share the risk associated with transnational book circulation and in 1887 provided loans and stock so that Petherick could launch the Colonial Booksellers' Agency.

5
The Colonial Booksellers' Agency[1]

A lover of books, and I hope 'a man of business' – having served twenty-five years with the largest of Colonial Booksellers, Messrs. George Robertson & Company, and therefore possessing knowledge and experience of the Trade at Home and Abroad – it will be my earnest endeavour so to hold my little candle that any who come within reach of its rays may find it a useful and helpful guide.[2]

Quoting Sir Richard Steele on how the '[k]nowledge of books is like ... [a] lantern', Edward Petherick described in the inaugural issue of *The Colonial Book Circular and Bibliographical Record* his desire to produce a journal that would provide a catalogue of primarily English-language fiction and non-fiction for readers at 'Home and Abroad' who wanted to purchase books but who had no idea what to buy. Once readers knew what to acquire and ordered the books, Petherick could then ship the books with his distribution company. Fittingly the symbol of the Colonial Booksellers' Agency and journal was a winged Mercury as Petherick offered to procure and deliver books 'to any part of the world'. In the first issue of the *Circular*, Petherick argued that 'English readers at Home and Abroad, probably number sixty or seventy millions, who year by year need "more light"' and Petherick believed his Colonial Booksellers' Agency and the *Circular* were the helpful guides that would provide that 'light'.

In September 1887, Edward Petherick launched the Colonial Booksellers' Agency in London and produced the first issue of the *Circular*. Loans from Australian banks and financing in the form of loans and stock from ten leading British publishers helped Petherick to open his business, and these firms and over 20 other publishers advertised their publications in the *Circular* and distributed their books via the

Colonial Booksellers' Agency.[3] Petherick's company and journal were initially conceived as a benefit 'for Booksellers in the Colonies and for Collectors of Colonial Literature'.[4] However, Petherick quickly realized that his firm was in a position to supply more than the colonial marketplace and book buyers interested in colonial publications because the demand for English-language books was increasingly international. The Colonial Booksellers' Agency and *Circular* could act as torches or guides for booksellers and individual international book buyers – hence the title change with the second issue of the journal to *The Torch and Colonial Book Circular*. Petherick's ambition was to build a business that could provide publications to book buyers wherever they might reside.

Two years after the first issue of the *Circular* was released, Petherick's company comprised distribution and advertising divisions and agents throughout North America, Europe, Australia, and elsewhere. Petherick also published his own imprint, E. A. Petherick & Co., and sold books in the Australian colonies under this name. The Colonial Booksellers' Agency supplied booksellers and buyers in the Australian colonies, Asia, India, Africa, Britain, Europe, and North America. Petherick boasted in his memoir that between 1888 and 1893 he 'disposed of £250,000 of high class literature'.[5] Still, his spectacular success in developing the first company to sell and distribute books on an international scale was fleeting. By 1894, the Colonial Booksellers' Agency was in bankruptcy.

While Petherick's biographies mention his career as George Robertson's London manager, he is primarily remembered in a national context as a bibliographer and as a collector of rare Australiana that would become a founding collection of the National Library of Australia.[6] Petherick's role in promoting the international book trade and the initial success of the Colonial Booksellers' Agency are all but forgotten. This chapter examines the rise and fall of the Colonial Booksellers' Agency between 1887 and 1894 and how the meteoric success of Petherick's company and its eventual failure illustrate the change in the last two decades of the nineteenth century from British publishers enthusiastically cooperating with their colonial and foreign counterparts to British, colonial, and foreign firms directly competing for access to and a portion of the international market in English-language books. In 1887, British publishers were eager to see Petherick succeed in launching the Colonial Booksellers' Agency as the company could distribute their publications in the colonies and internationally. However, when Petherick's outstanding bank loans came due in 1893, his financial backers refused to help him.[7] Bentley, Macmillan, Longman, and other investors realized that they no longer needed to work with middlemen like Petherick to gain access to colonial and foreign markets and so they allowed the Colonial Booksellers' Agency to fail.

Petherick first developed the idea for the Colonial Booksellers' Agency while working for George Robertson. During his tenure as Robertson's London manager between 1870 and 1887, shipments between Britain and the Australian colonies increased from a few cases of books every month to regular weekly shipments.[8] Robertson's business was buoyed by a rapidly expanding colonial reading public who demanded a regular supply of inexpensive English-language fiction and non-fiction. However, British publishers initially baulked at the expense of shipping and distributing books overseas and did not provide enough books to meet this growing demand, so the flow of books from Britain was irregular at best. Robertson established a London branch in 1857 in order to increase the quantity of books and improve the reliability of shipments. Robertson's success with his London agency, and the rapid growth of his colonial distribution, bookselling, and publishing business, encouraged British publishers to work with him to promote the sale of British books in the colonies. Convinced of the viability of selling books overseas, publishers were also increasingly eager by the 1870s – regardless of the expensive costs involved – to collaborate with Robertson and Petherick in the creation of editions specifically for the colonial market.

A business arrangement with Petherick and his employer could result in a publisher's access to bookstore shelves throughout the Australasian region, including Tasmania, New Zealand, and Fiji. Petherick and Robertson positioned the company as an important broker for publishers who wanted to expedite the sale of their books in the colonies. Petherick also tried to situate the firm as an international distributor and lobbied Robertson to develop contacts in new markets. Initially, Robertson supported Petherick's ambitions and Petherick negotiated on Robertson's behalf and opened accounts with European and American publishers. By 1878, Robertson and Company was regularly importing books from Britain, Europe, and the United States and producing in partnership with British publishers colonial editions of popular works, as well as exporting colonial publications to Britain and Europe. However, Petherick feared that if the firm rested on its laurels for even a moment Robertson would lose ground in a competitive business.[9] He believed that the firm needed to take advantage of the Pacific trade route between North America and Australia and the growing interest American publishers had in the Australian market. Petherick thought the future of the business lay in the international arena and Robertson and Company needed to expand in order to stay ahead of its competitors.

In 1878, Petherick travelled to the United States and Canada meeting with publishers in 'Chicago, Toronto, Boston ... New York, Philadelphia and Washington'.[10] Petherick wanted to secure the direct exportation to Australia of American books, which had previously had to be ordered through London, and investigate the possibility of a new distribution route to Asia and the Pacific colonies that took advantage of the port of San Francisco – a route that other firms like Macmillan would not cultivate until the mid 1880s.[11] After visiting the United States, Petherick returned to Britain as manager of the London office eager to implement his ideas to move the firm one step closer to being a full-fledged international distributor; however, Robertson was uninterested in expanding his company further. Petherick continued to work for Robertson but complained in his memoir that after 1878 Robertson pursued 'a retrogressive policy which eventually wrecked a grand business'.[12] The idea for the Colonial Booksellers' Agency can be traced back to Petherick's thwarted plans for Robertson's company. The Colonial Booksellers' Agency allowed Petherick to put into practice many of his bold ideas regarding the international sale and distribution of books and filled the breach left when Robertson abandoned his once thriving distribution business.

Edward Petherick gave notice in the summer of 1887, as the 5 August 1887 issue of *The Publishers' Circular* reported under 'Trade and Literary Gossip' that he was to leave George Robertson's company and to start his own business as a 'general colonial agent and export bookseller'.[13] While he may have continued working for Robertson in some capacity until February 1888, he produced in September 1887 the first number of the *Circular* and started the Colonial Booksellers' Agency that autumn. In a letter to the Agent General for New South Wales, Thomas A. Coghlan, dated 26 July 1905, he wrote that '[a]fter Robertson ruthlessly and without notice closed [branches] ... I resigned and organized a new business'.[14] Robertson had also downsized the London agency and let 14 men go 'without notice'.[15] Petherick found the strain insufferable as his budget was cut and employees fired.[16] However, he wrote that he 'was too far away to complain', and he had no option other than to quit.

While Robertson continued with his Australian bookselling operation, reports circulated that he also wanted to sell this business.[17] In 1887, Maurice Macmillan learned that George Robertson was failing to distribute his house's publications within the colonies.[18] Macmillan was in a bind, as were other London firms that had previously entrusted the distribution of their Australian book orders to Robertson; publishers needed to secure the wholesale distribution of their books both to and within the Australian colonies. Certainly, other wholesale distribution agencies existed, such as Simpkin and Marshall and Gordon and Gotch, but Robertson had over the preceding two decades distributed the majority of the British houses' publications in the Australian colonies. Moreover, Robertson had discouraged competitors by threatening to shut his London office; he warned Petherick that he would leave London publishers without a colonial distributor 'if any other person is supported and assisted by the British publishers to rival' the firm.[19] Consequently, when Robertson, who had a monopoly on the Australian book distribution system, downsized his business in 1887 there were no firms that could quickly replace him as an Australian distributor. Furthermore, starting over and developing new business relationships with other wholesale firms would take time, and as London publishers struggled to meet the growing colonial demand for books, American publishers and others might capitalize on the inability of British publishers to supply the Australian market.

As Robertson's London manager, Petherick was the individual with whom most London firms had done business and whom they had come to trust. Publishers valued Petherick's advice on producing and selling books for overseas markets because of both his enthusiasm for the international book trade and his experience as an ambitious distribution agent for Robertson. Consequently, with Petherick leaving Robertson's employment, an opportunity arose both for Petherick to replace Robertson's wholesale business with his own distribution company and for the London publishers to support Petherick financially, and in doing so gain a level of control over the Colonial Booksellers' Agency. In his letters to his father, Petherick made it clear that he aspired to operate his own book distribution and publishing firm.[20] However, his memoirs and his correspondence do not disclose whether, in 1887, he approached London publishers about sponsoring his new company or whether Macmillan and other firms proposed that he run a distributing agency underwritten by them. What is clear is that Petherick credited London publishers with supporting the Colonial Booksellers' Agency by providing stock on credit and 'small Capital, all guaranteed'.[21] While London publishers were increasingly competing with one another and other colonial and foreign firms in the international arena, they still preferred to share the risk and financially back a knowledgeable – and respected – individual like Petherick, who knew the colonial marketplace and could run a business that could distribute their books in Australia, New Zealand, and other overseas markets.

Petherick opened the Colonial Booksellers' Agency with £800 in capital and loans from Australian banks.[22] In 1888, Blackwoods, Clowes and Sons, Longman, Macmillan, and Smith Elder provided a further £500 each in loans and stock, for a total investment of £2500 in Petherick's business.[23] In 1889, another four firms, John Murray, Kegan Paul, Routledge, and Warne and Co., offered a further £1750 injection of capital. While Richard Bentley and Son is listed as contributing £500 in 1892, Petherick's letters to George Bentley in 1888 suggest that the publisher also provided starting capital and stock. In a letter dated 3 October 1888, Petherick thanked George Bentley for 'kindly help[ing] at my starting … and add[ed] the expression of my hope that the personal interest which you … have always taken in my welfare, may be fully justified, and in time meet with its recompense and reward'.[24] Other investors in Petherick's business included British merchant S. W. Silver, who founded the India Rubber, Gutta Percha, and Telegraph Works Company.

Petherick acknowledged the financial help he received from the London publishing houses and implied in his memoir that to a certain degree he ran the Colonial Booksellers' Agency – and companion periodical – for the London firms: 'I ~~had~~ was started, by the London Publishers, as a distributing Agent.'[25] Still, while London publishers provided Petherick with start-up capital and stock, the publishers did not control the new firm. He acted, much as Robertson had, as a middleman who purchased, typically on credit, stock from the publishers, only reimbursing them when the customer paid the firm on delivery of the book or books ordered. While Petherick boasted in his memoir that he superintended 'every detail of the work himself', he employed his brothers and others to help run the business that quickly grew to include not only the London branch, from where Petherick supervised the running of the Colonial Booksellers' Agency and produced the *Circular*, but also offices and bookstores in Melbourne, Sydney, and Adelaide – markets where George Robertson had either closed or scaled back his operations.[26]

Petherick published the *Circular*, which was a quarterly periodical issued in connection with the Colonial Booksellers' Agency and his imprint E. A. Petherick & Co., as an ordering guide to selected British, European, American, and colonial publishers' new and old publications. Petherick wrote in his memoir that '[t]he Publishers advertisements paid for the cost of the publication' and publishers were eager to include their publication lists in the *Circular*, which he produced between 1887 and 1892.[27] He was able to bring together over 30 different publishing companies from Australia, North America, Britain, Europe, and elsewhere and present their fiction and non-fiction publications in the first number of the journal.

The idea of the *Circular* was not new as it followed in the footsteps of other publishers' catalogues and trade journals. Moreover, the journal was not the first to target the transnational marketplace. Hedeler's *Export Journal: International Circular for the Book, Paper and Printing Trades*, which was first published one month before the debut of the *Circular*, was another periodical aimed at the flourishing international book trade. The *Export Journal*, which was written in English, French, and German, listed new English and European book and music publications, and it included a digest of copyright laws and other topics of interest to the international book trade. However, the *Export Journal* was an industry journal whereas the *Circular* was aimed at both those in the trade and private consumers. The *Circular* incorporated a select list of new English-language books and a list of new and old English and foreign-language publications on the colonies or published in the colonies, with both catalogues providing the book prices. The journal also included articles on the colonial and overseas book trades and publishers' advertisements. Unlike the *Circular*, the *Export Journal* was not a buying guide through which potential customers – both booksellers and individual book buyers – could order books and the *Export Journal* was not backed by a distribution agency.

While 'colonial' was in the title of Petherick's journal and he wrote in the first issue that he expected that the majority of his business would be in supplying the colonial trade, in the same issue he offered to find foreign-language books for potential clients, reported that he retained the services of a 'French and German correspondent', and promised to deliver books to readers worldwide.[28] In the second issue as he noted the change to the title to *The Torch and Colonial Book Circular*, he also reported that he had heard 'from Booksellers, Publishers, Librarians, and book-lovers all over the world' who had applauded the launch of the journal.[29] Petherick conceived of the *Circular* and the Colonial Booksellers' Agency as advertising, selling, and distributing books internationally and in the second issue of the journal he observed that his efforts were not going unnoticed. His emphasis on the colonial trade was simply a case of practicality as the colonial markets, particularly Australia, made up a large percentage of the emerging international trade in English-language books. Robertson had stopped distributing British publishers' books in Australia and Petherick had taken over the distribution network that he had helped to develop and his former employer had abandoned. Consequently, he recognized the importance of this particular market to his fledgling company's bottom line.

Petherick considered the colonial markets as part of the international book trade. He argued that the world conceptually was a network made up of 'a lot of ante-rooms in which we dodge about before entering the next. In that we can all meet, be it soon or late.'[30] The colonial sphere was simply another 'ante-room', albeit an important one, that was linked to and a part of the larger construct. Initially, Petherick had thought to focus on only the Australian market and acknowledged that 'the title first chosen for this publication was "The Australasian Book Circular," but at the suggestion of friends, and with their aid, its scope will be enlarged'.[31] He realized quite quickly as Robertson's London manager that the 'ante-rooms' of the colonial world connected to other rooms and book buyers who wanted access to a regular supply of books. The colonial world was not isolated and it was a part of the international book trade. In developing the distribution routes between Britain and the Australian colonies while working for George Robertson, he had also been building the infrastructure necessary for transnational book circulation. Consequently, the *Circular* advertised books and the Colonial Booksellers' Agency distributed them not only to buyers from the colonies and those interested in publications produced in or about the colonies but also to 'book-lovers all over the world'.[32]

Every issue of the journal included Select Lists of Recent Publications that consisted of non-fiction and fiction books. Non-fiction categories included Dictionaries and Encyclopaedias; History and Biography; Economics, Politics and Topics of the Day; Law and Jurisprudence; Trade and Commerce; Religion and Philosophy; Education; Geography, Topography, Voyages and Travels; Natural and Physical Science; Medicine; Industrial and Applied Arts; and Rural and Domestic Economy. Fiction was organized by Novels: Circulating Library Editions; Novels: Cabinet Editions, 3/6 to 6/-; Novels: Florin and Half Crown; Novels: Shilling and Eighteenpenny; Novels: Sixpenny and Threepenny; and Novels: Colonial Editions. Not every *Circular* included all the categories and the emphasis in the journal's first two volumes was on non-fiction publications. Analysing the first two volumes of the *Circular*, produced between 1887 and 1889, reveals the majority of these books were from the British houses that had provided backing for the Colonial Booksellers' Agency. However, American publishers' books occasionally appeared and by the fifth issue (volume two) the general catalogues regularly listed works published by the American firms Ticknor, Putnam, Harper Brothers, Lippincott, Houghton, and McClurg.

The second part of each issue of the *Circular* was devoted to a catalogue of primarily non-fiction Colonial Publications and Books Relating to the Colonies, which ranged from immigrant guides and travel narratives to government documents. For example, the first issue of the *Circular* included the fourth edition of James Hector's *Hand-Book of New Zealand*, published in Wellington, New Zealand, and George A. Koch's technical *Report on the Cariboo Quartz Ledges of British Columbia*, published in Victoria, BC, Canada.[33] While the majority of the publications catalogued provided practical historical, political, social, or scientific information, Petherick also listed novels, plays, and poetry by colonial authors or about the colonies. The second issue included Toronto publisher Blackett Robinson's publication of Sarah Anne Curzon's *Laura Secord the Heroine of 1812: Drama, and Other Poems* as a notable work about Canada.[34] In the second issue Petherick reported that his 'old friend and *confrère* Mr. James Bain, now of the Toronto Public Library' had supplied him with information of 'many new Canadian Publications', which had allowed him to expand the Canadian section of the list.[35]

Besides a catalogue of books about or published in the Dominion of Canada, this section of the *Circular* also included lists of general books about the colonies and books about or published in Australasia, which included New Zealand, Fiji, and Polynesia. With the fifth issue, the volume of books relating to the Australian colonies necessitated the division of the Australasian category into three separate groups: Australia; New Zealand; and New Guinea, Fiji, and Polynesia. Other colonies warranted separate categories and were incorporated in the *Circular* when there were publications Petherick thought might be of interest to the reader; consequently, books about or published in the South African colonies, West Africa, Mauritius and the Seychelles, West Indies, and British Guiana were also included in some of the issues.

While many of the books listed in the Colonial Publications and Books Relating to the Colonies section were produced by the major British houses, Petherick also added books published by his own imprint, as well as smaller foreign and colonial firms, including material from publishers and printers in Hong Kong, Singapore, Cape Colony, India, and Australia. While the vast majority of publications found in the *Circular* were English-language books, Petherick also listed German, French, and Italian books about the colonies and overseas possessions that the Colonial Booksellers' Agency was responsible for distributing, including the journal *Revue Coloniale Internationale* published by J. H. De Bussy in Amsterdam.[36] The Colonial Publications and Books Relating to the Colonies portion of the *Circular* offered a miscellany of non-fiction and fiction for sale and it demonstrated Petherick's extensive connections that allowed him to report on and distribute a diversity of British, European, American, and colonial English and foreign-language publications.

Initially, this diversity was not readily apparent as the first issues of the *Circular* principally listed British publications and included advertisements of the firms that provided Petherick with financial support. Moreover, these issues opened with articles on the Australian and colonial book trades that further promoted the impression that the *Circular* was primarily, if not exclusively, for a colonial audience. The inaugural issue included a short overview of '"The Trade" in Australasia' and notices of forthcoming Australian books, as well as a couple of notable British publications.[37] Besides Petherick's opening message to colonial book buyers and collectors of colonial literature, he also briefly addressed the need for more British publishers to produce colonial book series and provided a history relating to the discoverer Abel Janszen Tasman for whom Tasmania was named.[38] The second issue, now renamed *The Torch and Colonial Book Circular*, included an announcement about the new title and notices about upcoming Australian and British publications. The third issue opened with a portion of Petherick's 'Bibliography of Australasia' that would continue to appear in future issues of the journal.

Petherick's preoccupation with colonial spaces, particularly Australia, in the *Circular*'s pages was a consequence of his initial plans to produce a journal specifically for the Australian market and did not preclude the wider reach of the *Circular* and his company. Even with the first issue, which included foreign and colonial publications, and certainly with later issues that increased the diversity of the catalogues and the number of publishers and places included in the journal, he demonstrated an understanding of the colonial world as part of a larger international sphere. His inclusion of French, German, Italian, and other foreign-language books about colonial and international places revealed his understanding of the interconnectedness of the world. A book buyer in the United States, Australia, or Fiji might want a copy of the *Revue Coloniale Internationale* or a bookseller in Britain might want to order publications from firms in Colombo, Ceylon, and/or Milwaukee who advertised in the *Circular*. The *Circular*'s collected second volume included a half-page advertisement for C. N. Caspar, Mikwaukee, announcing the availability of Caspar's *General Directory of American Book, News, and Stationery Trade* and a full-page advertisement for A. M. J Ferguson, Observer Press, Colombo, listing the *Ceylon Hand-Book and Directory*, *The Buried Cities of Ceylon*, and the *Coffee Planter's Manual*, as well as other Observer Press publications that were available through the Colonial Booksellers'

Agency.[39] Petherick recognized that both himself and book buyers were part of a larger network. Colonial spaces were a part of the international book trade, and in launching the journal and the Colonial Booksellers' Agency he provided the means of circulating books globally.

The *Circular* was a material artefact of the international book trade and the growing social network of book trade agents distributing and selling books overseas in the late nineteenth century. It was the result of the many contacts Petherick made while working for George Robertson to develop the distribution system between Britain and the Australian colonies and the additional connections he made in launching an international distribution company. The increasingly diverse array of publishers, including firms from Odessa and Singapore, whose publications were catalogued in the journal also attests to Petherick's continuing ability to make further connections and encourage firms to list books, as well as advertise, in the *Circular*. More than just an artefact of the international book trade, the journal was a site where book buyers, who could not easily access booksellers and larger markets, could connect with publishers and other agents, who had publications for sale but who did not necessarily have access to all potential consumers. In the inaugural issue, Petherick described the *Circular* as a torch that could direct readers but I think it is more accurate to say that he was the light bearer who offered guidance in the pages of the journal. While the 'ante-rooms' of the various markets in the international book trade were linked, book buyers and producers did not have equal levels of access and connection; the *Circular* was an intermediary through which Petherick facilitated the connections between book buyers and book producers and encouraged them to 'meet, be it soon or late' in the processes of buying books.[40]

One of Petherick's particular goals in publishing the *Circular* was to promote the development of publications for the colonial and overseas markets. He encouraged publishers to create series of inexpensive new books not only for the colonies but also for other overseas markets for readers who lacked access because of the often high cost of British publications in smaller markets. In the inaugural September 1887 issue, Petherick described his former employer's successful publication and sale of inexpensive colonial editions in the Australian market: 'It is now twenty-three or twenty-four years since Mr. George Robertson obtained editions of *Lady Audley's Secret* and *Eleanor's Victory* to retail in the Colonies ... Since the year 1872 over 120 of the most popular novels have been added to Mr. Robertson's list.'[41] In the article, Petherick implied that Robertson's success persuaded British firms to follow suit and he observed that '[o]f late years British Publishers have awakened to a knowledge of the requirements of the Colonies, and occasionally have been induced to prepare cheap early editions for sale'. He noted that four firms – Richard Bentley and Son, Macmillan, Sampson and Low, and Kegan Paul – were presently producing colonial editions but many publishers still refused to entertain proposals for colonial editions: 'British publishers have not always been ready to entertain proposals for cheap special editions – indeed some have been most adverse to it.' Consequently, there was a need for an international buying guide that offered publications that could be 'posted to any part of the world'.[42] He considered the Colonial Booksellers' Agency and *Circular* as filling a gap since the distribution company and journal would aid colonial and foreign individual book buyers and booksellers to order books without having to wait for inexpensive special editions to be produced.

Following his own advice to British publishers to produce inexpensive series of new and popular books, Petherick started his own imprint, E. A. Petherick & Co., and published Petherick's Collection of Favourite and Approved Authors for Circulation in the Colonies Only. E. A. Petherick & Co. bought sheets from or jointly produced editions of British, American, and colonial fiction for the colonial markets with various British publishers; firms with whom Petherick worked include: William Heinemann; James R. Osgood, McIlvaine and Company; Kegan Paul, Trench, Trübner and Co.; Smith Elder; Oliphant, Anderson and Ferrier; Longman; Ward and Downey; Chatto and Windus; Fisher Unwin; and George Allen. Petherick bound his books in distinctive red covers that incorporated on the back four images of animals that represented the major markets where he sold his publications: an elephant represented India, a lion represented Africa, a kangaroo represented the Australian colonies, and a beaver represented Canada. Graeme Johanson observes that 'never before had a publisher relied entirely for all colonial editions on binding others' sheets, and no publisher (before or afterwards) relied entirely on colonial editions to support a publishing business'.[43] While the vast majority of the publications were colonial editions, E. A. Petherick & Co. also occasionally produced books either by colonial authors or about the British colonies, which were for the colonial, British, American, and other markets. For example, in 1889, Petherick published *A Journey to Lake Taupo and Australian and New Zealand Tales and Sketches* by Percy Russell without a British partner. In 1890, he started producing *E. A. Petherick & Co's Monthly Catalogue* that listed literary, artistic, and scientific books, with an emphasis on his imprint's publications, available for sale in his Melbourne and Sydney bookstores and through the Colonial Booksellers' Agency.[44]

Petherick boasted in his memoir that his distribution, advertising, and publishing divisions initially thrived and that in the first three years of the Colonial Booksellers' Agency's existence the firm grew rapidly as the demand for books escalated.[45] While no supporting financial documentation survives or has been found that clarifies the true extent of Petherick's success, what is known is that in order to meet the growing demand for books, expand his transnational distribution capabilities, and develop his imprint, he took out loans and any success was tempered by increasing levels of debt.[46] In 1892, the Colonial Booksellers' Agency's liabilities were £50,000, and this high level of debt precipitated a crisis that eventually led to bankruptcy.

A number of letters and legal documents in the Petherick Collection and British publishers' archives that have recently come to light illustrate the Colonial Booksellers' Agency did not fail simply because of Petherick's mismanagement or misfortune; the business was a victim of its own success and of some of its creditors and debtors who realized that they no longer needed a middleman like Petherick to distribute their publications overseas and in the colonies. As publishers not only produced financially successful colonial series but also explored distributing their own publications overseas, the knowledge gap that had led the firms to seek Petherick's advice and assistance regarding international book distribution narrowed.[47]

Even before the launch of the Colonial Booksellers' Agency, some firms like Macmillan hedged their bets and provided Petherick with loans while also developing their own distribution routes.[48] As they became aware of the financial benefits of selling English-language books to an international clientele, publishers educated themselves about the emerging overseas marketplace. By 1892, publishers no longer needed to keep Petherick's business afloat. Moreover, whereas the Colonial Booksellers' Agency initially supported and worked with British publishers to distribute their books in colonial and foreign markets, Petherick's foray into publishing his own inexpensive series led to him being in direct competition with publishing houses that were financing his company. Consequently, when the rapid escalation of debts led to a credit crisis, some of Petherick's guarantors could not see the value in propping up a competitor and refused to help refinance the company in order to rebalance liabilities and assets, which pushed the Colonial Booksellers' Agency into bankruptcy.

Publishing was a business of slim profit margins, more so in the realm of the international distribution of books; even though Petherick believed there was a demand for an international distributor and bookseller, the Colonial Booksellers' Agency was plagued by cash-flow problems from the outset. Initially, Petherick bought books on credit and only paid the publishers when the books were sold and payment was received from his customers. Petherick faced the same problems as Macmillan and other publishers and distributors who had transnational business dealings in the nineteenth century. Financial transfers between countries, especially over long distances, were difficult, if not non-existent. One of the reasons colonial and foreign firms, like George Robertson and Company, opened London offices was that there was no delay in the firm paying bills for books and texts. For example, Robertson received favourable terms from London publishers because his local office could pay them without delay. Similarly, Petherick based the Colonial Booksellers' Agency in London in order to reap the advantages of location. Still, he often had to wait months for payments from clients because of the lack of an international monetary system and the delays caused by distance and/or transportation problems. Moreover, while publishers extended him a line of credit, he, like other borrowers, was expected to pay within a certain period; many publishers either did not want to extend their due dates on promissory notes or did not factor in the extended time that Petherick would need to collect money owed from clients that lived overseas.

The overhead costs of maintaining the firm's global scale were also not adequately redistributed: even though the shipping costs were quite high, it does not seem that Petherick marked up the price of his books accordingly. In the inaugural edition of the *Circular*, he noted that '[a]s to the prices quoted; now that the means for forwarding books are so frequent and regular, and rates of freight so low, most of the new English books are retailed in the Colonies at the published prices'.[49] Petherick only made allowances for an additional charge to be levied on books imported from the colonies for customers: 'for Colonial Publications a small advance will sometimes be necessary to cover the cost of postage, that being at present, the only practicable means of importing them while the demand is limited'.[50] Petherick mistakenly assumed that the economies of scale that applied to the large shipments he had previously dispatched, while working for George Robertson, that allowed the Melbourne-based bookseller to offer books at British prices would also permit the Colonial Booksellers' Agency to offer books at reasonable prices. While Petherick was very much aware that books shipped overseas had to be packed 'in zinc-lined cases' and he had the outlay for 'freight, insurance, dock charges, cartage, commission agents, and other expenses incidental to shipping', he seemed not to realize that transportation costs would be magnified because the Colonial Booksellers'

Agency offered to distribute books anywhere mail could be sent and received and because the firm shipped smaller and more numerous packages to individual book buyers and booksellers.[51]

Even as Petherick's costs soared, the demand for English-language books increased and he took on further loans in order to finance further expansion of the Colonial Booksellers' Agency. In a letter dated 30 April 1892, Petherick wrote to Richard Bentley, George Bentley's son, about 'the present position of this business, which is steadily progressing'.[52] He reported that he was looking for a partner but had 'not yet met with a partner willing to embark in colonial business, but I am getting liberal aid from my London Bankers'. According to Petherick, his business had increased 'steadily month by month, until our purchases are £50,000 a year, and this year, will probably be £60,000'. He required an influx of capital, as he was buying books on credit to fill the escalating demand for English-language books. Consequently, he was taking on more and more debt in order to fill his orders. As he could not find a single business partner, he proposed that Richard Bentley and Son join with 13 other London publishers who had each offered Petherick a further £500 or more 'so that I [could] have at present a working capital of £8000'. He hoped that Bentley would add his firm to the list – 'the only first-class firm which is not yet included' – and provide the Agency with a minimum of £500. In a second letter sent to Bentley on 1 May 1892, Petherick thanked him for agreeing to his plan: '[I am] sure it will result profitably and be mutually beneficial.'[53]

However, Petherick's cash-flow problems continued; three months after receiving the infusion of capital, he already needed more money to pay off mounting debts. In a letter to Bentley dated 12 August 1892, he wrote that 'I have to face the difficulty … and, God giving me strength, I will overcome it. The difficulty must be got over <u>permanently</u>.'[54] Petherick asked his 'sympathizing' friend's advice and pleaded with him 'not [to] lose confidence in us'. The 'us' Petherick is referring to is both the Colonial Booksellers' Agency and the economically depressed Australian book trade: 'Surely I am not to be allowed to fail! … we are ourselves sustaining so many there [in Australia] perhaps and probably to our own detriment.' In continuing to supply books to booksellers and readers who could not immediately reimburse Petherick for their purchases, he was left with escalating debts that he could not pay; nevertheless, he argued with Bentley that the firm had to support the trade; otherwise, the entire market could collapse. Petherick added that just '[b]ecause we have used Bank money or received Banker's accommodation instead of invested capital, the business is not less legitimate, or profitable'. Sensitive to the fact that he did not have family capital to invest in his own firm and had to rely on bank and publishers' loans and credits to fund the launch of the company, he noted that George Robertson had also been granted a great deal of bank and publishers' credit in the past, and he 'was not doing more "book" business than we are doing at present – and that [previous] accommodation was given by Bankers and Publishers upon no security at all'. However, unlike Robertson, Petherick had mounting bank loans at a time when a series of severe depressions in Australia, the United States, Canada, and Europe occurred that affected the international economy. Banks were calling in loans in order to avoid bankruptcy and Petherick was in no position to pay any of them off, especially as he was allowing customers to delay payment so their own businesses would not collapse.

While Petherick assumed Richard Bentley was a sympathetic friend, who wanted to help him and his firm, Bentley argued against the London publishers propping up the Colonial Booksellers' Agency any further in letters to George Hubert Longman: 'the proposition seemed to <u>defer</u> the crisis but not to <u>cope</u> with it'.[55] Interestingly, Bentley worried that if the publishers loaned any more money to Petherick, they would in effect own the Colonial Booksellers' Agency, and they would be in direct competition with other wholesale firms. However, Bentley's objection, which would become clearer in successive letters to Longman, was not that the London firms should not compete directly for market share but that they did not need to invest and potentially risk any more money on Petherick's venture.[56] The firm had outlived its usefulness as an international distributor of British publications. Robertson, Petherick, and others had established the channels of distribution between Britain and distant book markets, like Australia, as well as pioneered the use of new communication and transportation technologies to advance the international book trade. Their actions had paved the way for the London publishers to market, sell, and distribute their own publications overseas.

In a letter dated 20 August 1892, Richard Bentley wrote to George Hubert Longman about Petherick's proposal to 'shift the burden from the shoulders of the Australian firm to those of the guarantors', arguing that the plan was flawed as it would result in creditors sinking 'further capital into the venture' with little chance of recovery.[57] He stated that the creditors could only recoup their investments if 'there were a surplus in winding up the estate'. However, a surplus was unlikely and Bentley contended 'that the creditors cannot increase their capital in the Colonial Booksellers' Agency when the company is in so much financial difficulty'. Furthermore, Bentley believed that the firm's future was in doubt, regardless of whether the London publishers offered Petherick a further infusion of capital, because '[s]o many different interests are concerned that other complications are likely'. For example, he pointed out that the Federal Bank of Australia 'owing to the tightness in the Australian Market (just now depressed) might call in its overdraft'. Bentley's letter to Longman ends with an addendum that 'news of the suspension of the Federal Bank reached England by telegraph January 30 1893'.

Bentley responded to Petherick's request, on 16 September 1892, stating that he had written to Mr Longman about both asking the creditors to increase their holdings in the Colonial Booksellers' Agency and passing a binding resolution on the creditors to accept a schedule for payment of debt.[58] Bentley and Longman wanted neither to antagonize the other creditors by forcing their hands nor did they wish to increase their holdings in the firm and become Petherick's guarantors. While Bentley's response to Petherick stressed his intention of working with him and the firm's creditors, his letters to Longman made no mention of trying to find a solution to Petherick's mounting debt. Bentley's first letter to Longman was primarily concerned about whether the creditors would be able to recover the money they had lent to Petherick to start the business.

In January 1893, Petherick agreed to relinquish ownership in favour of the firm becoming 'a Limited Company with £50,000 capital', in which investors could purchase shares.[59] Bentley reported to Longman that 'the majority of the guarantors favour ... the scheme' and that the resolution passed at the January meeting of the creditors and guarantors of the Colonial Booksellers' Agency. However, Bentley argued in a letter to Longman that with 'special knowledge at our command of the status of Mr. Petherick's affairs' neither publisher should lend their names to the formation of a company without assets.[60] He doubted that any prospective shareholders would come forward and asked Longman how much longer 'are we warranted in keeping the general creditors in the dark'. Apparently the creditors had not been apprised of Petherick's complete lack of funds at previous meetings. Bentley added that five months had passed since the start of the crisis and there was little expectation of benefit arising from the latest attempt to save the firm. Finally, Bentley wrote that he was going to take independent action and send Petherick a claim for the amount owing his firm, £500.[61] In January 1893, Bentley sent Petherick a formal claim for monies owed and a letter that warned that until the bill was paid the firm could no longer supply him with any more books.[62]

While Bentley argued that the 'difficulties of the firm cannot be overcome', other publishers initially supported Petherick.[63] In an account of Petherick's financial problems, Richard Bentley, or one of his employees, reported that 'from July to December [1892] we alone advised caution in dealing with the matter, all the other houses taking a different view ... In February 1893 they however adopted a common mode of action similar to our own.'[64] Initially, Longman and Heinemann wanted to protect Petherick from bankruptcy. In a letter dated 8 October 1892, Richard Bentley wrote to George Hubert Longman asking to defer his official response to the proposal of the other London firms to refinance the Colonial Booksellers' Agency in order to give him time to confer with his father.[65] Richard Bentley was 'very reluctant to cause even the appearance of any hindrance to the favourable progress of a matter upon which so much time and consideration have been bestowed', but he was not going to agree to the proposal that he and his father felt would only delay the inevitable failure of Petherick's business. While Bentley argued that the publishers could only postpone Petherick's bankruptcy, Longman and Heinemann attempted to broker a deal to protect Petherick and his firm from economic failure. William Heinemann was one of the publishers who favoured loaning Petherick further capital, and he suggested 'floating a company' or reorganizing the existing firm as a limited company so that the London publishers became the sole owners and Petherick their employee.[66] In a letter dated 25 January 1893, Richard Bentley promised William Heinemann that his firm would not 'take any stringent step against him [Petherick] unless, indeed, some circumstances ... arose to compel action on our part in defence of our interests'.

At the end of January 1893, Longman and other publishers realized that Petherick's 'total want of capital' left the Colonial Booksellers' Agency in a precarious position, which was made worse when Petherick's largest creditor, the Federal Bank of Australia, failed.[67] Suddenly, Petherick lost his main line of credit, his loan of approximately £10,000 was called in, and his company was spun further into crisis. By late 1893, the Agency had for all intents and purposes ground to a halt because of a lack of stock. Also, the *Circular* had ceased publication in 1892 because of Petherick's lack of capital and growing debts, but he was still producing colonial editions under the E. A. Petherick & Co. imprint, although as part of his bankruptcy proceedings he sold his colonial library to one of his creditors, George Bell, 'who expanded it for another fourteen years'.[68]

At a later meeting of guarantors and creditors, on 5 July 1894, Petherick stated that 'they had no stock; for the last 8 months they had positively no supplies, and for the last 22 [months] very scanty. The stock at Melbourne had run down from £40,000 to £20,000: £2,000 or £3,000 of which were on sale or return.'[69] Moreover, publishers demanded Petherick return any of their books that he had still not sold. By February 1893, the London publishers reluctantly supported Richard Bentley's assertion that the firm could probably not be saved. Negotiations between Petherick, guarantors, and creditors continued for another year before other publishers forced the Agency into bankruptcy. A claim for monies owed was sent on 23 April 1894, from Longman, Routledge, Macmillan, Warne and Co., George Bell, and other publishers, who appointed representatives with instructions to use 'all legal and effectual means to recover and receive all of the assets of the said debtor in Victoria or elsewhere in Australia'.[70] The document ends with a schedule of creditors that includes Longman who was owed approximately £1903 and Macmillan who was owed the most at slightly over £2111. Longman, Macmillan, and the other publishing houses sought not only to secure their initial investments but also to claim Petherick's Australian assets through Edward Dickson and John Kiddle, their Australian solicitors.

However, at the meeting of guarantors and creditors in July 1894, Petherick desperately sought a last-minute reprieve from bankruptcy, asking creditors to delay bills for six months or to give him £5000 to attempt to get the company back up and running.[71] There had already been delays in the process as a committee of creditors and guarantors, including representatives for Longman, Routledge, and Macmillan, charged with issuing a report on the Agency's financial status and the means by which Petherick could refinance or repay his debts, struggled to come to a consensus.[72] Also, Petherick reported that he had tried again to refinance his debt and re-establish a line of credit at the Federal Bank of Australia, but the bank gave 'no satisfactory answer' to the question of the £10,000 still owed and he could only estimate his total liabilities at £47,000. Both numbers were speculative as neither Petherick nor the committee of creditors were sure how much was left owing. In 1894, *The London Times* reported that the bank was actually owed 'between £14,000 and £15,000' and 'gross liabilities are returned at £55,986, of which £53,103 are unsecured, with assets estimated to produce £21,360'.[73]

According to Bentley's notes of the July meeting, Petherick made a statement in which he argued that 'the Backers had told him only yesterday that it was only necessary for him to get the business taken over by a syndicate of 12 leading London Publishers to admit of every facility being afforded to him'.[74] In other words, Petherick felt that the Colonial Booksellers' Agency was still viable, if ownership was transferred to a syndicate that included his largest creditors and guarantors. However, none of the guarantors or creditors were willing to follow up on any of his suggestions and after hearing that George Allen intended to file proceedings against Petherick, they unanimously moved to file a petition of bankruptcy in court.

A newspaper clipping in the *Richard Bentley and Son Archives* of a *Daily Chronicle* article reported that following the 5 July meeting, Petherick's creditors, represented by Longman, petitioned the court on 20 July 1894 for the Colonial Booksellers' Agency to be put into receivership.[75] Another clipping from *The Standard* on 6 April 1895 detailed Petherick's request for an order of discharge from bankruptcy and the ruling of the receiver.[76] The receiver stated that less than ten shillings to the pound would be paid to Petherick's creditors. The receiver also charged that 'the Bankrupt had traded after knowledge of insolvency', but Petherick's lawyer, Mr Trinder, argued that this allegation was just a case of 'excessive trading': Petherick had kept on selling books, even after it was apparent that he was insolvent, in an attempt to recover the capital needed to pay the creditors. The court accepted Petherick's defence regarding 'the offence of trading after knowledge of insolvency' and suspended the order of discharge from bankruptcy for 'the minimum statutory period of two years'.

While Longman, Heinemann, and other publishers initially resisted forcing Petherick into bankruptcy and preferred to utilize the wholesale business to distribute their books internationally, Richard Bentley argued that the inherent risk with continually loaning larger sums of money to the Colonial Booksellers' Agency was not balanced by the return on investment and suggested that publishers should not risk their own businesses for the sake of friendship. When the firm was established in September 1887, London publishers needed both to replace George Robertson as the chief distributor of British books in the Australian colonies and to find a figure who was knowledgeable of the distribution networks and the colonial and overseas markets. Petherick's initial success with the company only confirmed that even if the international economy was depressed, people continued to buy books. However, the Colonial Booksellers' Agency's success was offset by Petherick's repeated requests for further loans and guarantees in order to keep the business afloat. Therefore, London publishers were faced with the reality that their investments in the firm were not paying off: Petherick was irregularly collecting money from book buyers, and they were not getting paid for their publications.

Bentley argued that if publishers wanted to improve the flow of capital between colonial and foreign book buyers and British publishers, they would be better off dealing with the booksellers and book buyers directly. While he made the argument that British publishers could forego using middlemen like Petherick, Bentley actually re-employed George Robertson's company to distribute books in the Australian colonies. It is important to add at this point that unlike his father George Bentley, Richard Bentley was largely uninterested in selling books overseas. The firm did not stop selling books outside Britain upon Petherick's bankruptcy but, like George Robertson with his own business, Bentley gradually wound down 'a grand business'.[77] The house continued to work with other British publishers, and in 1896, Longman and Bentley engaged an Australian representative to sell and promote jointly their publications in the colonies.[78] However, whereas Macmillan employed, in 1895, the firm's own representative to sell the publisher's publications in Australia and was more aggressive in developing its own distribution network, Bentley chose to continue cooperating in an increasingly competitive market.[79] Regardless of Bentley's actions, other publishers like Macmillan utilized the distribution networks and infrastructure that Petherick had set up firstly under George Robertson's employment and secondly with the development of the Colonial Booksellers' Agency to wholesale their own publications in the international book trade.

When Robertson curtailed his distribution business in 1887, it was not surprising that British firms, like Bentley, Longman, and Macmillan, financially backed Petherick's Colonial Booksellers' Agency. Petherick had pioneered a faster British–Australian distribution network while working for Robertson, and British publishers, still lacking knowledge of the colonial markets and distribution practices, readily offered Petherick loans, credit, and stock. However, by the early 1890s, many British publishers also had representatives and, in the case of Australia and the United States, branches in overseas markets. Their activities mirrored the earlier actions of their colonial counterparts, who had, in the 1850s and 1860s, opened London offices to facilitate the distribution of books for the overseas markets, as well as their collaboration with British publishers in the production of books and series for the colonies. Just as George Robertson and others had found their London offices to be effective in improving the supply of books for the Australian colonies, British publishers discovered that having local representatives and agencies in the United States, Canada, Australia, India, and Africa helped the firms to tailor their production and distribution practices to meet the needs of the local markets. A result of British publishers engaging representatives, or opening foreign and colonial branches, was that they no longer needed the wholesale firms and middlemen like Edward Petherick to sell and distribute their publications overseas.

As Petherick's financial losses increased and loans were called in, it was easier for Bentley and other British publishers to let the Colonial Booksellers' Agency fail rather than continue to prop it up with further financial aid. Even publishers who initially supported Petherick like Heinemann eventually accepted the fact that there was no material benefit to keeping the Colonial Booksellers' Agency financially afloat. In general, British publishers were no longer unfamiliar with the major colonial and foreign markets and could forego the cost of a middleman distributor like Petherick. Petherick offered in the inaugural issue of the *Circular* to be a guide and through the journal and Colonial Booksellers' Agency provide a light for book buyers that 'would show the "bewildered the way which leads to their prosperity and welfare"'.[80] By 1895, a publisher like Macmillan felt the firm could provide its own light to guide book buyers to their publication lists that would better secure the house's 'prosperity and welfare'.

Petherick's ambitious plans to sell and distribute books internationally with the Colonial Booksellers' Agency are no less daring because his company failed. Petherick dreamed of running a company that could successfully deliver books anywhere that mail and packages could be sent and received. While he could not traverse the limits of a fledgling global economy, the Colonial Booksellers' Agency showed other book trade agents the potential of the international marketplace. Petherick persuaded colleagues, perhaps to his own firm's detriment, that the world was not so vast that they could not distribute books internationally. Even when a series of economic depressions in the 1890s affected the development of the field of international literary production and distribution, the book trade's enthusiasm for a global market dampened but did not disappear. Heinemann and other British publishers did not stop producing colonial editions and series for sale in the colonial marketplace.[81] British, American, and colonial publishers and booksellers would continue to use the distribution networks pioneered by Petherick, though those networks would not see international trade return to pre-1895 levels until the second half of the twentieth century.

Conclusion

> The outward trade of London to Australia is not only an important one, but has made enormous strides of late years ... When I came here nearly all goods were shipped to Australia in sailing vessels: we had the opportunity of shipping about once in three months by direct auxiliary steamer, and once a month limited supplies in small packages could be sent by the Overland Mail. Now in January of this year twenty full powered Steamers left London for Australia and New Zealand, with an aggregate tonnage of sixty thousand tons, besides thirty sailing vessels representing nearly another sixty thousand gross tonnage of goods carried.[1]

Thirteen years after arriving in London, Edward Petherick reminisced about the tremendous increase in trade between Australia and Britain and the changes he had witnessed as manager of George Robertson's London branch. During his career first with Robertson and then later with his Colonial Booksellers' Agency, Petherick participated in the expansion of trade routes between the colonies and Britain and used new technologies and transportation methods to improve the circulation of books. In supplying the growing demand for English-language books in the colonies, Petherick helped to develop the infrastructure and distribution routes of an international book trade.

In the same document, written between 1883 and 1884 while still working for George Robertson, in which he recounted the improvement in British–Australian trade, Petherick described 'London [as] the centre of the publishing world' and his role in the city as helping 'in a small way to satisfy the great and increasing demand for books' in the Australian colonies.[2] Ten years earlier, Petherick had also remarked in a letter to his father that he sometimes found the city to be an overwhelming 'vortex', yet he was grateful to be in a position to engage directly with publishers and other agents who inhabited a city that he felt was a book trade hub.[3] While Petherick regarded London as a centre, he never relegated Australia to the margins or periphery of Empire. He imagined the colonies as another centre of the international book trade. A market that was part of a developing line of a larger network where there were many centres and nodes. When Petherick wrote about Australia as an important emerging market he was very much aware of distance as a barrier to increased trade but it did not stop him envisioning the colonies and himself as nodes in a network where London was just another meeting point, albeit an important one, where agents could intersect and connect.

In the late nineteenth century, Petherick and other agents in the social network challenged and crossed both real and imagined boundaries that had previously constrained the development of the international book trade. The first boundary Petherick traversed was the physical distance that separated himself and his family. He recognized that an immense distance separated London and Melbourne; still, he comforted himself with the thought that distance only temporarily separated him from his siblings and parents in Melbourne.[4] As communication and transportation improved and new distribution routes developed, distance became less of a concern to Petherick and book trade agents in general. In 1885 George E. Brett suggested to Frederick Macmillan that his son, George P. Brett, should visit Australia the next time he was out West: 'Would you let me remind you that Australia is not a great distance from San Francisco.'[5]

This physical boundary was then also an imaginary one as Edward Petherick, George E. Brett, and other agents had to think about the world not as a vast geographical expanse with isolated pockets of humanity but as a network of linked and negotiable spaces. Book trade agents needed to conceptualize the world as a series of interconnected 'ante-rooms' through which they could exchange ideas and commodities.[6] San Francisco was in terms of the network only a node away from Sydney. Instead of thinking of the thousands of miles of water that separated the two cities, Brett focused on the relative proximity brought about by faster ships and a Pacific distribution route. London, New York, Melbourne, and Calcutta were all centres or 'ante-rooms' in a larger network – the international book trade – where distance was relative. The importance Petherick initially placed on being in a certain place or location where it would be easier for him to connect with other agents would start to lessen as the geography of the network reduced the distances that separated agents and markets. In the network, Melbourne was a letter or telegram away from London, and Sydney was 'not a great distance' from San Francisco.

Petherick's and Brett's respective correspondence also reveals that both men realized that books circulated internationally irrespective of distance or borders. Petherick explained to his father in 1877 that George Robertson had to develop his American business and export American books directly to the colonies otherwise the firm would not be able to compete with other companies already distributing American books in the colonies.[7] Similarly, George E. Brett in 1885 wrote to Macmillan that other publishers were already developing their Australian business.[8] Petherick and Bretts were aware that their companies were not operating in a vacuum and that agents were already distributing books far and wide, and that to ignore this growing international book trade and network would be foolhardy and potentially disastrous to a business's bottom line.

In particular, Petherick recognized he was an agent within this network and had a choice: he could be passive or he could manoeuvre to improve his respective position in the international book trade and his ability to connect to and with other agents and companies. Petherick made the most of his personal advantage, positioning himself as a distribution middleman who could use his knowledge of colonial and overseas markets and transnational distribution channels to benefit his business partners and clients. He believed he was so successful in his endeavours that he repeatedly boasted that his hard work had resulted in Australians viewing him as important as 'a Colonial Governor' and the trade considering him an influential figure in an emerging international print economy.[9] Putting aside Petherick's arrogance, he imagined himself as a node or centre: a person other agents wanted to connect to because of his knowledge of overseas markets and experience as a colonial and transnational distributor.

Paul Eggert contends that '[w]hile economic power remained in London, there is little doubt that the empire did indeed write back', and a colonial firm like George Robertson and Company had influence with British firms on what was produced for colonial markets.[10] I would go farther than Eggert and argue that 'economic power' decentralizes during the late nineteenth century and coalesces in the network in terms of individual agents. In other words, perhaps the agents are the centres, not the places, and the agent one interacted with mattered more than the physical location of oneself or the other agent. Instead of imagining London as a centre, perhaps in terms of a social network it was an interchange; London was an important intersection in the international book trade because of all the agents or nodes found there, which facilitated engagement. However, it was not the only junction in the network, and technology expedited the linking of agents and made it less important for an agent to be located at a particular crossing within the system. Petherick's experiences as George Robertson's London manager and later as head of his own distribution company taught him that he was an influential agent in the network. He lived in an increasingly connected world, and his work on the infrastructure of the British–Australian book trade aided in the crossing of boundaries that had once separated and isolated agents.

As agents became aware of and interested in the international book trade, the growth of social networks had a transformative effect on the literary field and enabled the further crossing of social, cultural, and political boundaries. Petherick in his memoir detailed the hectic pace of George Robertson's branch and later the Colonial Booksellers' Agency and this particular account in many ways dovetails with his earlier 'ante-room' metaphor as an apt description for the growth of the social network and the international book trade.[11] Petherick described the constant flow of mail and parcels monthly, weekly, daily, and hourly streaming in and out of the two London offices:

> Shipments, monthly, fortnightly, weekly; parcels of papers by post – by various routes overland and by sea – big cases and sometimes hundreds by each steamer and sailing vessel averaging six tons a day! ... This for 25 years occupied my attention besides the reading of reviews and perusal of all the new books, a daily and hourly work, selecting and ordering them, and apportioning them to our branches and correspondents – Mail in Monday morning with half a dozen or more big packets of orders, remittances from Melbourne, besides smaller dispatches from lesser correspondents ... Letters to write, answers and reports to get. Replies and acknowledgements, invoices, contents of every parcel by post or case, of every case – summaries of everything to 6. o'clock Friday with my own Official and Confidential Letters – Lists of all new books submitted, ordered or declined – This and a hundred details completed by 7 pm Friday, for post closing.[12]

Each book, parcel, and letter that he mentioned buying, sending, and writing was an agent or node and each one connected to other agents or nodes in the network. As Petherick's purchases, packages, and correspondence circulated, they were bought, received, and responded to by other agents. Books, parcels, and letters generated further books, parcels, and letters. One connection led to another and the international book trade expanded as books were produced, distributed, and consumed.

Petherick's recognition of the interconnectivity of the book trade was not that unusual. Hedeler's *Export Journal*, first published a month before the inaugural issue of Petherick's *Circular* in August 1887, also demonstrated an awareness of the various markets, publishers, and other agents being linked and a part of an international book trade in the late nineteenth century. Published monthly, the *Export Journal* and some of the advertisements were written in French, German, and English in order to communicate with as large an audience as possible.[13] With articles on expiring copyrights, copyright laws, and import duties, the *Export Journal* tried to facilitate the circulation of books, paper, and print materials in the international sphere. It also provided 'Sketches of Eminent Houses', based in Leipzig, Paris, Milan, London, New York, and Boston, and catalogues of new publications listed under German, English, French, Finnish, Greek, Dutch, Romance (Spanish and Italian), Scandinavian, and Slavonic headings.[14] Petherick even wrote an article entitled 'Australasia: Bookselling and Stationery Trades' for the first issue in which he 'doubt[ed] if any other country in the world [could] ... show so large a consumption of books and stationery for so limited a population'.[15] The trade journal attempted to educate the trade about foreign and colonial markets. While the first volume of the *Export Journal* concentrated on the European and colonial trades, this limited focus was a consequence of the markets thought to be of interest to subscribers and did not preclude the fact that the journal positioned itself as an international journal that considered the various trades as not isolated but connected.

The *Export Journal* also provided assistance to subscribers trying to overcome or circumvent the numerous impediments to the transnational circulation of books and commodities. The table of contents for the collected first volume of the *Export Journal* included listings for Post Tariffs and Postal and Custom Notes, as well as a Comparative Money Scale.[16] Moreover, through a Trade Directory, the journal provided the means by which agents could learn about and connect to other agents in the book industries. Short articles on issues of interest to the various book and stationery trades also appeared in the journal. For example, Dr S. R. Millar, United States Consul in Leipzig, provided a brief overview of American import duties on books and stationery goods in the first issue of the *Export Journal* that reminded subscribers that '[i]t is important to comply with the regulations, because ignorance of them is not accepted as an excuse, and noncompliance entails trouble and sometimes expense to consignees'.[17] While some of the difficulties and 'expense[es]' surrounding international trade could be avoided if agents educated themselves about another country's rules and regulations, not all of the problems associated with the transnational circulation of books could be so easily surmounted.

George P. Brett wrote to Frederick Macmillan in a letter dated 6 March 1894 stating that he regretted to learn that the colonial edition of Mrs Humphry Ward's *Marcella* would be sold in Canada: 'I am a little sorry to learn from your cable of this morning that you cannot withhold the Colonial Library edition of "Marcella" from Canadian sale as it will be so much cheaper than ours [American edition] that we shall have a number of copiers coming across the American borders.'[18] The logistics of selling books and different editions of books in multiple locations could not always be easily arranged. Brett reported that he would have to cancel 'the sale of one thousand sets [copies] to the Toronto News Co.' as the more expensive American edition would not sell if the colonial edition was also available in Canada. Moreover, even if an agent managed to overcome many of the boundaries and impediments that constrained the transnational circulation of print matter, there was no guarantee the agent would be successful in the international book trade. Brett in another letter written to Macmillan in 1894 worried about 'the condition of the trade' and if booksellers were 'squeezed out of business' how it would affect the company.[19] A host of factors influenced the success or failure of a business, including the overall 'dull times' Brett described that were depressing the American and British markets and economies.

While Petherick often wrote about the growing demand of colonial and foreign readers for English-language books in his correspondence, the history of the Colonial Booksellers' Agency further illustrates that supplying the increasing demand for books was not a guarantee of success. When Petherick opened the Colonial Booksellers' Agency in September 1887, he was confident about the business's future because of the escalating demand for books overseas, and he boasted in his memoir that all the major London publishing houses were eager to finance the transnational distribution firm.[20] George Bentley, Herbert Longman, and others lent Petherick capital and provided his company with stock because they needed to replace George Robertson, who had drastically downsized his distribution network. Desire to preserve their share of the Australian colonial market and/or enter the international market played a large role in the publishers financing Petherick's company. However, his friendship with Bentley, Longman, and other publishers also influenced their decision both to inject capital into the distributing firm and to ignore their growing trepidation regarding the Colonial Booksellers' Agency's questionable finances and lack of profit.

While Petherick claimed his business was profitable, in order to meet the growing demand for books overseas and expand his business capabilities, he repeatedly asked for and received large loans from his financial backers; thus, increasing levels of debt mitigated the success of the Colonial Booksellers' Agency.[21] In 1893, Petherick, realizing that his creditors had lost patience with his requests for further capital and for time to turn the business around, presented a business plan to restructure the Colonial Booksellers' Agency as a limited-liability joint-stock company – the forbearer of the modern corporation.[22] Petherick recognized, too late, that a traditionally organized business with a single owner who owed money to a circle of family, friends, and colleagues could not raise the funds necessary to continue operating internationally. Moreover, Petherick's centralized control of the Colonial Booksellers' Agency and his imprint E. A. Petherick & Co. did not allow his employees at the three offices and bookstores in the Australian colonies, as well as his other agents, the necessary autonomy to deal with problems affecting one market and not another. When he proposed altering the structure of the company, he was willing to give up control to his creditors who would become stockholders in the new business and to decentralize the command structure, providing his employees with a degree of autonomy, in order to avoid bankruptcy. Initially, the majority of Petherick's creditors supported his proposal; however, Petherick could not find new investors willing to risk their funds on a deteriorating business and the Colonial Booksellers' Agency failed. He realized too late that the international book trade demanded a business structure that could more easily adjust to the demands of a global market.

A deterrent to international trade was the traditional centralized organization of business, which could not always adapt to or account for the distance that often separated one office from another and a company from its overseas markets. The use of the telegraph had improved overseas communication but instant and inexpensive communication still did not exist. Both Edward Petherick and George P. Brett regularly received and sent telegrams, using the technology to communicate with their respective offices and agents. While the overseas telegraph sped up communication, it could not always overcome the distance that separated offices. The decision made in London as to the publication date and distribution of Mrs Humphry Ward's *Marcella* was not communicated to the New York office in time to avoid the problem of the cheaper colonial edition circulating in the Canadian market and undercutting Macmillan's more expensive American edition.[23] While conceptualizing the world as a linked network helped agents to shrink distance, agents still had to contend with tangible obstructions to the transnational flow of products, such as the lack of an international system to transfer funds. Furthermore, firms operating in the international sphere often needed large reserves of capital in order to weather downturns in the various local, regional, and national economies within which the company had investments or business. Brett worried that Macmillan's New York branch would be 'much worse off', if a depressed economy led to a number of American booksellers going out of business, than the branch in London, where the economic downturn might not be so severe.[24] It was difficult for a company to account and plan for the disparities between markets and economies in which it did business.

The transnational circulation and sale of books and other goods required a company with a decentralized and flexible organization that could adapt to the variable economic conditions agents faced in the international sphere. While Macmillan started as a family-run house, the firm hired a professional manager in George E. Brett to run their American branch and gave Brett a certain amount of autonomy to run the business. Macmillan adapted and diversified as commerce changed in the nineteenth century and as international trade demanded a company be flexible enough to both accommodate multiple markets and finance large capital flows. Macmillan New York became a joint-stock company in 1891 when the American branch became a separate business: 'George Craik, Alexander and Frederick Macmillan each retaining a 20 per cent share in the New York business, and George and Maurice Macmillan 15 per cent each. [George P.] Brett was taken into partnership with a 10 per cent share' of the 'increasingly buoyant American operation'.[25] In 1894, Brett worried about the impact a slump in the economy might have on the American branch, but the independence of the New York office provided the needed flexibility to weather and accommodate the downturn in one market and not another.

In 1896, Macmillan was additionally restructured and the New York agency was incorporated as a joint-stock limited-liability 'American company, owned mostly by the London Macmillans but managed by Brett as its president'.[26] A limited-liability joint-stock company is a business in which capital is raised through the sale of stocks to a group of shareholders who are liable for company debts but their limit of liability only extends to the amount they initially invested in the firm.[27] A network of investors in which one stockholder can be replaced by another stockholder, a limited-liability joint-stock company can quickly raise the large financial investments that were often necessary to operate successfully in the international field. The restructuring of Macmillan in the 1890s, or rupture in the social network, resulted in two companies that were still linked but largely autonomous. This reorganization facilitated Macmillan's expansion into international markets. The publishing house adapted as commerce changed in the late nineteenth century, allowing the firm to continue expanding and diversifying even during a period of global economic downturn.

In the 1880s and 1890s, a series of economic depressions in Australia, North America, and Europe occurred that eventually affected the international book trade.[28] George P. Brett in his letters to Maurice Macmillan first remarked on the severity of the financial slump battering the Australian economy in 1887.[29] Surprisingly, neither Petherick nor his backers discussed the impact of this decline on the Colonial Booksellers' Agency. Petherick was clearly aware of the problem as he wrote at times of the need for his company to be lenient in requiring customers to pay as the Colonial Booksellers' Agency was, to a certain degree by not forcing a number of colonial booksellers to pay their outstanding debts, keeping the colonial firms financially afloat.[30] He did not want to call in debts and his backers certainly did not seem worried about the lack of payments; when Petherick repeatedly requested further infusions of capital, between 1888 and 1892, his supporters complied. In contrast to Petherick's actions, Macmillan was not willing to support the Australian book trade to the detriment of the company, though the firm provided Petherick with financial aid when asked.

While Macmillan was interested in enlarging the firm's share of the international book trade in 1887, the company did not want to jeopardize its existing branches in Britain and the United States for the sake of further expansion. Instead of opening an Australian distribution agency, Macmillan invested in Petherick's Colonial Booksellers' Agency. The firm's shrewd and pragmatic calculation was that it was cheaper and safer to invest a smaller amount in another distribution company rather than risk a larger sum of capital in establishing the publishing firm's own branch in the Australian colonies. Macmillan succeeded where Petherick failed for a number of reasons. Macmillan was better capitalized and positioned than the Colonial Booksellers' Agency and the firm was able to split into two companies, which provided the needed flexibility necessary for transnational commerce. While not all of the barriers or boundaries that impeded the free flow of books would disappear until the mid twentieth century, Macmillan, unlike Petherick's company, was in a position to sell books successfully first in the international sphere by the end of the nineteenth century and later as part of a global book trade.

International, transnational, global – the words are synonyms on one level yet on another each one potentially defines a different type of network or sphere. In writing about companies like Macmillan and the Colonial Booksellers' Agency that operated across borders, I have had to think about a particular problem or impediment that historians constructing histories about book trades outside the local or national fields face: what labels do I use and how do I define and/or differentiate (if there is even a need to differentiate) these terms such as international, transnational, and global? Sydney Shep nicely illustrates the debate in 'Books Without Borders' when she notes, for example, the concern Bill Bell and others have around the imbedding of national within the words international and transnational and the suggestion that words like intercultural and transcultural might be more inclusive labels to use when describing the circulation of print materials between different cultural groups or areas.[31] Intercultural or transcultural might be fitting terms to use in certain contexts, but in others, global, international, or transnational might be more appropriate.

Certainly, this discussion surrounding terminology mirrors the ongoing debate regarding whether the field should be referred to as book history or print culture, or by another label. Laurel Brake argues that the name of the field is currently under debate because certain names imply inclusion or exclusion of certain areas of study.[32] For example, she contends that naming the field 'book history' suggests the primary area of study is the book, which excludes other print matter. I do not believe we necessarily require one label or sign for either the field or in referencing the movement of print materials but fluency and flexibility, as well as critical awareness, of the host of terms and signposts we might choose to employ in different contexts. Perhaps instead of trying to come to a consensus, the field needs to maintain a level of debate that acknowledges the need for the continual examination of both the acts of naming and the power we imbue labels with, as well as the relationship between these labels and the boundaries and assumptions that organize and sometimes marginalize our field.

Brake asserts that technology has reshaped book history, increasing the scope of potential research beyond the traditional object of study and challenging the 'national boundaries' that often lead to an insular focus on the relationship between a nation and books.[33] Still, print historians, influenced by the work of Benedict Anderson, often accept as a given the connections between the growth of the nation and the growth of the book trade.[34] While Brake, Shep, and others have written about the pervasiveness of Anderson in the field and examined the problems, which I also address in the introduction to this book, of negating critical inquiry regarding the relation between print and nation, Andersen's influence remains.[35] It is the continuing impact of Anderson's idea on the field, even though he has since *Imagined Communities* revised his argument and other academics have 'explored the limits of Anderson's model of the imagination', that probably makes Bell and others wary of using words like international and transnational.[36] These labels are not ideologically neutral and academics are correct to be cautious because we still continue to apply them without thinking about all the associated baggage and assumptions that come with this terminology. This continuing lack of critical examination of the labels, as well as focus, theory, and methodology, that the field uses then leads Shep to wonder if planned international histories of the book will be 'anything more or different from what is already embodied in the national histories of the book'.[37]

Shep and Bell raise valid concerns but I think international and transnational are the right words in the context of my study to use to describe the trade at the end of the nineteenth century and the circulation of books. The book trade was not yet global, as books did not have a universal circulation and the markets I examine were primarily concerned with the trade in English-language books. Moreover, the necessary financial infrastructure was not yet in place to facilitate a global book trade, which could spread print materials to every corner of the world, and would not develop until the second half of the twentieth century. However, the trade was by the late nineteenth century transnational or international in scope as it extended across national borders and oceans. One could argue that the trade was international before the nineteenth century as well, since books had moved between countries for centuries. However, the quantity and speed of English-language book circulation increased in the late nineteenth century. It also stretched past the borders of the British Empire, including Japan and other Asian markets.

The second issue of Petherick's *Circular*, published December 1887, demonstrated the scale of the international book trade with the range of books catalogued in the Recent Colonial Publications and Books Relating to the British Colonies section of the journal, which customers could purchase through the Colonial Booksellers' Agency: books listed included N. Cantley's *Strait Settlements: Annual Report on the Botanic Gardens* published in Singapore in 1886; A. Klaus' *Unsere Kolonien: Studien und Materialiet zur Geschichte und Statistik der Ausländischen*

Kolonisation in Russland published in Odessa in 1887; copies of issues of the *Revue Française de l'Etranger et des Colonies* published in Paris; F. M. Bailey and P. R. Gordon's *Plants Reputed Poisonous and Injurious to Stock* published in Brisbane in 1887; and James D. Davis' *Contribution toward a Bibliography of New Zealand* published in Wellington (no date provided).[38] In the context of this particular study that examines the Colonial Booksellers' Agency and the *Circular*, labels that embed nation are appropriate because I focus on and stress the circulation and movement of books and people *across* boundaries, and I illustrate how agents had to contend with physical and imaginary boundaries, including the sometimes contradictory desire for stronger and weaker national borders, as they sought a wider distribution for their books and engaged with each other in the social network.

Petherick and his contemporaries were concerned about the impediment of national borders to the free flow of their publications and printed matter. Conversely, when it was not to the publisher's advantage, Macmillan and other firms worried about how to stop books from drifting across borders from one nation into another. In 1886, George E. Brett reported the rumour that one of Macmillan's publications was about to be illegally printed in Canada and told Frederick Macmillan that he had sent his son across the border to discover the truth.[39] In 1894, George P. Brett informed Macmillan that F. Marion Crawford was concerned about the effect the cheaper colonial editions were having on the sale of the American editions of his novels: 'I find that Mr. Crawford is not quite satisfied as to the Colonial editions. He thinks that they interfere slightly with his American market, coming in in considerable numbers into the northern states along the Canadian border.'[40] Brett suggested that one possible remedy for this problem was that Macmillan could 'exclude the Canadian market' and remove the colonial editions of Crawford's novel from circulation. Books may have been '[h]eedless of borders', but publishers tried to limit transmission when it was not to their advantage to have books circulate internationally.[41] Moreover, when agents did seek a wider distribution for publications they then had to contend with import and export duties and taxes that were further obstructions to the transnational flow of books. While Britain championed free trade in the late nineteenth century, trade was not unencumbered whether that trade was between the United States and Canada or between Britain and its colonies. Even if duties were not an issue, sometimes books would be 'delayed en route' or lost in transit.[42]

There is also an observable tension in Edward Petherick's memoir and in *The Torch and Colonial Book Circular* between overlapping and sometimes competing national, colonial, and international identities. Petherick imagined himself as an Australian national and colonial citizen, as well as an inhabitant of a connected world. These first two identities were largely complementary. Petherick considered himself an Australian: he was satisfied by the fact that Australians 'possess rights and privileges equal to that of any other country, glory in their origin, and the history of Britain'.[43] He was particularly concerned about supplying books and supporting his 'home's' book trade when he started the Colonial Booksellers' Agency. He then conceived of this Australian identity in connection with the larger British Empire. Petherick's *Circular* illustrates his particular belief of belonging to and being a citizen of an Imperial world. In the journal and his memoir he emphasized the connections that linked Britain with the rest of the Empire. He viewed his efforts first with George Robertson and later with the Colonial Booksellers' Agency as his patriotic duty to help spread English-language books worldwide and put books into the hands of British and colonial subjects at 'Home and Abroad'.[44]

Initially, the structure of the *Circular* – with the collected lists of books published in or about each of the main colonies – illustrated Petherick's particular view of a cohesive Imperial world. The journal seemed to demonstrate 'a deep, horizontal comradeship' or shared imagining of colonial identity with Petherick's insistence on a universal colonial reader for which he was producing the journal.[45] However, the diverse number of English and foreign-language books catalogued in the journal presented competing social, cultural, and political views of the colonies and Empire. A survey of the journal's contents and the books listed in the journal reveals potentially rival constructions of national, imperial, and international identities. At the same time that Petherick identified himself as an Australian and a British colonialist, he also acknowledged the ties that linked Australia, Britain, and consequently himself to the rest of the world. He thought of himself as a citizen of the world where everyone was part of an interconnected system of 'ante-rooms' in which 'we can all meet'.[46] This third identity intersected and was in tension with the first two, and Petherick navigated in the journal and his writing between national, imperial, and international imaginings. National affiliations overlapped and competed in a larger field of discourse with other identities. In the context of this history of the international book trade, nation was not absent.

In order to avoid flawed histories, we need to be critically aware of both any labels we choose to employ, as well as flexible in our usage, and the assumptions that shape the narratives we write. When I started this project, I viewed writing about the international book trade as an occasion to think about some of the field's theoretical and methodological limitations. In particular, inspired by Petherick and some of his contemporaries who envisioned a connected world in which books and people circulated, I saw an opportunity to develop a decentred model of book production and distribution. A social network emphasizes the principles of connection, multiplicity, and rupture and avoids centre/periphery dynamics and binary power relations. Consequently, it is capable of mapping a multifaceted trade that spanned the globe and the fluid complexity of interactions between agents without prescribing the nature of the relations between agents. However, a social network model can only represent a segment of the system at a time, as it simply cannot capture the entire complexity of the network because of all the agents, lines, and branches involved. The social network is a never-ending narrative. A history of the network is then fragmentary and at best is suggestive of the larger system as it traces lines and agents. The limited number of agents and the restricted temporal and spatial scope of a social network model that this book examines might admittedly then cause some concern.

Both an explanation of a social network and a history of specific agents in this system at the end of the nineteenth century, this study weaves together a narrative that includes Petherick, both Bretts, Macmillan, Bentley, Robertson, the Colonial Booksellers' Agency, and other agents and firms. I emphasize the dynamic complexity of 'relationships, interactions, and circulation' of a limited number of agents and entangle their accounts in order to exemplify the transnational sphere in which agents operated and connected.[47] The small section of the social network that I highlight in this book is then hopefully illustrative of the larger network of interactions that made up the international book trade. However, it is important to stress that I make no claims to an exhaustive or definitive history, which I think is impossible given the scope and density of the system. The various markets in North America, Europe, Asia, and Australia at the end of the nineteenth century collectively comprised a *sui generis* entity – the international book trade – that amounted to more than its disparate parts. I do not need to write about the trade in its entirety, and do not believe one study can do so, in order to demonstrate the existence of the social network and the international book trade. Moreover, I view my book in the context of a larger body of work. It is a node in an academic network and needs to be read in relation to Robert Fraser's *Book History through Postcolonial Eyes*, the edited two-volume *Books Without Borders*, and other books and projects that explore globally 'the transforming potential of print' in English and other languages and Western and non-Western markets that were all a part of the international print economy.[48]

Sydney Shep argues that '[i]t is imperative that we start rearranging book history's furniture, consider its existing and potential frames of reference, and look beyond the national to contemplate the ... mobilities and modalities of those material objects we call books'.[49] Robert Fraser adds that the field 'require[s] a number of drastic readjustments of vision'.[50] While Edward Petherick crossed and challenged boundaries that initially limited the transnational circulation of books, academics need to make visible the field's boundaries, as well as sites of exchange and discussion. If we cannot see what surrounds us, we can hardly debate alternative approaches to examining books and print matter and rearrange 'book history's furniture'. Petherick described the development of new transnational distribution routes as 'a vast amount of trouble' and one could argue that wrestling with the field's theoretical and methodological limits is similarly problematic.[51] However, just as Petherick felt his efforts were 'worthwhile', I believe joining this furniture-rearranging discussion is not only necessary but also equally 'worthwhile'.

I would like to think that I offer a possible alternative 'furniture' plan with the social network, while illustrating the boundary crossing of a number of agents like Petherick who pioneered distribution systems in order to secure and improve the transnational flow of books in the late nineteenth century. However, it is important to stress that agents could not traverse all the boundaries they faced: otherwise I risk replacing one problematic assumption or boundary with another relating to the speed and rate of progress. The flow of people, books, and ideas increased in intensity and velocity in the late nineteenth century but progress was not inevitable. The international book trade did not automatically develop into a global one. Following a series of economic depressions, the international economy contracted. Moreover, a number of the political, economic, and financial structures necessary for a global economy would not appear until the middle of the twentieth century. Global book flows would not circulate until the latter half of the twentieth century.

The international book trade is not just about growth and intensification: social networks expand *and* contract. Still, while one branch may shrink, other parts of the social network can continue to develop because the network is made up of multiple branches and a multitude of agents. A social network might contract or rupture because of changing social, cultural, and political realities, but it rarely disappears. There is an inherent stickiness associated with a rhizomorphic model because connection is the principal component of a social network and 'any point of a rhizome can be connected'.[52] While Petherick boasted of his importance in the international book trade, he also acknowledged that he was replaceable: 'Never under value yourself – nor think no one else can fill your place.'[53] No one agent is so central that the network will fail if that individual agent cannot make connections or leaves the network. New agents join, new connections are made, and new centres and nodes develop in the network; one connection leads to another. Even if an entire line or branch within the network withers, it is unlikely all parts of a network will do so.

Economic depressions in the 1890s impeded the growth of the international book trade but did not completely stop development. The idea or intellectual infrastructure of the international book trade had gained a certain currency by the 1890s. As agents' letters and shipments circulated, the trade deterritorialized and reterritorialized the idea of selling and distributing books as part of an international print economy: 'from sign to sign, a movement from one territory to another, a circulation assuring a certain speed of deterritorialization'.[54] The idea of an international book trade engaged the imaginations of too many authors, publishers, and distributors to disappear; books circulated transnationally, and later globally, because the idea of an international book trade had been widely disseminated in the late nineteenth century by Petherick, the Bretts, and their contemporaries.

Notes

Introduction

1. This book is based on Rukavina, 'Circulating Commodities'.
2. George E. Brett to Frederick Macmillan, 3 Apr. 1885, *Macmillan Archives*, Reel 3/12/146.
3. Askew and Hubber, 'The Colonial Reader Observed', 116.
4. George E. Brett to Frederick Macmillan, 3 Apr. 1885, *Macmillan Archives*, Reel 3/12/145.
5. George P. Brett to Frederick Macmillan, 22 June 1886, *Macmillan Archives*, Reel 3/13/54–5.
6. Ibid.
7. Chatterjee, 'Macmillan in India', 156.
8. Bentley to Alexander Macmillan, 22 Oct. 1886, *Archives of Richard Bentley*, Reel 42/86/119.
9. Chatterjee, 'Macmillan in India', 156.
10. Ibid.
11. George P. Brett to Frederick Macmillan, 11 Oct. 1886, *Macmillan Archives*, Reel 3/13/90.
12. George P. Brett to Frederick Macmillan, 11 Oct. 1886, *Macmillan Archives*, Reel 3/13/92.
13. Petherick to Peter Petherick, 9 Jan. 1873, Petherick Collection, MS 760/1/189.
14. Petherick to Peter Petherick, 10 May 1877, Petherick Collection, MS 760/1/320–1.
15. Steinburg, *Five Hundred Years of Printing*, 58.
16. Scholte, *Globalization*, 65–6.
17. Ibid., 72.
18. O'Brien and Williams, *Global Political Economy*, 87.
19. Ibid., 86.
20. Ibid., 88.
21. Ibid., 89.
22. Ibid., 94.
23. Scholte, *Globalization*, 68–9.
24. George P. Brett to Frederick Macmillan, 14 Mar. 1890, *Macmillan Archives*, Reel 4/15/323.
25. Shep, 'Books Without Borders', 16.
26. Fleming, Gallichan, and Lamonde, *History of the Book in Canada*, 3.
27. Wirtén, 'Surveying the (Battle)field', 3–4. Emphasis is in the original article.
28. Ibid., 4.
29. Anderson, *Imagined Communities*, 108.
30. Ibid., 7.
31. Bhabha, *Nation and Narration*, 310.
32. Eliot, 'An International History of Popular Fiction.'

33. Wirtén, 'Surveying the (Battle)field', 3–4.
34. Ibid., 4.
35. Michon, Introduction, *Les Mutations du Livre*, 14–15.
36. Gross, 'Books, Nationalism, and History', 116.
37. Eliot, 'An International History of the Book?', 7.
38. Burmester, 'Petherick, Edward Augustus (1847–1917)', 438. Also, see Biscup, 'Edward Augustus Petherick and the National Library of Australia, 1909–1917', 75–99; Fanning, 'Edward Augustus Petherick, 1847–1917: Bibliographer, Bookseller, Publisher, Book Collector', 30–2; and Thompson, 'Petherick's Australian Legacy', 3–5.
39. Wirtén, 'Surveying the (Battle)field', 3–4.
40. Darnton, 'What is the History of Books?', 11.
41. Gross, 'Books, Nationalism, and History', 110.
42. Petherick to Peter Petherick, 13 June 1872, Petherick Collection, MS 760/1/120.
43. Petherick, Unpublished memoir, Petherick Collection, MS 760/13/157. There seem to be two memoirs, as well as drafts, that are bundled together in the Petherick Collection: one memoir written in 1883 and a second memoir written between 1907 and 1909. It is not always clear which memoir is which as not all the pages are dated, so subsequent citations will only refer to the unpublished memoir.
44. Wirtén, 'Surveying the (Battle)field', 4.
45. Shep, 'Books Without Borders', 29–31.
46. Kocka, 'Comparison and Beyond', 42.
47. Ibid.
48. Ibid., 44.
49. Werner and Zimmerman, 'Beyond Comparison', 38. Italicization in the original article.
50. Ibid., 43.
51. Ibid., 44.
52. Ibid., 43.
53. Ibid.; Fan, 'Macmillan', 289.
54. Petherick to Peter Petherick, 10 May 1877, Petherick Collection, MS 760/1/320–1.

1 Social Networks

1. A shorter version of this chapter is Rukavina, 'Social Networks'.
2. Petherick to his siblings, 3 Sept. 1870, Petherick Collection, MS 760/2/4.
3. Petherick to Peter Petherick, 15 Nov. 1875, Petherick Collection, MS 760/1/261–2.
4. Petherick to Peter Petherick, 10 May 1877, Petherick Collection, MS 760/1/320–1.
5. Petherick to Peter Petherick, 13 June 1872, Petherick Collection, MS 760/1/120.
6. Darnton, *The Kiss of Lamourette*, 107, 110.
7. Darnton, 'What is the History of Books?', 17.
8. Ibid., 11.

9. Darnton, *The Kiss of Lamourette*, 113.
10. Adams and Barker, 'A New Model for the Study of the Book', 15.
11. Ibid., 39.
12. Winship, *American Literary Publishing in the Mid-Nineteenth Century*.
13. Petherick to Richard Bentley and Son, 12 Sept. 1873, *Archives of Richard Bentley and Son*, Reel IU 49. The microfilmed archives from the University of Illinois (IU) section are not indexed.
14. For a history of George Robertson see Holroyd, *George Robertson of Melbourne, 1825–1898*.
15. Petherick to Peter Petherick, 15 Nov. 1875, Petherick Collection, MS 760/1/261.
16. Mathers to Edward Petherick, July 1881 (day obscured), Petherick Collection, MS 760/2/87.
17. Askew and Hubber, 'The Colonial Reader Observed', 116.
18. Mathers to Edward Petherick, 25 Mar. 1883, Petherick Collection, MS 760/2/126.
19. Darnton, *The Kiss of Lamourette*, 111.
20. Jordan and Patten, *Literature in the Marketplace*, 11.
21. Ibid., 13.
22. Ibid., 12.
23. Rak, 'Double-Wampum, Double-Life, Double Click', 160–1.
24. Foucault, *The Archaeology of Knowledge and The Discourse on Language*, 23.
25. Jordan and Patten, *Literature in the Marketplace*, 11.
26. Deleuze and Guattari, *A Thousand Plateaus*, 7.
27. Petherick to Peter Petherick, 9 Jan. 1873, Petherick Collection, MS 760/1/189.
28. George P. Brett to Frederick Macmillan, 22 June 1886, *Macmillan Archives*, Reel 3/13/54–5.
29. Deleuze and Guattari, *A Thousand Plateaus*, 4.
30. Ibid., 21.
31. Ibid., 25.
32. Ibid., 5.
33. Ibid., 7–12.
34. Ibid., 7.
35. Petherick to Richard Bentley and Son, 12 Sept. 1873, *Archives of Richard Bentley*, Reel IU 49.
36. Hartley to George Robertson, 3 Apr. 1879, Petherick Collection, MS 760/2/53.
37. Petherick to George Bentley, 25 Nov. 1875, *The Archives of Richard Bentley*, Reel IU 49.
38. Deleuze and Guattari, *A Thousand Plateaus*, 4.
39. Adams and Barker, 'A New Model for the Study of the Book', 39.
40. Benton, 'From the World Systems Perspective to Institutional World History', 261–95.
41. Ibid., 285.
42. Ibid., 289.
43. Darnton, 'What is the History of Books?', 22.
44. Bourdieu, *The Field of Cultural Production*, 47.
45. Ibid., 56.

46. Ibid., 68.
47. McDonald, *British Literary Culture and Publishing Practice 1880–1914*, 18; Benton, 'From the World Systems Perspective to Institutional World History', 285.
48. Petherick to Richard Bentley, 12 Aug. 1892, *Archives of Richard Bentley*, Reel IU 49.
49. Petherick to Peter Petherick, 11 June 1874, Petherick Collection, MS 760/1/215.
50. Deleuze and Guattari, *A Thousand Plateaus*, 8.
51. George E. Brett to Macmillan, April 1885, *Macmillan Archives*, Reel 3/13/48–9.
52. Petherick, Unpublished memoir, Petherick Collection, MS 760/13/25.
53. Deleuze and Guattari, *A Thousand Plateaus*, 9.
54. Ibid., 126.
55. Draft of a publication catalogue, Richard Bentley and Son, Richard Bentley and Son Collection, British Library, London, Add. 59629/40.
56. Rutherford described the original *Broad Arrow* as 'an 847-page moral tract'. Rutherford, 'The Wages of Sin', 248.
57. Jordan and Patten, *Literature in the Marketplace*, 11.
58. Petherick to Peter Petherick, 13 June 1872, Petherick Collection, MS 760/1/120.
59. Petherick to Peter Petherick, 29 Sept. 1873, Petherick Collection, MS 760/1/172; Petherick to Peter Petherick, 16 Apr. 1874, Petherick Collection, MS 760/2/206.

2 Developing Distribution Channels and the Social Network

1. A version of this chapter appeared as Rukavina, 'This is a Wonderfully Comprehensive Business.'
2. Petherick, 'Bookselling in Australia', 466.
3. Petherick to Peter Petherick, 21 Jan. 1874, Petherick Collection, MS 760/1/186.
4. Kirsop, 'Bookselling and Publishing in the Nineteenth Century', 32.
5. Petherick, Unpublished memoir, Petherick Collection, MS 760/13/157.
6. Holroyd, *George Robertson of Melbourne*, 19.
7. 'Shippers of Books', 119.
8. Barnes, 'Depression and Innovation in the British and American Booktrade, 1819–1939', 209, 214.
9. Petherick to Peter Petherick, 13–16 June 1871, Petherick Collection, MS 760/1/86; Petherick to Peter Petherick, 14 July 1871, Petherick Collection, MS 760/1/90; Petherick to Peter Petherick, 11 Aug. 1871, Petherick Collection, MS 760/1/92.
10. Cullen, 'Edward Augustus Petherick', 99.
11. Petherick to Peter Petherick, 22 Feb. 1871, Petherick Collection, MS 760/1/77.
12. Petherick to Peter Petherick, 18 Jan. 1871, Petherick Collection, MS 760/1/72.
13. Petherick to Peter Petherick and family, 3 Nov. 1871, Petherick Collection, MS 760/1/102.

14. Robertson quoted in a letter from Edward Petherick to Peter Petherick, 16 June 1871, Petherick Collection, MS 760/1/87.
15. Petherick to Peter Petherick, 30 Dec. 1870, Petherick Collection, MS 760/1/67.
16. Holroyd, *George Robertson of Melbourne*, 37.
17. Petherick to Peter Petherick, 8 Sept. 1871, Petherick Collection, MS 760/1/96.
18. Petherick to Peter Petherick, 28 Nov. 1871, Petherick Collection, MS 760/1/104.
19. Petherick to Peter Petherick, 10 June 1874, Petherick Collection, MS 760/1/213.
20. Petherick to Peter Petherick, 13 June 1872, Petherick Collection, MS 760/1/120.
21. Petherick, 'Bookselling in Australia', 466.
22. Petherick to Peter Petherick, 10–12 June 1874, Petherick Collection, MS 760/1/214.
23. Petherick, Unpublished memoir, Petherick Collection, MS 760/13/58.
24. Petherick to his siblings, 3 Sept. 1870, Petherick Collection, MS 760/2/4.
25. Petherick to Peter Petherick, 10 May 1877, Petherick Collection, MS 760/1/320.
26. Petherick, 'Bookselling in Australia', 465.
27. Ibid., 465–6.
28. Petherick, Unpublished memoir, Petherick Collection, MS 760/13/58.
29. Petherick to Peter Petherick, 18 Nov. 1870, Petherick Collection, MS 760/1/61.
30. George Robertson quoted in a letter from Petherick to Peter Petherick, 22 Mar. 1871, Petherick Collection, MS 760/1/79. The underlining and comments in parentheses are in the original letter.
31. Petherick to Peter Petherick, 9 Jan. 1873, Petherick Collection, MS 760/1/189.
32. Petherick to Peter Petherick, 18 Jan. 1871, Petherick Collection, MS 760/1/68. Underlining in the original document.
33. Lee, *Linking a Nation*.
34. Petherick to George Robertson, n.d., Petherick Collection, MS 760/1/66.
35. Petherick to Peter Petherick, 31 Aug.–1 Sept. 1876, Petherick Collection, MS 760/1/293; Petherick to Peter Petherick, 10 May 1877, Petherick Collection, MS 760/1/320–1.
36. Petherick, 'The Book-Trade in Melbourne', 4.
37. Fenn to Edward Petherick, 27 Jan. 1876, Petherick Collection, MS 760/2/17–18.
38. Petherick to Peter Petherick and family, 3 Nov. 1871, Petherick Collection, MS 760/1/102.
39. Petherick, Unpublished memoir, Petherick Collection, MS 760/13/166.
40. Petherick to Peter Petherick, 16 June 1871, Petherick Collection, MS 760/1/86.
41. Petherick, 'Bookselling in Australia', 465.
42. Blainey, *The Tyranny of Distance*, 218.
43. Petherick to Stevenson Blackwood, British Secretary of the General Post Office, 21 Mar. 1882, Petherick Collection, MS 760/13/90–1.

44. Petherick, 'Bookselling in Australia', 465. Emphasis in the original letter.
45. Petherick to Peter Petherick, 16 May 1872, Petherick Collection, MS 760/1/119.
46. Blainey, *The Tyranny of Distance*, 223.
47. Petherick to Peter Petherick, 29 Sept. 1873, Petherick Collection, MS 760/1/172.
48. Petherick to Peter Petherick, 16 Apr. 1874, Petherick Collection, MS 760/2/206.
49. Petherick to Peter Petherick, 15 Nov. 1875, Petherick Collection, MS 760/1/261.
50. Petherick to Richard Bentley and Son, 17 July 1880, *Archives of Richard Bentley and Son*, Reel IU 49.
51. Petherick to Peter Petherick, 18 Feb. 1875, Petherick Collection, MS 760/1/233.
52. Holroyd, *George Robertson of Melbourne*, 39.
53. Allan Dooley argues that of particular importance to the portability of book moulds was the adoption of stereotyping because it allowed plaster – and later paper – moulds to be made that could be easily transported or stored for later use. Dooley, *Author and Printer in Victorian England*, 56.
54. Petherick to George Bentley, 8 Apr. 1876, *Archives of Richard Bentley*, Reel IU 49.
55. Petherick, 'The Book-Trade in Melbourne', 4.
56. Petherick to Peter Petherick, 10 May 1877, Petherick Collection, MS 760/1/320–1.
57. Ibid.
58. Petherick to Peter Petherick, 15 Nov. 1875, Petherick Collection, MS 760/1/261.
59. Petherick, Unpublished memoir, Petherick Collection, MS 760/13/92.
60. Fraser, 'John Murray's Colonial and Home Library', 339.
61. Askew and Hubber, 'The Colonial Reader Observed', 116.
62. Petherick, Unpublished memoir, Petherick Collection, MS 760/13/92. Graeme Johanson notes that historians 'have been over-eager to attribute the beginning of colonial editions' to George Robertson but there is no proof to support this claim. Similarly, there is no evidence to support Petherick's boast regarding being the 'projector' of colonial editions. Johanson, *A Study of Colonial Editions*, 46.
63. Young to Edward Petherick, 12 Aug. 1879, Petherick Collection, MS 760/2/38.
64. Young to Edward Petherick, 13 Aug. 1879, Petherick Collection, MS 760/2/40. Underlining in the original letter.
65. Holroyd, *George Robertson of Melbourne*, 47; Accounts Ledgers, *Archives of the House of Longman*, Reel 16/B14/512; Reel 19/B17/67.
66. La Nauze, 'William Edward Hearn (1826–1888)', 370–2.
67. Accounts Ledgers, *Archives of the House of Longman*, Reel 21/B19/40.
68. Holroyd, *George Robertson of Melbourne*, 53; Accounts Ledgers, *Archives of the House of Longman*, Reel 19/B17/67.
69. Parkes, Title page, *Speeches on Various Occasions*.
70. Commission Ledgers, *Archives of the House of Longman*, Reel 18/B16/558.
71. The history of George Robertson's business dealings with Richard Bentley and Son and Robertson's involvement in Bentley's development of the

Australian Library are examined in greater detail in Rukavina, 'Fabricating a National Canon'. The section on Petherick's negotiations with Bentley also draws on research from Rukavina, 'Cultural Darwinism and the Literary Canon', 56–63.

72. Petherick to Richard Bentley and Son, 12 Sept. 1873, *Archives of Richard Bentley*, Reel IU 49.
73. Ibid.
74. Petherick to George Bentley, 25 Nov. 1875, *Archives of Richard Bentley*, Reel IU 49.
75. Petherick to George Bentley, 8 Apr. 1876, *Archives of Richard Bentley*, Reel IU 49.
76. Petherick to George Bentley, 15 Mar. 1876, *Archives of Richard Bentley*, Reel IU 49.
77. Petherick to George Bentley, 8 Apr. 1876, *Archives of Richard Bentley*, Reel IU 49.
78. Petherick to Richard Bentley and Son, 12 July 1880, *Archives of Richard Bentley*, Reel IU 49.
79. Robertson and his attorney, C. Newberry, Letter to the Collector of Customs, Christchurch, New Zealand, 15 May 1880, *Archives of Richard Bentley*, Reel IU 49.
80. Dzwonkoski, 'George Munro', 315.
81. Robertson and his attorney, C. Newberry, Letter to the Collector of Customs, Christchurch, New Zealand, 15 May 1880, *Archives of Richard Bentley*, Reel IU 49.
82. Richard Bentley and Son to Edward Petherick, 16 July 1880, *Archives of Richard Bentley*, Reel 41/85/200.
83. Petherick to Richard Bentley and Son, 12 Sept. 1873, *Archives of Richard Bentley*, Reel IU 49.
84. Johanson, *A Study of Colonial Editions*, 143.
85. McLeod to Richard Bentley and Son, 4 Oct. 1881, *Archives of Richard Bentley*, Reel 31/61/96.
86. George Bentley to Hamilton Mackinnon, 19 Apr. 1882, *Archives of Richard Bentley*, Reel 31/61/101.
87. Richard Bentley and Son to Hamilton Mackinnon, 29 Mar. 1883, *Archives of Richard Bentley*, Reel 41/85/389.
88. Richard Bentley and Son to Edward Petherick, 15 Dec. 1877, *Archives of Richard Bentley*, Reel 41/85/61.
89. Richard Bentley and Son to Hamilton Mackinnon, 29 Mar. 1883, *Archives of Richard Bentley*, Reel 41/85/389.
90. Richard Bentley and Son to Hamilton Mackinnon, 24 June 1884, *Archives of Richard Bentley*, Reel 41/85/452.
91. Richard Bentley and Son to Hamilton Mackinnon, 13 Feb. 1885, *Archives of Richard Bentley*, Reel 42/86/50.
92. Ibid.; Richard Bentley and Son to Hamilton Mackinnon, 3 Oct. 1885, *Archives of Richard Bentley*, Reel 42/86/80.
93. Petherick to Richard Bentley and Son, 17 July 1880, *Archives of Richard Bentley and Son*, Reel IU 49.
94. A one-volume edition of Clarke's *Natural Life* was part of this series and all the books in the collection were priced at six shillings.

95. Draft of a publication catalogue, Richard Bentley and Son, Richard Bentley and Son Collection, British Library, London, Add. 59629/40.
96. Petherick to George Bentley, 3 Oct. 1888, *Archives of Richard Bentley*, Reel IU 49.
97. *Colonial Book Circular*, 10. The title page for the 1892 issue of Leakey's *The Broad Arrow* only has Bentley's imprint.
98. Petherick, Letter to Peter Petherick, 24 Jan. 1872, Petherick Collection, MS 760/1/108.
99. Petherick, Unpublished memoir, Petherick Collection, MS 760/13/60.
100. Robertson qtd in a letter written by Petherick to Peter Petherick, 19 Apr. 1872, Petherick Collection, MS 760/1/118.
101. Petherick to Peter Petherick, 11 June 1874, Petherick Collection, MS 760/1/215.
102. Johanson, *A Study of Colonial Editions*, 66.
103. Petherick to Peter Petherick, 10 May 1877, Petherick Collection, MS 760/1/320–1.
104. Petherick, Unpublished memoir, Petherick Collection, MS 760/13/100.
105. Petherick to Peter Petherick, 21 Jan. 1874, Petherick Collection, MS 760/1/186.
106. Petherick to Peter Petherick, 18–19 Jan. 1877, Petherick Collection, MS 760/1/313.
107. Petherick to Peter Petherick, 13 Apr. 1877, Petherick Collection, MS 760/1/316–17. Underlining in the original document.
108. Petherick, Unpublished memoir, Petherick Collection, MS 760/13/124.
109. Petherick to Peter Petherick, 10 May 1877, Petherick Collection, MS 760/1/320.
110. Swan Sonnenschein and Co., Letter to George Robertson, 2 Jan. 1887, *The Archives of Swan Sonnenschein & Co.*, Reel 1/2/339.
111. Cusack to Edward Petherick, 10 Dec. 1880, Petherick Collection, MS 760/2/62. Underlining in the original letter.
112. Holroyd, *George Robertson of Melbourne*, 58.
113. Petherick to Peter Petherick, 10 May 1877, Petherick Collection, MS 760/1/320–1.
114. Petherick to Stevenson Blackwood, British Secretary of the General Post Office, 21 Mar. 1882, Petherick Collection, MS 760/13/90–1.
115. Petherick to Peter Petherick, 13 June 1872, Petherick Collection, MS 760/1/120.

3   Piracy, Copyright, and the International Book Trade

1. Feather, *Publishing, Piracy and Politics*, 154.
2. Ibid., 150.
3. Ibid.,154.
4. Ibid.
5. Parker, *The Beginnings of the Book Trade in Canada*, 106.
6. Fraser, 'John Murray's Colonial and Home Library', 339–408.
7. Johanson, *A Study of Colonial Editions*, 221.
8. Kirsop, 'From Colonialism to the Multinationals', 325.

9. Kirsop, 'Bookselling and Publishing in the Nineteenth Century', 34; Hubber, 'A "Free Trade" in the Antipodes', 22.

10. Robertson, Letter, 115–16.

11. Ibid.

12. Ibid.

13. Howitt, Letter, 148.

14. 'Copy of a Correspondence', 234; Robertson, Letter, 234.

15. Petherick to George Bentley, 15 Mar. 1876, *Archives of Richard Bentley*, Reel IU 49.

16. Holroyd, *George Robertson of Melbourne*, 27.

17. Petherick to George Bentley, 12 July 1880, *Archives of Richard Bentley*, Reel IU 49.

18. Richard Bentley and Son to Edward Petherick, 16 July 1880, *Archives of Richard Bentley*, Reel 41/85/200.

19. Petherick to George Bentley, 17 July 1880, *Archives of Richard Bentley*, Reel IU 49.

20. In 1886, Macmillan's adoption of a plan to release 'a colonial library of new British novels, often using U.S. or U.K. stereotype plates for printing,' marked the first instance of a colonial series of new books. Johanson, *A Study of Colonial Editions*, 144.

21. Parker, *The Beginnings of the Book Trade in Canada*, 94.

22. Ibid.

23. Kirsop, *Books for Colonial Readers*, 8–9.

24. Parker, *The Beginnings of the Book Trade in Canada*, 109.

25. Ibid., 115.

26. Feather, *Publishing, Piracy and Politics*, 170.

27. Ibid., 170–1.

28. The Canadian book trade was accused 'of ignoring native writers "because they made good sales and large profits on British and American works, which were already popular, and seldom pushed Canadian books." He [E. H. Dewart] concluded that "our colonial position … is not favourable to the growth of an indigenous literature".' Parker, *The Beginnings of the Book Trade in Canada*, 91. Ellipses in Parker's text.

29. Adam, Stevenson, and Company to William Kirby, 8 July 1873, Kirby Collection, F1076, MS 542, A6 I.

30. Adam to William Kirby, 25 May 1875, Kirby Collection, F1076, MS 542, A6 I.

31. Trubner and Co. to William Kirby, 5 May 1873, Kirby Collection, F1076, MS 542, A6 I.

32. Richard Bentley and Son to William Kirby, 19 Dec. 1884, Kirby Collection, F1076, MS 542, A6 II.

33. Parker, *The Beginnings of the Book Trade in Canada*, 177.

34. Adam to William Kirby, 12 July 1875, Kirby Collection, F1076, MS 542, A6 II.

35. Parker, *The Beginnings of the Book Trade in Canada*, 169.

36. Ibid., 172.

37. Parker, 'English-Canadian Publishers and the Struggle for Copyright', 152.

38. Stern, *Imprints on History*, 262.

39. Ibid., 260.

40. Adam to William Kirby, 5 Oct. 1875, Kirby Collection, F1076, MS 542, A6 II.

41. Adam to William Kirby, 24 May 1876, Kirby Collection, F1076, MS 542, A6 II.
42. Adam to William Kirby, 29 Jan. 1877, Kirby Collection, F1076, MS 542, A6 II.
43. Robert Lovell to William Kirby, 1 Apr. 1877, Kirby Collection, F1076, MS 542, A6 II.
44. Parker, *The Beginnings of the Book Trade in Canada*, 191.
45. John Lovell to William Kirby, 2 Apr. 1878, Kirby Collection, F1076, MS 542, A6 II.
46. John Lovell to William Kirby, 11 Apr. 1878, Kirby Collection, F1076, MS 542, A6 II.
47. Adam to William Kirby, 21 Nov. 1884, Kirby Collection, F1076, MS 542, A6 II.
48. John W. Lovell to William Kirby, 22 Nov. 1884, Kirby Collection, F1076, MS 542, A6 II.
49. Elizabeth Brady describes other pirated issues and editions. Brady, 'A Bibliographical Essay on William Kirby's *The Golden Dog* 1877–1977', 24–48.
50. Withrow to William Kirby, 7 May 1885, Kirby Collection, F1076, MS 542, A6 II.
51. Kirby to Richard Worthington, 12 Apr. 1880, Kirby Collection, F1076, MS 542, A6 II.
52. Macmillan to William Kirby, 16 Apr. 1885, Kirby Collection, F1076, MS 542, A6 II.
53. Dawson to William Kirby, 29 Oct. 1887, Kirby Collection, F1076, MS 542, A 6 II.
54. Parker, *The Beginnings of the Book Trade in Canada*, 215.
55. Ibid., 171.
56. Collins to Hunter Rose, 13 July 1872, Morris L. Parrish Collection of Victorian Novelists, NJ, MS C0171.
57. Papers Relating to Colonial Copyright, Imperial Blue Book, 1872, Box 20/287/75.
58. Adam to William Kirby, 21 Oct. 1884, Kirby Collection, F1076, MS 542, A6 II.
59. Rose, Letter, 64–5.
60. 'The Copyright Question', 518–20.
61. Papers Relating to Colonial Copyright, Imperial Blue Book, 1872, Box 20/287/46.
62. 'The Copyright Problem', 2.
63. O'Brien and Williams, *Global Political Economy*, 89–90.
64. Feather, *Publishing, Piracy and Politics*, 156.
65. 'The Copyright Problem', 2.
66. 'Canadian Wickedness', 8.
67. Putnam, 'International Copyright', 351.
68. 'The Canadian Book Trade and the Post Office', 882–3.
69. Randolph, 'Free Trade in Books', 512.
70. George E. Brett to Frederick Macmillan, 14 Jan. 1885, *Macmillan Archives*, Reel 3/12/118a.
71. George E. Brett to Frederick Macmillan, 23 June 1885, *Macmillan Archives*, Reel 3/12/168a.

72. Parker, *The Beginnings of the Book Trade in Canada*, 185.
73. George E. Brett to Frederick Macmillan, 23 June 1885, *Macmillan Archives*, Reel 3/12/167.
74. George E. Brett to Frederick Macmillan, 23 June 1888, *Macmillan Archives*, Reel 3414/53.
75. Another reason for the proliferation of cheap books was new printing technology, such as power presses, and new paper-making technology that saw paper made from wood pulp rather than rags, reduced production costs. Parker, *The Beginnings of the Book Trade in Canada*, 184.
76. 'The Canadian Incursion', 439.
77. Lovell, Letter, 470.
78. Estes and Lauriat, Advertisement, 827, 844.
79. 'Decisions in the United States Affecting the Book Trade', 26–7.
80. Bentley to Harper Bros., 16 May 1881, *Archives of Richard Bentley*, Reel 41/85/265.
81. George E. Brett to Frederick Macmillan, 11 Feb. 1885, *Macmillan Archives*, Reel 3/12/122.
82. George E. Brett to Frederick Macmillan, 11 Feb. 1885, *Macmillan Archives*, Reel 3/12/124a.
83. 'Questions on International Copyright', 197.
84. Lippincott, Letter, 197.
85. Carleton, Letter, 197.
86. Cooke, Letter, 239.
87. Habberton, Letter, 262–3.
88. Lovell, Letter, 470.
89. 'The "Monopoly" of Copyright', 508–9.
90. Feather, *Publishing, Piracy and Politics*, 168.
91. George E. Brett to Frederick Macmillan, 23 Oct. 1885, *Macmillan Archives*, Reel 3/12/205.
92. George E. Brett to Frederick Macmillan, Feb. 1888, *Macmillan Archives*, Reel 4/14/5a.
93. George E. Brett to Macmillan and Co., 28 Dec. 1870, *Macmillan Archives*, Reel 3/12/103–6.
94. Madison, *Book Publishing in America*, 262.
95. Frederick Macmillan to George P. Brett, 10 Apr. 1891, *Macmillan Archives*, Reel 10/498/60; Frederick Macmillan to George P. Brett, 15 Apr. 1891, *Macmillan Archives*, Reel 10/498/60; George E. Brett to Frederick Macmillan, 23 Apr. 1887, *Macmillan Archives*, Reel 3/13/176.
96. George P. Brett to Frederick Macmillan, 30 Aug. 1890, *Macmillan Archives*, Reel 4/15/111–12.
97. Towheed, 'Rudyard Kipling's Literary Property, International Copyright Law and the *Naulahka*', 426–7.
98. George P. Brett to Frederick Macmillan, 22 Apr. 1892, *Macmillan Archives*, Reel 10/498/285–6.
99. George P. Brett to Frederick Macmillan, 11 Apr. 1890, *Macmillan Archives*, Reel 5/15/47.
100. Feather, *Publishing, Piracy and Politics*, 168.
101. George P. Brett to Frederick Macmillan, 6 Mar. 1894, *Macmillan Archives*, Reel 4/17/55.

102. 'English Authors and the Colonial Book Market', 111.
103. Ibid., 112.
104. Ibid., 113.
105. Ibid., 114.

4   The International Book Trade

1. 'Literary Notes', 2.
2. Petherick to George Bentley, 15 Mar. 1876, *Archives of Richard Bentley*, Reel IU 49; Petherick to George Bentley, 12 July 1880, *Archives of Richard Bentley*, Reel IU 49.
3. Chatterjee, 'How India Took to the Book', 102.
4. Joshi, 'Trading Places: The Novel, the Colonial Library, and India', 17.
5. Chatterjee, 'Macmillan in India', 158; Joshi, 'Trading Places: The Novel, the Colonial Library, and India', 20–1.
6. Winship, 'The Transatlantic Book Trade and Anglo-American Literary Culture in the Nineteenth Century', 99.
7. Parker, *The Beginnings of the Book Trade in Canada*, 169.
8. Petherick, 'Bookselling in Australia', 465.
9. Askew and Hubber, 'The Colonial Reader Observed', 113.
10. Victoria was the first colony to introduce free, compulsory, and secular education with the Education Act 1872. However, compulsory religious education in Victoria and the other colonies had existed since the early nineteenth century.
11. Petherick to Stevenson Blackwood, British Secretary of the General Post Office, 21 Mar. 1882, Petherick Collection, MS 760/13/90–1.
12. Askew and Hubber, 'The Colonial Reader Observed', 116.
13. Finklestein, 'Book Circulation and Read Responses in Colonial India', 105; Condie, 'Thacker, Spink and Company', 113.
14. 'The Approaching Book Season', 26.
15. James, 'Letters from America', 171.
16. Petherick to George Bentley, 8 Apr. 1876, *Archives of Richard Bentley*, Reel IU 49.
17. Gettman, *A Victorian Publisher*, 77.
18. Brantlinger, *The Reading Lesson*, 12.
19. Gettman, *A Victorian Publisher*, 23.
20. Bentley to J. B. Lippincott, 14 Feb. 1868, *Archives of Richard Bentley*, Reel 41/84/112.
21. Bentley to J. B. Lippincott, 8 Feb. 1870, *Archives of Richard Bentley*, Reel 41/84/155.
22. Lippincott to Richard Bentley, 14 Aug. 1879, *Archives of Richard Bentley*, Reel 31/60/151.
23. Richard Bentley and Son to Henry Holt, 12 July 1878, *Archives of Richard Bentle*, Reel 41/85/ 93–4.
24. Jordan to Henry Holt, 12 Nov. 1880, *Archives of Richard Bentley*, Reel 41/85/219–20.
25. Jordan to Appleton and Co., 10 Mar. 1880, *Archives of Richard Bentley*, Reel 41/85/179.

26. Richard Bentley and Son to Henry Holt, 19 Mar. 1885, *Archives of Richard Bentley*, Reel 42/86/55–6.
27. Bentley to Henry Holt, 3 Feb. 1885, *Archives of Richard Bentley*, Reel 42/86/48–9. Capitalization in the original letter.
28. Bentley had first published Thisted's novel in 1866. The new edition contained a preface by novelist and poet George MacDonald.
29. Feather, *Publishing, Piracy and Politics*, 168.
30. Richard Bentley and Son to Henry Holt, 19 Mar. 1885, *Archives of Richard Bentley*, Reel 42/ 86/55–6; Richard Bentley and Son to Henry Holt, 13 Feb. 1892, *Archives of Richard Bentley*, Reel 42/86/453.
31. Richard Bentley and Son to Henry Holt, 13 Feb. 1892, *Archives of Richard Bentley*, Reel 42/86/453.
32. Stern, *Imprints on History*, 266.
33. Richard Bentley and Son to Wolcott Balestier, 19 Feb. 1890, *Archives of Richard Bentley*, Reel 42/86/323.
34. Richard Bentley and Son to Wolcott Balestier, 10 Apr. 1890, *Archives of Richard Bentley*, Reel 42/86/335.
35. Bentley had previously sold Lovell the unbound sheets to Rosa Nouchette Carey's melodramatic novel *Lover or Friend*.
36. Contract for Rhoda Broughton's *Alas!*, 11 Apr. 1890, *Archives of Richard Bentley*, Reel 33/64/266.
37. Richard Bentley and Son to Wolcott Balestier, 1 Aug. 1890, *Archives of Richard Bentley*, Reel 42/86/352. Quotation marks and underlining in the original letter.
38. Foreign and Colonial Department Review, 1889, *Archives of Richard Bentley*, Reel IU 1.
39. Ibid. Braces in the original document.
40. Petherick to George Bentley, 25 Nov. 1875, *Archives of Richard Bentley*, Reel IU 49.
41. Pembroke, *South Sea Bubbles*, title page and back cover.
42. Petherick to Richard Bentley and Son, 12 Sept. 1873, *Archives of Richard Bentley*, Reel IU 49.
43. Petherick, Unpublished memoir, Petherick Collection, MS 760/13/25.
44. Ibid., 160.
45. Official Advice Form: detailing a telegram from Mrs (Rosa) Campbell Praed, 7 May 1886, *Archives of Richard Bentley*, Reel IU 2/6B/208.
46. Richard Bentley and Son to Hamilton Mackinnon, 29 Mar. 1883, *Archives of Richard Bentley*, Reel 41/85/389.
47. Richard Bentley and Son to Edward Petherick, 15 Dec. 1877, *Archives of Richard Bentley*, Reel 41/85/61.
48. Author's name obscured, letter to Richard Bentley and Son, 29 Aug. 1884, *Archives of Richard Bentley*, Reel 32/62/249–51.
49. Accounts Ledger, 31 Mar. 1888, *Archives of Richard Bentley*, Reel 16/35/120; Accounts Ledger, 31 Mar. 1888, *Archives of Richard Bentley*, Reel 16/35/ 128.
50. Foreign and Colonial Department Review, 1889, *Archives of Richard Bentley*, Reel IU.
51. Ibid.
52. Joshi, 'Trading Places: The Novel, the Colonial Library, and India', 22–3, 27.

53. Ibid., 39.
54. Johanson, *A Study of Colonial Editions*, 58.
55. Ibid., 63; Petherick to Richard Bentley and Son, 17 July 1880, *Archives of Richard Bentley and Son*, Reel IU 49.
56. *Colonial Book Circular*, Bentley advertisement in the collected first volume, 25; *Torch and Colonial Book Circular*, Macmillan advertisement in the collected first volume, 3. The advertisements in both collected volumes are separately numbered from the rest of the journal.
57. Bentley to Macmillan, 22 Oct. 1886, *Archives of Richard Bentley*, Reel 42/86/119.
58. Bentley to Macmillan, 6 June 1894, *Archives of Richard Bentley*, Reel 42/87/220.
59. Bentley to Macmillan, 8 June 1894, *Archives of Richard Bentley*, Reel 42/87/221.
60. Richard Bentley and Son to Macmillan, 12 Jan. 1895, *Archives of Richard Bentley*, Reel 42/87/292.
61. Richard Bentley and Son to Macmillan (New York), 4 Oct. 1897, *Archives of Richard Bentley*, Reel 43/88/353.
62. George E. Brett to Frederick Macmillan, 3 Apr. 1885, *Macmillan Archives*, Reel 3/12/146.
63. George E. Brett to Frederick Macmillan, 3 Apr. 1885, *Macmillan Archives*, Reel 3/12/145; Chatterjee, 'Macmillan in India', 156.
64. George P. Brett to Frederick Macmillan, 22 June 1886, *Macmillan Archives*, Reel 3/13/54–5; George P. Brett to Frederick Macmillan, 11 Oct. 1886, *Macmillan Archives*, Reel 3/13/90.
65. Morgan, *The House of Macmillan*, 163.
66. George E. Brett to Frederick Macmillan, 23 June 1885, *Macmillan Archives*, Reel 3/12/168a.
67. James, 'Letters from America', 171.
68. Ibid.
69. West, 'Book-Publishing 1835–1900', 372.
70. Ibid., 369.
71. Nowell-Smith, *The House of Cassell*, 265.
72. Living, *Adventures in Publishing: The House of Ward Lock*, 55.
73. Eyre, *Oxford in Australia*, 5.
74. Chatterjee, *Empires of the Mind*, 20.
75. Joshi, 'Trading Places: The Novel, the Colonial Library, and India', 21.
76. Chatterjee, 'Every Line for India', 82.
77. Joshi, 'Trading Places: The Novel, the Colonial Library, and India', 21.
78. George P. Brett to Frederick Macmillan, 22 June 1886, *Macmillan Archives*, Reel 3/13/54–5.
79. George P. Brett to Frederick Macmillan, 1 Mar. 1894, *Macmillan Archives*, Reel 4/17/37.
80. Fan, 'Macmillan', 291.
81. George P. Brett to Frederick Macmillan, 11 Oct. 1886, *Macmillan Archives*, Reel 3/13/90.
82. Ibid., 92.
83. George P. Brett to Frederick Macmillan, 22 June 1886, *Macmillan Archives*, Reel 3/13/54.
84. Winship, 'The International Trade in Books', 154.

85. George P. Brett to Frederick Macmillan, 22 June 1886, *Macmillan Archives*, Reel 3/13/54.
86. George P. Brett to Frederick Macmillan, 15 Nov. 1886, *Macmillan Archives*, Reel 3/13/104.
87. George P. Brett to Frederick Macmillan, 24 Dec. 1886, *Macmillan Archives*, Reel 3/13/120.
88. George E. Brett's note attached to George P. Brett's letter to Frederick Macmillan, 24 Dec. 1886, *Macmillan Archives*, Reel 3/13/122.
89. George E. Brett to Maurice Macmillan, 10 May 1887, *Macmillan Archives*, Reel 3/13/190.
90. George E. Brett to Maurice Macmillan, 30 Mar. 1887, *Macmillan Archives*, Reel 3/13/158.
91. George E. Brett to Maurice Macmillan, 9 Apr. 1887, *Macmillan Archives*, Reel 3/13/164.
92. George E. Brett to Maurice Macmillan, 19 Apr. 1887, *Macmillan Archives*, Reel 3/13/170.
93. George E. Brett to Maurice Macmillan, 17 June 1887, *Macmillan Archives*, Reel 3/13/210.
94. George E. Brett to Maurice Macmillan, 19 Apr. 1887, *Macmillan Archives*, Reel 3/13/172. Underlining in the original letter.
95. George E. Brett to Maurice Macmillan, 16 May 1887, *Macmillan Archives*, Reel 3/13/191. Underlining in the original letter.
96. George E. Brett to Maurice Macmillan, 9 Apr. 1887, *Macmillan Archives*, Reel 3/13/164–5.
97. Ibid., 165.
98. Ibid., 166.
99. George E. Brett to Maurice Macmillan, 24 Mar. 1887, *Macmillan Archives*, Reel 3/13/153–4.
100. James, 'Introduction', 2.
101. George E. Brett to Maurice Macmillan, 24 Mar. 1887, *Macmillan Archives*, Reel 3/13/154.
102. Ibid., 156.
103. George E. Brett to Maurice Macmillan, 16 May 1887, *Macmillan Archives*, Reel 3/13/191.
104. George E. Brett to Maurice Macmillan, 24 Mar. 1887, *Macmillan Archives*, Reel 3/13/154–5.
105. George E. Brett to Maurice Macmillan, 19 Apr. 1887, *Macmillan Archives*, Reel 3/13/171.
106. George E. Brett to Maurice Macmillan, 24 Mar. 1887, *Macmillan Archives*, Reel 3/13/157.
107. George E. Brett to Maurice Macmillan, 28 May 1887, *Macmillan Archives*, Reel 3/13/203.
108. George E. Brett to Maurice Macmillan, 24 Mar. 1887, *Macmillan Archives*, Reel 3/13/154.
109. Petherick, Unpublished memoir, Petherick Collection, MS 760/13/79.
110. George E. Brett to Maurice Macmillan, 9 Apr. 1887, *Macmillan Archives*, Reel 3/13/166, 168.
111. George E. Brett to Maurice Macmillan, 3 June 1887, *Macmillan Archives*, Reel 3/13/206.

112. George E. Brett to Maurice Macmillan, 10 May 1887, *Macmillan Archives*, Reel 3/13/190.
113. Ibid.
114. George E. Brett to Maurice Macmillan, 19 Apr. 1887, *Macmillan Archives*, Reel 3/13/172.
115. Ibid., 172, 174.
116. George E. Brett to Maurice Macmillan, 16 May 1887, *Macmillan Archives*, Reel 3/13/192.
117. George E. Brett to Maurice Macmillan, 17 May 1887, *Macmillan Archives*, Reel 3/13/194.
118. George E. Brett to Maurice Macmillan, 28 June 1887, *Macmillan Archives*, Reel 3/13/212.
119. George E. Brett to Maurice Macmillan, 24 Mar. 1887, *Macmillan Archives*, Reel 3/13/154–5.
120. George E. Brett to Maurice Macmillan, 19 Apr. 1887, *Macmillan Archives*, Reel 3/13/170.
121. George E. Brett to Maurice Macmillan, 17 June 1887, *Macmillan Archives*, Reel 3/13/212.
122. George E. Brett to Maurice Macmillan, 16 May 1887, *Macmillan Archives*, Reel 3/13/191.
123. Ibid., 192.
124. Handford, 'Macmillan Chronology', xxvi.
125. James, 'Letters from America', 175.
126. Bourdieu, *The Field of Cultural Production*, 68.

5   The Colonial Booksellers' Agency

1. A shorter draft version of this chapter appeared as Rukavina, 'A Victorian Amazon.com.'
2. Petherick, 'Opening Letter', 1.
3. Burmester, 'Petherick, Edward Augustus (1847–1917)', 439.
4. Petherick, 'Opening Letter', 1.
5. Petherick, Unpublished memoir, Petherick Collection, MS 760/13/124.
6. Burmester, 'Petherick, Edward Augustus (1847–1917)', 438.
7. Petherick, Unpublished memoir, Petherick Collection, MS 760/13/3, 17, 25, and 79.
8. Petherick, 'Bookselling in Australia', 465–6.
9. Petherick to Peter Petherick, 10 May 1877, Petherick Collection, MS 760/1/320–1.
10. Petherick, Unpublished memoir, Petherick Collection, MS 760/13/100.
11. George E. Brett to Frederick Macmillan, 3 Apr. 1885, *Macmillan Archives*, Reel 3/12/145–6.
12. Petherick, Unpublished memoir, Petherick Collection, MS 760/13/25.
13. 'Trade and Literary Gossip', 759.
14. Petherick to Thomas A. Coghlan, 26 July 1905, Petherick Collection, MS 740/6/14.
15. Petherick, Unpublished memoir, Petherick Collection, MS 760/13/160.
16. Ibid., 161.

17. George P. Brett to Maurice Macmillan, 9 Apr. 1887, *Macmillan Archives*, Reel 3/13/166, 168; Unpublished memoir, Petherick Collection, MS 760/13/79.
18. George P. Brett to Maurice Macmillan, 24 Mar. 1887, *Macmillan Archives*, Reel 3/13/154.
19. Petherick to Peter Petherick, 13 June 1872, Petherick Collection, MS 760/1/120.
20. Petherick to Peter Petherick, 10 May 1877, Petherick Collection, MS 760/1/320–1.
21. Petherick, Unpublished memoir, Petherick Collection, MS 760/13/25.
22. Burmester, 'Petherick, Edward Augustus (1847–1917)', 439.
23. Richard Bentley and Son, List of Guarantors on a Colonial Account, *Archives of Richard Bentley*, Reel 42/87/80.
24. Petherick to George Bentley, 3 Oct. 1888, *Archives of Richard Bentley*, Reel IU 49.
25. Petherick, Unpublished memoir, Petherick Collection, MS 760/13/124. Word struck out in the original.
26. While Petherick mentions his relatives and alludes to other employees in his memoirs, he never actually states how many men worked for him. Ibid., 33.
27. Petherick, Writings, printed and unprinted, Petherick Collection, MS 760/13/1425.
28. Petherick, 'Opening Letter', 1.
29. Petherick, 'Torch', 37.
30. Petherick to Peter Petherick, 13 June 1872, Petherick Collection, MS 760/1/120.
31. Petherick, 'Opening Letter', 1.
32. Petherick, 'Torch', 37.
33. *Colonial Book Circular*, 28, 33.
34. Ibid., 85.
35. Petherick, 'Torch', 37.
36. *Colonial Book Circular*, 24.
37. Petherick, '"The Trade" in Australasia', 2. Interestingly, the article on the Australasian bookselling and stationery trades had been written for the first issue of Hedeler's *Export Journal* and reprinted by Petherick in the *Circular*.
38. Petherick, 'Cheap Editions for the Colonies', 3; 'The Growth of a Tasmanian Myth', 4.
39. *Torch and Colonial Book Circular*, advertisements in the back pages. The advertisements in the collected second volume are separately numbered from the rest of the journal. The Ferguson advertisement is on page 16 and the Caspar advertisement is on page 29 of the back pages.
40. Petherick to Peter Petherick, 13 June 1872, Petherick Collection, MS 760/1/120.
41. Petherick, 'Cheap Editions for the Colonies', 3.
42. Petherick, 'Opening Letter', 1.
43. Johanson, *A Study of Colonial Editions*, 62–3.
44. *Petherick and Co's Monthly Catalogue*, 1.
45. Petherick, Unpublished memoir, Petherick Collection, MS 760/13/124.
46. Ibid.; Bentley, Notes Re: Petherick & Co. Bankruptcy, 5 July 1894, *Archives of Richard Bentley*, Reel 42/87/234–5.

47. See Johanson's *A Study of Colonial Editions* for an overview of the various colonial series produced by British publishers for the Australian market at the end of the nineteenth century.
48. George E. Brett to Maurice Macmillan, 9 April 1887, *Macmillan Archives*, Reel 3/13/164.
49. Petherick, 'Opening Letter', 1.
50. Ibid.
51. Petherick, 'Bookselling in Australia', 465.
52. Petherick to Richard Bentley, 30 Apr. 1892, *Archives of Richard Bentley*, Reel IU 49.
53. Petherick to Richard Bentley, 1 May 1892, *Archives of Richard Bentley*, Reel IU 49.
54. Petherick to Richard Bentley, 12 Aug. 1892, *Archives of Richard Bentley*, Reel IU 49. Underlining in the original letter.
55. Bentley to George Hubert Longman, 10 Aug. 1892, *Archives of Richard Bentley*, Reel IU 49. Underlining in the original letter.
56. Bentley, Meeting Resolution and Notes Re: Mr. E. A. Petherick, 20 Dec. 1892, *Archives of Richard Bentley*, Reel 42/87/71.
57. Bentley to George Hubert Longman, 20 Aug. 1892, *Archives of Richard Bentley*, Reel 42/87/41.
58. Bentley to Edward Petherick, 16 Sept. 1892, *Archives of Richard Bentley*, Reel 42/87/48–50.
59. Bentley, Memorandum with Regard to a Colonial Account, 20 Jan. 1893, *Archives of Richard Bentley*, Reel 42/87/81.
60. Bentley to George Hubert Longman, 6 Jan. 1893, *Archives of Richard Bentley*, Reel 42/87/78–9.
61. Bentley, Memorandum with Regard to a Colonial Account, 20 Jan. 1893, *Archives of Richard Bentley*, Reel 42/87/81.
62. Bentley, Memorandum with Regard to a Colonial Account, 20 Jan. 1893, *Archives of Richard Bentley*, Reel 42/87/82.
63. Bentley to George Hubert Longman, 13 June 1893, *Archives of Richard Bentley*, Reel 42/87/127.
64. Bentley, Notes Re: E. A. Petherick & Co., *Archives of Richard Bentley*, Reel 42/87/115.
65. Bentley to George Hubert Longman, 8 Oct. 1892, *Archives of Richard Bentley*, Reel 42/87/52.
66. Bentley to William Heinemann, 25 Jan. 1893, *Archives of Richard Bentley*, Reel 42/87/84.
67. Bentley, Meeting Resolution and Notes Re: E. A. Petherick, 20 Dec. 1892, *Archives of Richard Bentley*, Reel 42/87/71.
68. Johanson, *A Study of Colonial Editions*, 63.
69. Bentley, Notes Re: Petherick & Co. Bankruptcy, 5 July 1894, *Archives of Richard Bentley*, Reel 42/87/234–5.
70. Longman, Power of Attorney Contract and Debt Owing Claim, 23–25 Apr. 1894, *Archives of the House of Longman*, Reel 65/N132.
71. Bentley, Notes Re: Petherick & Co. Bankruptcy, 5 July 1894, *Archives of Richard Bentley*, Reel 42/87/234–5.
72. Bentley to Edward Petherick, 16 Mar. 1894, *Archives of Richard Bentley*, Reel 42/87/203.

73. 'Heavy Failure', 14–15.
74. Bentley, Notes Re: Petherick & Co. Bankruptcy, 5 July 1894, *Archives of Richard Bentley*, Reel 42/87/234–5.
75. *Daily Chronicle* Clipping, 20 July 1894, *Archives of Richard Bentley*, Reel 42/87/238.
76. *Standard* Clipping, 6 Apr. 1895, *Archives of Richard Bentley*, Reel 42/87/213.
77. Petherick, Unpublished memoir, Petherick Collection, MS 760/13/25.
78. Longman, Power of Attorney Contract and Debt Owing Claim, 23–25 Apr. 1894, *Longman Archives*, Reel 65/N132.
79. Handford, 'Macmillan Chronology', xxvi.
80. Petherick, 'Opening Letter', 1.
81. Johanson, *A Study of Colonial Editions*, 76.

Conclusion

1. Petherick, Unpublished memoir, Petherick Collection, MS 760/13/58.
2. Ibid.
3. Petherick to Peter Petherick, 10 June 1874, Petherick Collection, MS 760/1/213.
4. Petherick to his siblings, 3 Sept. 1870, Petherick Collection, MS 760/2/4.
5. George E. Brett to Frederick Macmillan, 3 Apr. 1885, *Macmillan Archives*, Reel 3/12/146.
6. Petherick to Peter Petherick, 13 June 1872, Petherick Collection, MS 760/1/120.
7. Petherick to Peter Petherick, 10 May 1877, Petherick Collection, MS 760/1/320–1.
8. George E. Brett to Frederick Macmillan, 3 Apr. 1885, *Macmillan Archives*, Reel 3/12/146.
9. Petherick to Peter Petherick, 21 Jan. 1874, Petherick Collection, MS 760/1/186.
10. Eggert, 'Robbery Under Arms', 142.
11. Petherick, Unpublished memoir, Petherick Collection, MS 760/13/157.
12. Ibid.
13. The advertisement for Trübner & Co. is written in English, French, and German. The *Export Journal*, 14.
14. Ibid., 2.
15. Ibid., 8–9.
16. Ibid., Table of Contents.
17. Ibid., 6.
18. George P. Brett to Frederick Macmillan, 6 Mar. 1894, *Macmillan Archives*, Reel 4/17/55.
19. George P. Brett to Frederick Macmillan, 30 Mar. 1894, *Macmillan Archives*, Reel 4/17/79–80.
20. Petherick, Unpublished memoir, Petherick Collection, MS 760/13/25.
21. Ibid., 124; Bentley, Notes Re: Petherick & Co. Bankruptcy, 5 July 1894, *Archives of Richard Bentley*, Reel 42/87/234–5.
22. Bentley, Memorandum with Regard to a Colonial Account, 20 Jan. 1893, *Archives of Richard Bentley*, Reel 42/87/81.

23. George P. Brett to Frederick Macmillan, 6 Mar. 1894, *Macmillan Archives*, Reel 4/17/55.
24. George P. Brett to Frederick Macmillan, 30 Mar. 1894, *Macmillan Archives*, Reel 4/17/79–80.
25. James, 'Letters from America', 176.
26. Madison, *Book Publishing in America*, 263.
27. Micklethwait and Wooldridge, *The Company*, 52.
28. Macintyre, *A Concise History of Australia*, 129.
29. George E. Brett to Maurice Macmillan, 10 May 1887, *Macmillan Archives*, Reel 3/13/190.
30. Petherick to Richard Bentley, 12 Aug. 1892, *Archives of Richard Bentley*, Reel IU 49.
31. Shep, 'Books Without Borders', 16.
32. Brake, 'On Print Culture: The State We're In', 125. Also, see Hudson, 'Challenging Eisenstein: Recent Studies in Print Culture', 83–95.
33. Brake, 'On Print Culture: The State We're In', 127.
34. Anderson, *Imagined Communities*, 110.
35. Shep, 'Books Without Borders', 13–35; Wirtén, 'Surveying the (Battle)field', 3–4.
36. Shep, 'Books Without Borders', 25.
37. Ibid., 15.
38. *Colonial Book Circular*, 78–81.
39. George P. Brett to Frederick Macmillan, 12 Feb. 1886, *Macmillan Archives*, Reel 3/13/14–15.
40. George P. Brett to Frederick Macmillan, 10 Aug. 1994, *Macmillan Archives*, Reel 4/17/177.
41. Gross, 'Books, Nationalism, and History', 110.
42. Fenn to Edward Petherick, 27 Jan. 1876, Petherick Collection, MS 760/2/17–18.
43. Petherick, Unpublished memoir, Petherick Collection, MS 760/13/58.
44. Petherick, 'Opening Letter', 1.
45. Anderson, *Imagined Communities*, 7.
46. Petherick to Peter Petherick, 13 June 1872, Petherick Collection, MS 760/1/120.
47. Werner and Zimmerman, 'Beyond Comparison', 38.
48. Fraser, *Book History through Postcolonial Eyes*, 7.
49. Shep, 'Books Without Borders', 34.
50. Fraser, *Book History through Postcolonial Eyes*, x.
51. Petherick to Peter Petherick, 10 May 1877, Petherick Collection, MS 760/1/320–1.
52. Deleuze and Guattari, *A Thousand Plateaus*, 7.
53. Petherick to Peter Petherick, 21 Jan. 1874, Petherick Collection, MS 760/1/186.
54. Deleuze and Guattari, *A Thousand Plateaus*, 126.

Bibliography

Adams, Thomas R. and Nicholas Barker. 'A New Model for the Study of the Book.' In *A Potencie of Life: Books in Society*, edited by Nicholas Barker, 5–43. London: Oak Knoll, 1993.

Anderson, Benedict. *Imagined Communities*. Revised Edition. London: Verso, 1996.

'The Approaching Book Season.' *The Canadian Bookseller: Miscellany and Advertiser* 2, no. 4 (Oct. 1872): 25–7.

Askew, Marc and Brian Hubber. 'The Colonial Reader Observed: Reading in its Cultural Context.' In *The Book in Australia: Essays Towards a Cultural and Social History*, edited by Wallace Kirsop and D. H. Borchardt, 110–37. Melbourne: Australian Reference Publications, 1988.

Barnes, James. 'Depression and Innovation in the British and American Booktrade, 1819–1939.' In *Economics of the British Booktrade 1605–1939*, edited by Robin Myers and Michael Harris, 209–31. Cambridge: Chadwyck-Healey, 1985.

Bentley, Richard and Son. *The Archives of Richard Bentley and Son 1829–1898*. Cambridge: Chadwyck-Healey, 1976.

——. Richard Bentley and Son Collection. Add. 59629. British Library, London.

Benton, Lauren. 'From the World Systems Perspective to Institutional World History: Culture and Economy in Global Theory.' *Journal of World History* 7, no. 2 (1996): 261–95.

Bhabha, Homi K. *Nation and Narration*. New York: Routledge, 1990.

Biscup, Peter. 'Edward Augustus Petherick and the National Library of Australia, 1909–1917.' *Australian Library History: Papers for the Second Forum on Australian Library History*, edited by P. Biskup and M. K. Rochester, 75–99. Canberra: College of Advanced Education, 1985.

Blainey, Geoffrey. *The Tyranny of Distance: How Distance Shaped Australia's History*. Melbourne: Sun Books, 1969.

Bourdieu, Pierre. *The Field of Cultural Production: Essays on Art and Literature*. Edited and Introduced by Randal Johnson. New York: Columbia University Press, 1993.

Brady, Elizabeth. 'A Bibliographical Essay on William Kirby's *The Golden Dog* 1877–1977.' *Papers/Cahier of the Bibliographical Society of Canada* 15 (1976): 24–48.

Brake, Laurel. 'On Print Culture: The State We're In.' *Journal of Victorian Culture* 6, no. 1 (2001): 125–36.

Brantlinger, Patrick. *The Reading Lesson: The Threat of Mass Literacy in Nineteenth Century British Fiction*. Indianapolis: Indiana University Press, 1998.

Burmester, Clifford. 'Petherick, Edward Augustus (1847–1917).' In *Australian Dictionary of Biography*, Vol. 5, edited by Bede Nairn, Geoffrey Serle, and Russel Ward, 438. Melbourne University Press. 1974.

'The Canadian Book Trade and the Post Office.' *Publishers' Weekly* 16, no. 26 (27 Dec. 1879): 882–4.

'The Canadian Incursion.' *Publishers' Weekly* 15, no. 15 (12 Apr. 1879): 439.

'Canadian Wickedness.' *Publishers' Weekly* 15, no. 1 (4 Jan. 1879): 8.

Carleton, G. W. Letter. *Publishers' Weekly* 15, no. 7 (15 Feb. 1879): 197.

Chatterjee, Rimi B. 'How India Took to the Book: British Publishers at Work Under the Raj.' In *Les Mutations du Livre et de l'Edition dans le Monde*, edited by Jacques Michon and Jean-Yves Mollier, 100–21. Quebec: University Press Laval, 2001.

——. 'Macmillan in India: A Short Account of the Company's Trade with the Sub-continent.' In *Macmillan: A Publishing Tradition*, edited by Elizabeth James, 153–69. London: Palgrave Macmillan, 2002.

——. '"Every Line for India": The Oxford University Press and the Rise and Fall of the Rulers of India Series.' In *Print Areas: Book History in India*, edited by Abjhijit Gupta and Swapan Chakravorty, 65–99. Delhi: Permanent Black, 2004.

——. *Empires of the Mind: A History of the Oxford University Press in India under the Raj.* Oxford University Press, 2006.

Collins, Wilkie. Letter. Morris L. Parrish Collection of Victorian Novelists. MS C0171. Princeton University, Princeton, NJ.

Colonial Book Circular and Bibliographical Record, The 1, nos 1–4 (1887–88).

Condie, Victoria. 'Thacker, Spink and Company: Bookselling and Publishing in Mid-Nineteenth-Century Calcutta.' In *Books Without Borders*, Vol. 2, edited by Robert Fraser and Mary Hammond, 112–23. London: Palgrave Macmillan, 2008.

Cooke, Joseph. Letter. *Publishers' Weekly* 15, no. 8 (22 Feb. 1879): 239.

'Copy of a Correspondence Between George Robertson, Bookseller, Melbourne, and the Hon. The Collector of Customs for the Colony of Victoria, in Reference to the Importation of Pirated Editions of English Copyright Works.' *Athenaeum* 1426 (24 Feb. 1855): 234.

'The Copyright Problem.' *New York Times*, 24 Sept. 1881, 2.

'The Copyright Question.' *Bystander* 1, no. 9 (Sept. 1880): 518–20.

Cullen, Marie. 'Edward Augustus Petherick: A Bio-Bibliographical Study to August 1887.' PhD diss., Monash University, 2000.

Darnton, Robert. *The Kiss of Lamourette: Reflections in Cultural History.* New York: Norton, 1990.

——. 'What is the History of Books?' In *The Book History Reader*, edited by David Finkelstein and Alistair McCleery, 9–26. London: Routledge, 2002.

'Decisions in the United States Affecting the Book Trade: Judge Wheeler's Decision in the Chatterbox Case.' *Books and Notions* 1, no. 2 (Sept. 1884): 26–7.

Deleuze, Gilles and Félix Guattari. *A Thousand Plateaus.* Trans. Brian Massami. Minneapolis: University of Minneapolis Press, 1987.

Dooley, Allan C. *Author and Printer in Victorian England.* Charlottesville: University Press of Virginia, 1992.

Dzwonkoski, David. 'George Munro.' In *American Literary Publishing Houses, 1638–1899 Part 1: A–M Dictionary of Literary Biography*, Vol. 49, edited by Peter Dzwonkoski, 315–16. Detriot: Gale, 1986.

Eggert, Paul. 'Robbery Under Arms: The Colonial Market, Imperial Publishers, and the Demise of the Three-Decker Novel.' *Book History* 6 (2003): 127–46.

Eliot, Simon. 'An International History of the Book?' *SHARP News* 12, no. 1 (2003): 7.

——.'An International History of Popular Fiction.' Plenary Session of Crossing Borders. Society for the History of Authorship, Reading, and Publishing Annual Conference. ENS, Lyon, 20 July 2004.

'English Authors and the Colonial Book Market.' *The Author*, Sept. 1890, 111–14.

Estes and Lauriat. Advertisement. *Publishers' Weekly* 18, no. 25 (18 Dec. 1880): 827, 844.

Export Journal: International Circular for the Book, Paper, and Printing Trades, The 1, nos 1–12 (1887–88).

Eyre, Frank. *Oxford in Australia*. Oxford University Press, 1978.

Fan, Ada M. 'Macmillan.' *American Literary Publishing Houses, 1638–1899 Part 1: A–M Dictionary of Literary Biography*, Vol. 49, edited by Peter Dzwonkoski, 289–94. Detriot: Gale, 1986.

Fanning, Pauline. 'Edward Augustus Petherick, 1847–1917: Bibliographer, Bookseller, Publisher, Book Collector.' *Canberra Historical Journal* 31 (1993): 30–2.

Feather, John. *Publishing, Piracy and Politics: An Historical Study of Copyright in Britain*. London: Mansell, 1994.

Finklestein, David. 'Book Circulation and Read Responses in Colonial India.' In *Books Without Borders*, Vol. 2, edited by Robert Fraser and Mary Hammond, 100–11. London: Palgrave Macmillan, 2008.

Fleming, Patricia, Gilles Gallichan, and Yvan Lamonde, eds. *History of the Book in Canada*. Vol. 1, *Beginnings to 1840*. University of Toronto Press, 2004.

Foucault, Michel. *The Archaeology of Knowledge and The Discourse on Language*. Trans. A. M. Sheridan Smith. New York: Pantheon Books, 1972.

Fraser, Angus. 'John Murray's Colonial and Home Library.' *Papers of the Bibliographical Society of America* 91, no. 3 (1997): 339–408.

Fraser, Robert. *Book History through Postcolonial Eyes*. London: Routledge, 2008.

Gettman, Royal A. *A Victorian Publisher: A Study of the Bentley Papers*. Cambridge University Press, 1960.

Great Britain. Papers Relating to Colonial Copyright. Imperial Blue Book. Box 20. No. 287, 1872.

Gross, Robert A. 'Books, Nationalism, and History.' *Papers of the Bibliographical Society of Canada* 36 (1998): 107–23.

Habberton, John. Letter. *Publishers' Weekly* 15, no. 9 (1 Mar. 1879): 262–3.

Handford, John. 'Macmillan Chronology, 1843–1970.' In *Macmillan: A Publishing Tradition*, edited by Elizabeth James, xxv–xxvi. London: Palgrave Macmillan, 2002.

'Heavy Failure.' *The London Times*, 29 Nov. 1894, 14–15.

Held, David, Anthony McGrew, David Goldblatt, and Jonathan Perraton. *Global Transformations: Politics, Economics and Culture*. Stanford University Press, 1999.

Holroyd, John. *George Robertson of Melbourne, 1825–1898*. Melbourne: Robertson and Mullens, 1968.

Howitt, William. Letter. *Athenaeum* 1423 (3 Feb. 1855): 148.

Hubber, Brian. 'A "Free Trade" in the Antipodes: American Reprints in the Australasian Colonies.' *Bibliographical Society of Australia and New Zealand Bulletin* 16, no. 1 (1992): 19–22.

Hudson, Nicholas. 'Challenging Eisenstein: Recent Studies in Print Culture.' *Eighteenth-Century Life* 26, no. 2 (2002): 83–95.

James, Elizabeth. 'Introduction.' In *Macmillan: A Publishing Tradition*, edited by Elizabeth James, 1–10. London: Palgrave Macmillan, 2002.

——. 'Letters from America: The Bretts and the Macmillan Company of New York.' In *Macmillan: A Publishing Tradition*, edited by Elizabeth James, 170–91. London: Palgrave Macmillan, 2002.

Johanson, Graeme. *A Study of Colonial Editions in Australia, 1843–1972.* Sydney: Eliabank Press, 2000.

Jordan, John O. and Robert L. Patten, eds. *Literature in the Marketplace: Nineteenth-Century British Publishing and Reading Practices.* Cambridge University Press, 1995.

Joshi, Priya. 'Trading Places: The Novel, the Colonial Library, and India.' In *Print Areas: Book History in India*, edited by Abjhijit Gupta and Swapan Chakravorty, 17–64. Delhi: Permanent Black, 2004.

Kirby, William. The William Kirby Collection. F1076 MS 542 A-6. Archives of Ontario, Toronto.

Kirsop, Wallace. 'Bookselling and Publishing in the Nineteenth Century.' In *The Book in Australia: Essays Towards a Cultural and Social History*, edited by Wallace Kirsop and D. H. Borchardt, 16–42. Melbourne: Australian Reference Publications, 1988.

——. *Books for Colonial Readers: The Nineteenth-Century Australian Experience.* Melbourne: Bibliographical Society of Australia and New Zealand, 1995.

——. 'From Colonialism to the Multinationals: The Fragile Growth of Australian Publishing and its Contribution to the Global Anglophone Reading Community.' In *Les Mutations du Livre et de l'Edition dans le Monde*, edited by Jacques Michon and Jean-Yves Mollier, 324–9. Quebec: University Press Laval, 2001.

Kocka, Jürgen. 'Comparison and Beyond.' *History and Theory* 42 (Feb. 2003): 39–44.

Lee, Robert. *Linking a Nation: Australia's Transport and Communications 1788–1970.* Canberra: Australian Heritage Commission, 2003. http://www.ahc.gove.au/publications/national stories/transport/index.html (accessed 1 May 2006).

Lippincott, J. B. Letter. *Publishers' Weekly* 15, no. 7 (15 Feb. 1879): 197.

'Literary Notes.' *George Robertson's Monthly Book Circular* 232 (Nov. 1881): 2.

Living, Edward. *Adventures in Publishing: The House of Ward Lock.* London: Ward Lock, 1954.

Longman, House of. *Archives of the House of Longman, 1794–1914.* Cambridge: Chadwyck-Healey, 1978.

Lovell, John. Letter. *Publishers' Weekly* 15.16 (19 Apr. 1879): 470–1.

Macintyre, Stuart. *A Concise History of Australia.* Cambridge University Press, 1999.

Macmillan and Co. *Macmillan Archives.* Cambridge: Chadwyck-Healey, 1982.

Madison, Charles A. *Book Publishing in America.* New York: McGraw-Hill, 1966.

McDonald, Peter. *British Literary Culture and Publishing Practice 1880–1914.* Cambridge University Press, 1997.

Michon, Jacques. Introduction. In *Les Mutations du Livre et de l'Edition dans le Monde*, edited by Jacques Michon and Jean-Yves Mollier, 11–15. Quebec: University Press Laval, 2001.

Micklethwait, John and Adrian Wooldridge. *The Company: A Short History of a Revolutionary Idea.* New York: Random, 2003.

'The "Monopoly" of Copyright.' *Publishers' Weekly* 15, no. 16 (3 May 1879): 508–9.

Morgan, Charles. *The House of Macmillan (1843–1943).* London: Macmillan, 1943.

La Nauze, J. A. 'William Edward Hearn (1826–1888).' In *Australian Dictionary of Biography*, Vol. 4, edited by Douglas Pike, 370–2. Melbourne University Press, 1972.

Nowell-Smith, Simon. *The House of Cassell.* London: Cassell, 1958.

O'Brien, Robert and Marc Williams. *Global Political Economy.* New York: Palgrave Macmillan, 2004.

Parker, George L. *The Beginnings of the Book Trade in Canada.* University of Toronto Press, 1985.

——.'English-Canadian Publishers and the Struggle for Copyright.' In *History of the Book in Canada,* Vol. 2, *1840–1918,* edited by Yvan Lamonde, Patricia Lockhart Fleming, and Fiona A. Black, 148–59. University of Toronto Press, 2005.

Parkes, Henry. *Speeches on Various Occasions.* Melbourne: George Robertson; London: Longman, 1876.

Pembroke, Earl of, and Doctor Kingsley. *South Sea Bubbles.* Melbourne: George Robertson, 1872.

Petherick, Edward. Petherick Collection. MS 760. National Library of Australia, Canberra.

——. 'The Book-Trade in Melbourne.' *The Argus* (Melbourne) 21 Feb. 1874: 4.

——. 'Bookselling in Australia.' *The Bookseller* 2 June 1874: 465–6.

——. 'Opening Letter.' *Colonial Book Circular and Bibliographical Record* 1, no. 1 (1887): 1.

——. '"The Trade" in Australasia.' *Colonial Book Circular and Bibliographical Record* 1, no.1 (1887): 2.

——. 'Cheap Editions for the Colonies.' *Colonial Book Circular and Bibliographical Record* 1, no. 1 (Sept. 1887): 3.

——. 'The Growth of a Tasmanian Myth.' *Colonial Book Circular and Bibliographical Record* 1, no. 1 (Sept. 1887): 4.

——. 'Torch.' *The Torch and Colonial Book Circular* 1, no. 2 (1887): 37.

——. 'Australasia: Bookselling and Stationery Trades.' *The Export Journal: International Circular for the Book, Paper and Printing Trades* 1, no. 1 (1888): 8–9.

E. A. Petherick and Co's Monthly Catalogue 1, no. 3 (May 1890): 1.

Putnam, George. 'International Copyright.' *Publishers' Weekly* 15, no. 12 (22 Mar. 1879): 351.

'Questions on International Copyright.' *Publishers' Weekly* 15, no. 7 (15 Feb. 1879): 197.

Rak, Julie. 'Double-Wampum, Double-Life, Double Click: E. Pauline Johnson by and for the World Wide Web.' *Textual Studies in Canada* 13/14 (Summer 2001): 155–70.

Randolph, A. D. F. 'Free Trade in Books', *Publishers' Weekly* 15, no. 18 (3 May 1879): 512.

Robertson, William. Letter. *Athenaeum* 1422 (27 Jan. 1855): 115–16.

——. Letter. *Athenaeum* 1426 (24 Feb. 1855): 234.

Rose, George Maclean. Letter. *Books and Notions* 1, no. 4 (Nov. 1884): 64–5.

Rukavina, Alison. 'Cultural Darwinism and the Literary Canon: A Comparative Study of Susanna Moodie's *Roughing It in the Bush* and Caroline Leakey's *The Broad Arrow.*' MA thesis, Simon Fraser University, 2000.

——. 'Circulating Commodities: The Role of George Robertson, Edward Petherick, George P. Brett, and Other Publishers and Distributors in the Late Nineteenth-Century Expansion of the International Book Trade.' PhD diss., University of Alberta, 2007.

——. '"This is a Wonderfully Comprehensive Business": The Development of the British–Australian and International Book Trades (1870–1887).' *Script and*

Print: Bulletin of the Bibliography Society of Australia and New Zealand 32, no. 1 (2008): 69–94.

——. 'Social Networks: Modeling the Transnational Distribution and Production of Books.' Special Issue, 'Moveable Type, Mobile Nations: Interactions in Transnational Book History', *Angles on the English Speaking World* 10 (2010): 73–83.

——. 'A Victorian Amazon.com: Edward Petherick and his Colonial Booksellers' Agency.' *Book History* 13 (2010): 104–21.

——. 'Fabricating a National Canon: The Role of Richard Bentley and Son and George Robertson in Developing and Marketing the Australian Library.' In *The Culture of the Publisher's Series*, Vol. 2, *Nationalisms and the National Canon*, edited by John Spiers. London: Palgrave Macmillan, forthcoming.

Rutherford, Anna. 'The Wages of Sin: Caroline Leakey's *The Broad Arrow*.' In *Commonwealth Writers Overseas: Themes of Exile and Expatriation*, edited by Alastair Niven, 245–54. Brussels: Didier, 1976.

Scholte, Jan Aart. *Globalization: A Critical Introduction*. New York: St Martin's, 2000.

Shep, Sydney. 'Books Without Borders: The Transnational Turn in Book History.' In *Books Without Borders*, Vol. 1, edited by Robert Fraser and Mary Hammond, 13–35. London: Palgrave Macmillan, 2008.

'Shippers of Books.' *The Bookseller* 28 Feb. 1862: 119.

Steinburg, S. H. *Five Hundred Years of Printing*. Harmondsworth: Penguin, 1961.

Stern, Madeleine B. *Imprints on History: Book Publishers and American Frontiers*. Bloomington: Indiana University Press, 1956.

Swan Sonnenschein and Co. *The Archives of Swan Sonnenschein & Co., 1879–1911*. London: Chadwyck-Healey, 1973.

Thompson, John. 'Petherick's Australian Legacy.' *National Library of Australia News* 7, no. 7 (1997): 3–5.

Torch and Colonial Book Circular, The 2, nos 5-8 (1888–89), Google Books. http://books.google.ca (accessed 10 Apr. 2010).

Towheed, Shafquat. 'Rudyard Kipling's Literary Property, International Copyright Law and the *Naulahka*.' *English Literature in Translation* 48, no. 4 (2005): 420–35.

'Trade and Literary Gossip.' *The Publishers' Circular*, 5 Aug. 1887, 759.

Werner, Michael and Bénédicte Zimmerman. 'Beyond Comparison: *Histoire Croisée* and the Challenge of Reflexivity.' *History and Theory* 45 (Feb. 2006): 30–50.

West, James. 'Book-Publishing 1835–1900: The Anglo-American Connection.' *Papers of the Bibliographical Society of America* 84, no. 4 (1990): 357–75.

Winship, Michael. *American Literary Publishing in the Mid-Nineteenth Century: The Business of Ticknor and Fields*. Cambridge University Press, 1995.

——. 'The Transatlantic Book Trade and Anglo-American Literary Culture in the Nineteenth Century.' In *Reciprocal Influences: Literary Production, Distribution and Consumption in America*, edited by Steven Fink and Susan Williams, 98–122. Columbus: Ohio State University Press, 1999.

——. 'The International Trade in Books.' In *A History of the Book in America*, Vol. 3, *The Industrial Book 1840–1880*, edited by Scott E. Casper, Jeffery D. Groves, Stephen W. Nissenbaum, and Michael Winship, 148–57. Chapel Hill: University of North Carolina Press, 2007.

Wirtén, Eva Hemmungs. 'Surveying the (Battle)field: Book History, SHARP, and the Guerilla Tactics of Research.' *SHARP News* 12, no. 1 (2003): 3–4.

Index